WINFIELD

Living in the Shadow of the Woolworths

Brick Tower Press
Habent Sua Fata Libelli

Brick Tower Press
Manhanset House
Shelter Island Hts., New York 11965-0342
Tel: 212-427-7139
bricktower@aol.com • www.BrickTowerPress.com
All rights reserved under the International and Pan-American Copyright Conventions. No part of this publication may be reproduced, stored in a retrieval system, or transmitted in any form or by any means, electronic, or otherwise, without the prior written permission of the copyright holder.
The Brick Tower Press colophon is a registered trademark of
J. T. Colby & Company, Inc.

The following story is true. The people, places, and events in this book are all real. Some of the names and details of certain persons have been changed to protect their privacy.

The Isadora Duncan quote on page 112 is from *Life into Art: Isadora and Her World* by Dorée Duncan, Carol Pratl, and Cynthia Splatt. W.W. Norton & Co., 1993.

Book design by James Sinclair.

Library of Congress Cataloging-in-Publication Data
Randall, Monica.
Winfield—Living in the Shadow of the Woolworths
p. cm.
Includes bibliographical references

1. Architecture / Historic Preservation.
2. Biography & Autobiography / Business.
3. History / United States / State & Local / Middle Atlantic (DC, DE, MD, NJ, NY, PA). I. Title.
ISBN: 978-1-899694-07-5, Trade Paper

Copyright © 2003 by Monica Randall

December 2022

PRAISE FOR MONICA RANDALL

"I know from personal experience that no one knows the social history of the North Shore of Long Island, the Aptly named Gold Coast, as well as Monica Randall does. Her book Winfield is a haunting and fascinating tale." —Dominick Dunne

"F. W. Woolworth's ornate and ominous Long Island mansion is the central character in this disquieting memoir, and the shadows it casts across Monica Randall's life linger disturbingly. This is a creepy and unsettling ghost story."
—J. P. Morrissey, author of *A Weekend at Blenheim*, on *Winfield*

"*Winfield* is a lovely creative treasure trove, memorably stocked with the Images, riches, adornments, and architectural wonders of the once opulent Gold Coast. Monica Randell, in poetic prose, has captured the essence and the excess of the age of F. Scott Fitzgerald and F. W. Woolworth with their oft tragic overtones."
—David D. Reed, author of *The President's Weekend*

"Her engaging text re-creates the glamorous era... Readers will be beguiled by photos of sumptuously decorated rooms and lavish formal gardens... The book is a rich evocation of a vanished time and lifestyle."
—*Publisher's Weekly* on *The Mansions of Long Island's Gold Coast*

"In spooky, sepia photographs and melodramatic text, Monica Randall captures her adventures roaming decrepit castles and foreboding Italianate abodes."
—*The New York Post* on *Phantoms of the Hudson Valley*

"Evocative."
—*The New York Times Book Review* on *Phantoms of the Hudson Valley*

"Brilliant... Extraordinary sepia-toned pictures and romantic words evocative of another time... A definitive— and unique—record of a long-forgotten era that is well worth remembering."
—Nancy Ruhlings, in *Victorian Homes*, on *Phantoms of the Hudson Valley*

The author photo on the back cover was taken in 1976
at Winfield's Showcase Ball. The gown, originally belonging to
Edna Woolworth and dating back to 1909,
was found by Monica in a greenhouse at Winfield.

WINFIELD

Living in the Shadow of the Woolworths

Monica Randall

Also by Monica Randall:

The Mansions of Long Island's Gold Coast

*Phantoms of the Hudson Valley:
The Glorious Estates
of a Lost Era*

In loving memory
To my dad and Sophie

Contents

1. Mrs. R. S. Reynolds *1*
2. Rescue Missions *22*
3. The Playhouse *35*
4. The Girls'-School Years *47*
5. The Auction *65*
6. André Von Brunner *71*
7. The Gold Rose *103*
8. Voices in the Night *114*
9. The Séance *131*
10. The Czar Comes to Winfield *145*
11. The Homecoming *156*
12. Pembroke *164*
13. The Greenhouse *173*
14. The Graphologist *181*
15. A Lion in the Ballroom *187*
16. The Halloween Party *195*
17. Gordon Merdock *208*
18. The Library *226*
19. Snowy Night in the City *240*
20. Woolworth's Vault *250*

Epilogue *267*
Author's Note *270*
Acknowledgments *271*
Selected Bibliography *274*

As a child I was haunted by a recurring dream. It came to me with visions, sounds, and sensations so vivid and compelling as to make my waking state pale by comparison. I dreamt that I came upon an abandoned palace in an undiscovered land, filled with the treasures of the ages. Its marble walls encompassed all that is beautiful in the world and created an effect so grand that the palace hardly seemed to be the work of human invention. Upon waking with its memory still fresh in my mind, I knew that I had been born in the wrong century.

WINFIELD

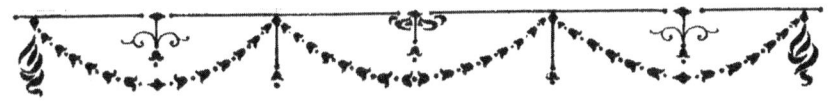

Chapter One

Mrs. R. S. Reynolds

Growing up on the North Shore of Long Island, I was surrounded by endless rolling hills and huge estates broken up occasionally by overgrown gardens, tennis courts, and towering rusting gates that were all that the outside world ever saw. You could walk for miles in this secretive land without encountering a single reminder of what century it was. Awesome manor houses seemed to brood atop their wooded bluffs. They stood there—empty ruins, haunting reminders of a time that will never come again. There were hundreds of them—the last survivors of what was known as the Gold Coast Era.

The faded remains of this flourish of Gilded Age creativity seemed endless. Miles of once-formal gardens surrounded by intricate mazes of topiary and clipped ilex had become a conquering jungle of weeds and vines that invaded greenhouses and long-abandoned swimming pools. Everywhere you turned, there were remnants of unique and unexpected things to delight the eye. On one property, a ruined Oriental pagoda with faded silk party lanterns stood moldering away at the far end of a lake.

Most of the estate properties were laid out without noticeable boundaries. One led to the other, and the interconnecting bridal paths were open to all who rode through on horseback. During the late 1950s, you could still hear the thundering hooves of a passing hunt and the wail of the bugle master's horn—the final generation of North Shore elite pursuing the all-but-extinct little fox.

The Gold Coast encompassed a twelve-mile ribbon of transplanted Europe. It reached its heyday during the 1920s. Italian villas, French châteaus, and feudal castles complete with moats were built without financial restrictions out of the profits of the industrial age from which they sprang. Once they built their mansions, the members of this elite society, regardless of where they came from, set out to play at being English. The Gold Coast was like a foreign country, and the old guard lived by a different set of rules and spoke with an unmistakable style and grace that were at times almost poetic. Ancestral portraits, bought at auction, covered their walls. Hunt clubs, polo games, and Edwardian teas became a way of life. Sprawling stables were built, even if the owners never set foot in them; horses were the thing.

To carry on this established tradition, as a teenager I took to horses with a passion. "No Trespassing" signs could be ignored if you cantered through the trails atop a fine thoroughbred. Each day after school I would escape into the wooded glades and follow the endless paths that led me back to those surreal and phantom realms that had long since cast their spell over me. In the days before development housing, you could gallop through the open fields in Old Westbury, past the long-abandoned Garvan and Winthrop estates, then past the massive racing stables of the Whitneys. Next over, on the Phipps estate, you could thunder down a mile long allée of towering linden trees. At its end there stood a great marble temple supported by eight life-sized stone Grecian goddesses. If you were careful, you could gallop through it, but you had to duck to clear the carved domed roof.

Ambrose Clarke's estate was every horseman's dream—thousands of acres surrounded by miles of split-rail fences. Horses of every kind and color grazed amid the bright yellow dandelions and daffodils in spring. Every day I took to those green fields and rode with soaring exhilaration, jumping the split-rail fences head-on as the sharp crackle of dead branches snapped under the horse's feet, and dry leaves flew up in clouds as we sped past.

During my long and restless wanderings, I took in the sumptuous spectacle of those crumbling architectural marvels—the flamboyant villas and turreted châteaus—as I rode by, believing they would stand forever. But no sooner had I found them than they began to be swept into oblivion. The era of development housing had begun.

My fascination with that lost world might not have become the all-consuming obsession that it was had I been to the manor born. But I was in fact an outsider, surrounded by a world that, had it still been flourishing, probably would not have accepted me. Though I longed to be one of them, this was never to be. But I took comfort in my secret knowledge and love of those places the old-guard families left behind. I loved them all and came to know their exotic-sounding names, and knew where they were hidden and how to get inside them.

Many of the empty manor houses stood on hilltops surrounded by towering black pine trees that swayed and resonated with the wilting sobs of mourning doves. It seemed they were always there, no matter what the weather or time of year. Day and night they droned on in a ghostly reign of grieving. That sound is inseparable from my memory of Farnsworth, a massive brick villa that once stood at the center of a glade of hemlock trees in Oyster Bay. Most of the locals knew about the place, and one way or another they had visited the site, ignoring the "No Trespassing" signs posted on the ancient trees that lined the long, winding drive. The estate's owner, Wallace C. Bird, had been killed in 1940 when his private plane crashed not far from his property. His grief-stricken wife ordered the plane wreckage crated and buried in the basement. Then she abandoned the house, leaving behind millions of dollars in furnishings and art treasures to molder over the next three decades. Her shocking death made headlines in 1962: it was discovered that her psychiatrist, who had stolen her fortune in jewels, had murdered her. Most of the locals agreed that the crumbling mansion had to be haunted, but there was no way to prove or disprove such tales. By that time all of the big houses had some kind of legend or scandal attached to them, including one house whose claim to fame was that its floors were paved with tombstones from children's graves. It seemed inevitable that rumors of ghosts wandering the shadowed corridors and cluttered attics would add to the melancholy mood of such places, but I only half listened, for I was not yet a believer in such things.

Farnsworth lay in ruins by the time the bulldozers arrived. The day demolition began, I watched in horror as plaster walls exploded and steel beams moaned before falling to earth. Within days, the building was reduced to a pile of rubble. Blackbirds passed swiftly over the site, making shrill cries as if in protest. I mourned the loss and wore black for a week. The destruction was devastating—not just because we were losing our old historic buildings; it went much deeper than that. As an artist, I found them the soul of inspiration, the be-all and end-all of everything I wanted to capture on film or to paint. They were the only things in life that moved me, and I was determined to breathe new life back into them and show the world their ruined, haunted beauty. There was something magical about the way light fell on ruins, the way the sun set on an overgrown garden. I was enchanted by the way the blue lunar light of the moon worked over the surfaces of marble statues in a deserted greenhouse, and there was something miraculous in the way that lilacs, cottage roses, and magnolias continued to burst forth for one last season, though no one was there to celebrate their last days on earth.

When I was fourteen, I was allowed to spend my weekends with an old school friend, Marian Crawford, who lived on one of the old estates off Piping Rock Road in Locust Valley. I reveled in that first experience of actually staying in one of the North Shore mansions and observing the comings and goings of the owners and their servants and gardeners as they went about their ordered tasks. On Saturday mornings, Marian and I would get up early and ride the estate's horses down to the nearby Creek Club. From there you could reach many of the grand places that were built along the water's edge. Vikings Cove, Ormston House, Peacock Point, and J. P. Morgan's Georgian manor house were all still in private hands. On any given day, you could observe the armies of men working feverishly to maintain them, but the keepers of that doomed enclave had been reduced to a handful of elderly members drawing their last breaths amid faded ballrooms that had not heard the sound of music since the Second World War. During the late fifties many of the Gold Coast's charming relics were still intact, and all along the waterfront, property lines were defined by neoclassic-style bath houses surrounded by long stretches of giant rocks that served as breakwaters. Many had private piers with gleaming white garden follies at the end. In their day, these ornate shore pavilions provided a perfect setting for yacht christenings and breezy summer picnics while seagulls and herons surged gloriously around their peaked rooftops. They're all gone now; the sea claimed them one by one.

One morning Marian and I packed a picnic lunch, then tacked up two of the quarter horses and headed out towards Welwyn, where a Gothic-styled pavilion stood precariously on a pile of jagged rocks. Years of storms and hurricanes had taken their toll, and the carved wooden balustrades that once surrounded the structure had long since tumbled into the salty depths. We left the horses on the beach, then made our way along the slippery three-hundred-foot rock jetty to reach the pavilion. We ate our modest lunch as the ceiling rafters creaked like an old ship and the sea crashed around us. The dramatic setting, the smell of the salt air, and the very real danger in being there were all part of the place's allure.

Marian, oblivious to danger, was quick to inform me that the estate's owner, the elderly Mrs. Harold Erving Pratt, no longer came down to the beach. But on a good day you would almost always find one of the colorful old-timers who worked for her fishing off the rocks—men who loved to spin tales about the glory days of rum-running and outrageous parties.

The beaches, though private, were generally visited by anyone who cared to wander by, and the sight of horses galloping along the water's edge was common. On that day we sat and talked in our Island hideaway for most of the afternoon and marveled at the occasional sight of old sailing yachts as they moved along the sound, their great white sails billowing in the wind. Marian recognized the *Matuta*, from nearby Peacock Point. It was followed by a massive yacht called the *Avosette*, which Marian claimed was owned by a prince. But grand as they were, The Long Island Sound was no longer resplendent with the great sailing ships, like the *Vigilante, Columbia,* and *Resolute* and J. P. Morgan's *Corsair*.

We watched the tide come in until the chilling water reached our bare feet as they dangled over the side of the pavilion's stone floor. Seagulls swooped and darted around us as we broke off pieces of bread and threw them out on the surrounding rocks. We were as happy as two teenagers could be as we talked about what we were going to make of our lives. My friend had sensible goals for her future, but I confessed to her that all I could think about were the ruins.

"There's not much call for ruin worshipers," she said good-naturedly.

"I guess not, but I want to capture all the ruins on film before it's too late," I said solemnly.

"Better move fast—I saw bulldozers over at the old Belmont place the other day," she said, reaching down into the water to pull up a piece of shiny green seaweed.

We began to make our way back to shore as a speedboat came barreling down the sound, creating fast-moving waves that headed towards us. Marion slipped and fell as a wave washed over her. She screamed with delight and giggled all the way back to the beach. Having been soaked to the skin, she took off on her horse and headed back to the house. I wanted to prolong what had been a perfect day and climbed back on the horse and headed west along the water's edge, then turned left, entering a forest of towering white pines and following an unfamiliar dirt path that eventually came out on Crescent Beach Road. Before long, I found myself standing before a huge marble arch that resembled the Arc de Triomphe in Paris. Etched into one of the stone blocks was the name "Winfield." The gate was locked and surrounded by an eight-foot iron fence, but in the distance I could make out the outline of a very large building standing in a thicket of trees. An old road appeared to go around the property line, and eventually I came upon a second gate, bound loosely with a rusty chain and padlock. The horse snorted when I climbed down and tied him to a nearby tree. He watched as if annoyed as I struggled with the chain and finally squeezed past the gate.

Inside there was a path of linden trees whose ancient branches formed an arch like a cathedral nave. The road looked as though no one had used it in decades, with knotty roots jutting up from open gullies and vines that stretched across the wide path and wound around some fallen branches. At the end of the allée, there was a long endless flight of wide marble stairs. I began to climb them, then looked up and caught sight of what appeared to be an abandoned palace.

From the bottom of those great marble stairs, the house rose up like a majestic phantom lost in time. It was late in the day, and liquid light gilded the marble in the west wing in shades of richest gold as it caught the last rays of sunlight. I continued to move as if something were pulling me towards it, then climbed another set of stairs flanked by a pair of giant stone lions. At the landing vines of ivy engulfed a tiled veranda that encircled the west wing of the house. A pair of tall French doors with thick red-velvet drapes pulled back with gold-tasseled braid stood open. Overcome with curiosity, I entered the room and caught sight of the most breathtaking ballroom. The ceiling was all fourteen-karat gold, and from its center a huge crystal chandelier was lit and seemed to explode in a shimmering rainbow of light. Mythological beasts, some snarling and sinister, danced amid the carvings of a towering alabaster fireplace.

Just then, some pigeons that had been roosting along a ledge of the veranda outside began to coo and flap their wings noisily. I quickly retreated from the open door and headed down the terrace steps, turning into a formal garden lush and fragrant with roses of every kind. There was a huge fountain surrounded by a limestone balustrade partly hidden under a blanket of moss. Streams of water played over a marble nymph perched high on a pedestal, where she seemed to hover between heaven and earth. Then I moved past a maze of clipped boxwood that led to an oval courtyard, and I was stunned by the sight of dozens of giant marble statues of Greek gods lining the long drive. They stood like sentries, casting dark shadows that stretched across the wide gravel drive. For a second I thought they might spring to life, leap from their pedestals, and chase me back to where I came from, but they stood there silent in their deserted park. It was getting late, but I was unable to turn away. A deathlike stillness hung over everything as I watched the last rays of light slip from the marble walls and stone gods. The house seemed strangely familiar, and I remembered my childhood dream.

The spell was suddenly broken when a water rat ran out from a garden wall and almost brushed past me, then turned sharply and headed up towards the house. It formed an unsettling dark spot against the frozen radiance of the scene, and I quickly made my way back down the long allée. I stopped and looked back once more at the lone chandelier that continued to blaze in the distance like a diamond against black velvet. The path, now dark, became a scary place as the mourning doves hidden in the black bowers of branches sang out like a chorus of forest angels. As I slipped out the rusting gate, I knew I'd be back, but I had no way of knowing then that I would one day live there.

A year or two passed before I returned to Winfield, having been content with the lingering memory of discovering it. From time to time I would ride past the house to reassure myself that it was still there. The lawns were manicured, the gardens flourished, and at night lights went on in the mansion. Each time I went past the property it was with the intention of trying to make contact with the owner. But I was timid about approaching the very rich.

In that private enclave of estates, the rules were different from elsewhere in the country. If you were a native of the area, lived on or near one of the large properties, rode horses, or took an interest in local worthwhile causes, then — rich or poor — you were accepted up to a point. Horses broke down the barriers between the classes, but only if you rode English, and proper attire was a must. My presence was somehow tolerated, though some thought it odd that I always carried a camera, even when riding on horseback. The horses allowed for a legitimate means of gaining access to the estates, and the camera was a way to keep a visual record of the doomed buildings at the same time. The two became my entrée into that privileged world.

On the day I finally wandered back to Winfield, I had neither a camera nor a horse. Purely on impulse I took a chance and entered the south gate, where a series of rambling greenhouses ran along an ivy-covered wall. To the right of the gate, there was a large stucco carriage house that overlooked the cutting garden where an old, frail-looking man in a straw hat was kneeling before a mound of dirt, intent on planting a shrub. He looked up, then pointed towards the building as though he thought I was expected. I smiled back at him and moved towards the greenhouse until I came to a tall arched door with intricate ironwork supporting a glass dome. I pressed my nose against the glass to get a better look inside, then wondered if I should go any farther. Suddenly from inside I heard a loud screeching noise, and, curious, I opened the door. In the center of the room, there stood a large ornate white Victorian cage with its door open. Perched on its roof was a parrot that was apparently free to come and go as it pleased. The bird was preening its lush green-and-peach feathers and contentedly making strange whistling sounds as I entered the room.

"Hello, you pretty thing," I said softly, and moved closer to it. It began to whistle excitedly, did a complete turn on the roof of its cage, and went back to smoothing its feathers with its large gray beak. I gazed about the room, which was diffused by layers of frosty white paint that had begun to peel off the glass walls and ceiling. At the far corner was a fountain made of fossil coral, with water trickling down it. All around were huge wooden tubs lush with ferns that flourished in the heavy humid air. It smelled of rich earth and growing plants that were alive and fragrant, and seemed to radiate with energy. At one end of the room, a glass-enclosed arbor led to another wing. When I reached it, I could hear the sound of clipping shears. Then I spotted an elderly woman with hair the color of carrots, cutting masses of pink carnations. At first glance, she appeared to be talking to someone who was either hidden from view by one of the large palm trees or crouched under one of the long plant counters. As I moved closer, I realized there was no one else there.

"Searching for stars through ceaseless rain," she said to herself softly; then she put the flowers down and reached over to grab a fountain pen, quickly writing something down on a notepad next to her. There was an imperceptible pause as she went back to cutting flowers.

"Through ceaseless rain," she repeated again to herself, "with face against the windowpane."

She had not seen me enter the room, and in that moment I almost turned back. She wrote some more lines on the paper, then looked up at the steel rafters in the ceiling, and her eyes followed the trail of a flowering vine that was clinging to it. She began to scan the room, then saw me.

"Hello," I said timidly, clearing my throat nervously. There was no response as she regarded me curiously, then smiled.

"Hello," she said, her voice faltering a bit, a faint flush on her cheeks. "Oh, you've come to pick up the orchids," she said placing her pen down on her writing pad.

"Orchids . . . no. Forgive my intruding this way, but are you the owner of . . . this lovely place?" I asked suddenly, at a loss for words.

She didn't answer at first but continued to stare in a quizzical way.

"You startled me. I thought you were . . . someone else," she said softly in what sounded like a Southern accent. Then she went back to clipping carnations. "I've owned the house since nineteen-twenty-nine."

"It's the most beautiful house I've ever seen," I said, relieved to find her so friendly.

"Oh, it was magnificent once, years ago when my husband and I first bought it. It was built by F. W. Woolworth, you know, the five-and-ten-cent-store man. It was quite the place then, but he had seventy-five gardeners. I'm glad I had a chance to see how it looked then, but each year it grows more and more unruly. I was just a bride when I first came here; the gardens were filled with all kinds of wonderful blooms—lemon of latana, pink verbena, and fancy trellises covered with gardenias. The scent would make your head swim. Angelo, who's almost eighty, takes care of the grounds now and just about everything else. It's too much—

too much for an old man; he's been here since Woolworth's day," she said sadly as she gazed down at her bouquet, touching it gently as though she were seeing flowers for the first time.

"Do you need help? I mean I'd be happy just to pick weeds in the garden — not for money or anything. I would be happy just to come by now and then, just to be surrounded by so much beauty."

"A lady gardener; I like that," she said, smiling. "Where do you come from, my dear?"

"I'm staying with friends for the weekend — the Crawfords in Locust Valley — so I rode over here on my bicycle."

"How nice," she said absently as she snipped and evened out the stems. She then bent down to cut some ferns to add to her bouquet. "I must go up to the house and put these lovely flowers in water before they wither." As she turned to walk towards the door, I took note of her dress. It was somewhat long, with the look and cut of decades past. She appeared to me to be a charming anachronism from a time of grander ways, with an eccentric bubbliness that matched her vibrant hair. Time had given her a softness and sweetness that conveyed an innocent, trusting nature. There were tiny webs of wrinkles around her eyes, but you could see by her high cheekbones that she must have been a beauty in her day. There was a naturalness and majesty about her that put me at ease.

"Have you been to the house yet?" she asked.

"Oh, no. It has always been my dream to go inside."

"Then you know the place?"

"Well, no. I was here some time ago and saw it from the gate," I said, not daring to admit I'd gone further than that.

"Come, I'll show you," she said as a faint smile played around her mouth. I think my heart skipped a beat at the suggestion, and I found I was more excited about seeing that house than I'd ever been about anything. I followed her as she started up across the sprawling lawn.

"That's the belvedere," she said as she pointed to a lavish fountain on the left, at the foot of the drive. "That marvelous creature in the center, rising from the shell surrounded by dolphins, is King Neptune." She continued to walk languidly across the emerald green lawn as though she had all the time in the world. As we neared the house, its brooding gray walls seemed to grow larger. Its atmosphere was that of a derelict grandeur. A pillared portico stretched out from the front door, which looked like a giant ornate bronze gate backed by thick glass so you could see through it. The door was open. As she entered it, I paused a bit too long before following her inside.

"Come, come child," she said suddenly, seeming impatient. The huge, ornate bronze door slammed shut behind us with jolting finality. Before I realized it, she had disappeared down one of the hallways. I was not sure if I should follow her, but something told me to wait for her to return. *The flowers,* I thought to myself. *She must have gone to put the flowers in water.* I stood there afraid to breathe, not sure just how to act in such a place. I looked up at the vast ceiling, which appeared to float up forever. For a second I felt dizzy just from the sight and vastness of it. The ceiling was lavishly carved and embellished with gold-and-blue designs. Above the polished marble staircase hung a gigantic chandelier supported by winged cherubim. I heard Mrs. Reynolds's voice again before I could see her.

"There was a time when we had fresh-cut flowers in all the rooms all year round—even when my husband and I were away in Europe. They made the house so fragrant and pretty," she said, her face hidden by the massive bouquet now arranged in a large Chinese vase. She glanced about the hall, looking from one table to the next. With a gentle nod of her head, she walked over to the far side of the room and placed the arrangement on top of a massive, carved-oak desk covered with a gold-fringed shawl. She stood back and regarded it for a moment, then removed a stem and placed it elsewhere amid the colorful blooms. I tried to take in the surroundings all at once.

"I've never seen anything so grand ever," I said, feeling my words were inadequate.

"Yes, I suppose it is. You get so . . . when you live in a place too long; you don't see the beauty as much. It takes a pair of fresh young eyes to remind you," she said with a welcoming smile. "Woolworth was quite a visionary. He designed most of the house himself. I'm told it cost him about nine million dollars—that was a king's ransom in those days. The first Winfield stood on this very spot, but a fire destroyed most of it in nineteen-sixteen. No one was really sure what caused it, but there were rumors that Mrs. Woolworth set fire to the drapes in a fitful rage. Come, I'll show you something very interesting," she said as she walked across the room towards a towering, medieval, marble fireplace flanked by a pair of gilt lion-headed thrones covered with red-velvet and gold-braided upholstery. "Look up there," she said, pointing up to a marble coat of arms. "Woolworth had the crest designed when he built the house. That's Mr. Woolworth up there on top, wearing a fancy plumed warrior's helmet. That poor creature below him is Mrs. Woolworth, in the iron helmet that completely covers her face."

She continued to stare up at it, then added in a contemplative tone, "One wonders about the character of a man who would do such a cruel thing to his wife, out there in the main hall for all to see. Below her on the shield are of course their three pretty daughters, Helena, Edna, and Jessie. Do you see the crack running through the face of the second one? That was Edna. They say she took her own life; no one knows why." There was a sense of drama and gravity in her voice as she went on to reveal: "On the night it happened, I heard that Woolworth was entertaining some guests in the music room. Suddenly a storm broke out, and from nowhere a bolt of lightning struck the mantel and caused it to crack. But you can see that the crack only runs through the image of the second girl, Edna. It wasn't until the next morning that she was found dead in her room."

I stared up at the mantel, fascinated by the cold, compelling eyes of its creator and the shameless arrogance it conveyed. Then I saw Mrs. Reynolds turn sharply and dart into the dark-paneled dining room to the right. She flicked on a switch, and the walls glittered with sterling silver and mirrored wall sconces and a pair of chandeliers that hung from an ivory, Elizabethan plasterwork ceiling. To the left was a glassed-in palm court with faun green trellised walls and a marble mythological beast spewing water into a fountain. The clicking of heels on the marble floor stopped suddenly as my guide walked across the lush green rug and into another large room with a huge, ornately carved billiard table in the center. Gazing down from the rich mahogany-paneled walls were several dusty mounted heads of deer, elk, and moose and one ferocious creature I didn't recognize as belonging to the known animal kingdom.

"What is that?" I asked, pointing up at it. Her face assumed a puzzled expression as though she'd never taken note of it.

"Lord knows," she said, dismissing it from her mind as she swept through a swinging door that led into the kitchen, where a man in uniform was chopping some vegetables. She quickly gave him some instructions in a language I did not understand; then, leaving him, she returned to the billiard room to resume the tour.

"The second floor is most unusual; I'll show you." She swept past the dining room and into the dining hall, then started up the wide marble stairs. Halfway up she paused to catch her breath. "The elevator is on the blink again, so we'll have to persevere on our own steam," she said with a moan.

A balustrade ran along the length of the staircase landing and along the top balcony to the second floor. When we finally reached the top, I was breathless with wonder. She pointed to a lavish room straight ahead.

"That's the Empress Josephine room; it belonged to Miss Salters, who was Mr. Woolworth's constant companion. She attended to all his needs. Her room connects to his; it is just as she left it." There was a long hallway that seemed to go on forever, finally ending with a screened-in summer porch decorated with large, comfortable rattan club chairs covered with pale, faded, floral chintz cushions.

"Mr. Woolworth's old room is here in the west wing," she said almost reverently as she gently opened the gold-trimmed door, as if not to disturb anyone who might be inside. "Woolworth was rather obsessed, I'm told, with Napoleon. It's an exact duplicate of one of Napoleon's rooms. All the furniture is original, including the sleigh bed," she said with an attitude of superiority and pride. I stood there fascinated by what was the grandest display of unfettered extravagance I'd ever seen. Most of the furnishings were embossed with distinctive laurel wreaths surrounding the letter N in the center. Hanging over the huge Empire bed was a round gold canopy with a fleur-de-lis design. From it hung a pair of red-and-gold drapes tied back with swags of braided, tasseled cords. She stood there long enough to see that I was duly impressed, then moved on to the bath. The all-marble bathroom blazed as mirrors reflected gold fixtures and upper wall moldings decorated with the imperial gold bees. The bathtub was made from a solid block of salmon pink Sienna marble and had a gold, swan-shaped faucet.

"In all the years I've been here, I've never dared to bathe in that tub," she said, staring down at its gleaming surface.

"Why?"

"I don't really know; I fear I'd be struck by lightning or something. . . . It's silly of me, I know," she responded. Then quickly she turned and was out the door and back in the hall, where she began opening each door in turn.

It was like floating through a time tunnel where you could visit every period in history. On the front of each door was a brass plaque that identified the name of each room. There was the Edwardian room, with its fine oak paneling; next to it was a room with a large painting of Alexander the Great. At the top of the stairs, in the Empress Josephine room, a long, balustraded terrace could be seen through a bank of tall glass doors.

On our left was the Elizabethan room, the Louis XVI room, and a dark and somber room replicating some objects once belonging to Charlemagne. The Gothic room had a high-vaulted ceiling with a carved stone mantel; further down, two rooms represented the Far East. She stopped to point out the value of a richly carved desk in a room labeled the Sheridan room.

As Mrs. Reynolds methodically went about the house, intent on not leaving out any details or points of intrigue, I wondered if she realized the effect that this spectacle was having on me. It seemed to nourish some inner chord of longing that had lain dormant for a long time. Yet as we wandered past this eerie tableau of history, she moved from room to room as though giving a tour in a wax museum. It did not appear as though she had any real feeling for her possessions, since they had not been of her own creation or design but someone else's. Nevertheless, she clearly enjoyed showing them to someone new. She stopped for a moment, her arms resting on the rail of the servants' staircase; with her free hand she smoothed down some strands of her red hair.

"Well, what do you think?" she asked with restless curiosity.

"It's like an incredible dream," I answered, caught off guard. She nodded her head and drew in a breath.

"Yes, it is a dream—Woolworth's dream. He was a lucky man to have realized so much in one lifetime," she said, moving quickly ahead but passing one door on the right.

"You skipped one," I said a little hesitantly.

"It's a replica of Marie Antoinette's room. I keep it locked. It's always so cold in that room, even in summer," she said, continuing to walk down the hall. I had the sense of something being withheld.

"Do you suppose anyone ever used these rooms?"

"Mr. Woolworth was a very curious man. . . . No one was ever sure of the exact purpose of these rooms. It seems to go beyond just a love of art and history. He was fascinated by things of a mystical nature. I'm told he spent most of his time in his library, studying ancient mysteries and the lives of famous historic figures. He was quite a scholar on the subject; it was a side of him that no one knew about."

"How did Mrs. Woolworth fit into all this?" I asked.

"Interesting question; her room is down here at the opposite end of the house, as far away from her husband as could be."

I followed as she walked to the end of the east wing; she waved her hand absently and pointed.

"That was Mrs. Woolworth's room. It's rather odd that it's so plain. There's no theme or representation of any great character in history; just a bed, a dresser, and an old rocking chair, and no draperies. From what I heard, she was a bit dotty and was rarely allowed to leave this room. Who wouldn't go mad locked up here year after year? When she was alive, there used to be a huge tapestry that hung over the outside of her door, so that anyone visiting the house wouldn't even know there was a room behind it. Kind of a replay on the coat of arms downstairs," she said with a degree of compassion.

"How did she survive?"

"There was a nurse who watched over her day and night. There was another entrance to the room around back," she murmured in a hushed tone.

"No one thought that strange? I mean, the servants must have known."

She looked at me inquisitively. "The servants wouldn't dare say anything. Most of them were immigrants; they knew their place," she said as she turned to leave.

I took one last look at the dreary room, then noticed a large glass dome standing on a pedestal in the corner. Inside there were several exotic birds; their frozen glass eyes seemed to stare out at us vacantly. *Poor Mrs. Woolworth*, I thought to myself. We were halfway down the hall when a voice called out from the bottom of the stairs.

"Mrs. Reynolds . . . if you please, Mrs. Babcock come. She need for you to pick out the orchids." It was the gardener; he was holding his hat with both hands respectfully as he spoke in broken English.

"Oh, I almost forgot. You must excuse me—I promised the orchids for the Red Cross fund-raiser. I won't be long. There's so much more to see yet," she said, rushing down the stairs.

"Oh, no. I've taken up too much of your time already. I must get back; my family doesn't know I'm here," I said quickly.

"Then you must come back and see me soon. Promise."

I thanked her for everything, then slipped out the way I came. Outside the gate I stood for a moment and had to pinch myself to be sure I hadn't been dreaming. There was a strange similarity between Winfield and the house I had dreamt about years before. The grand scale of it, architectural style, atmosphere, placement of objects, even the fragrant smell of flowers were all strangely familiar. Even then, a part of me knew I would become ensnared somehow in its melancholy beauty and enigma.

I waited several weeks before returning, as I wanted to bring Mrs. Reynolds some token of appreciation. At first I thought of flowers, but then I decided that anything from a commercial store would seem shabby after seeing her exotic greenhouse. Finally, at the local library, I came across a full-page ad that appeared in *Town & Country* magazine in 1929 that showed several photographs of Winfield taken during Woolworth's day. It listed the house and eighteen acres for sale for considerably less than what it had cost to build. Then I realized 1929 was the year of the great Wall Street crash. I had a copy made of the page, then took it home and framed it. I was excited about giving it to Mrs. Reynolds, but even more excited about returning to her Glen Cove estate.

I arrived to find Mrs. Reynolds alone, having tea on the massive west veranda, which was all but covered in vines. She appeared to be writing some more verses on her notepad when she saw me approaching the wide marble stairs. She was pleased with the magazine layout and said that she remembered seeing the house when it still looked that way, but that as the years passed, it became more and more impossible to keep things up.

"Places like this are beautiful to look at, but they can drain the life out of you unless you have an army to help," she said, seeming a little sad, perhaps at how much it had changed. For some time she did not look up but sat quite motionless, holding the framed layout in her hand; it seemed to evoke some long-buried memories of her early life there. But she surprised me and began to speak of Woolworth instead, saying that she had never actually met him. But some of the help stayed on after she and her husband bought the property, and with their former master dead and buried, they felt free to talk.

"You missed seeing the best room in the house when you were here last. Woolworth's treasure was his gilded music room." She waved her hand towards the open French doors that led off the porch. With her head held high, she stood up, set the frame down on the wicker tea tray, and moved into the house. The room was overpowering—even larger and grander than I remembered. It was filled with heavy gilt pieces of French furniture that gave the feeling of never having been used. At the far end of the room stood a gold baroque-rococo piano with heavenly scenes painted in panels all round it. Above, the massive chandelier caught the light of the sun and made fleeting patterns on the dark-patterned walls and fourteen-carat-gold ceiling. I felt strangely uneasy, as though I was invading a shrine meant for another; for all its grandeur, there was a feeling of desolation and emptiness about it.

Mrs. Reynolds, who was small in stature, seemed dwarfed by the room as she gazed about, taking note of the dust and cobwebs. "Woolworth was tone-deaf but loved music. I was told he had a live-in organist on hand to come and play for him whenever the spirit moved him. From what I understand, the room was somehow rigged like a sound stage, and he gave gala theatrical recitals here. Over there by the organ were huge, life-sized portraits of musical greats throughout history, and somehow the portraits were lowered down from the ceiling whenever those composers' compositions were being played. There were even colored stage lights that flashed and special effects—thunder and lightning and haunting chimes and gongs to enhance dramatic parts of the music. Of course, we had all that theatrical stuff removed." She turned and pointed up to the south wall. "Up there . . . behind those filigree panels, there are hidden rooms and chambers. The organ pipes run from the basement up to the third floor, but nobody knows about those rooms. You can look out from there and see everything going on in this room without anyone seeing you."

"How odd. How do you get up there?" I asked, wondering if it would be part of the tour.

"Oh, that's a secret; this house has lots of secrets," she said matter-of-factly.

"Do you play the organ?" I asked.

"A little. Years ago, when it worked properly, you could hear it all the way down to the beach. But the bellows are shot—it would cost a fortune to repair them."

I detected a nostalgic lilt in her voice as she moved slowly off to the left, then reached up to press something in the wall. Suddenly there was an unsettling rumble that shook the room slightly. Then, slowly, the entire wall began to move, its panels receding into a pocket. A moment later, a small stage or platform extended out into the room several feet; rising up from it was a Gothic organ console with long wooden slats extending from the base. With a graceful wave of her hand, she sat down before it and began running her fingers across the keyboard. She suddenly seemed electrified by the room and its curious wonders; her head began to move back and forth as though she were caught up in some private reverie. As she moved her fingers across the keys, she began to hum some obscure melody with a look of great concentration on her face, but no sound came out of the organ. I stood utterly still, hardly daring to breathe. I continued to watch her, not knowing what to think as her foot pressed and worked the pedals below. Her arms extended over the aged ivory keys as they clicked at the touch of her small, delicate fingers.

"I can feel the notes; the music is in my head," she said finally. "It's a sound you can never forget. The whole house would vibrate; there was a resonance, a richness to it that filled your soul," she said as she continued her phantom playing. But the only sound in the room was the plaintive ticking of the grotesquely ornate clock that stood on top of the mantelshelf. Finally, she gave a deep sigh as if to signal her return to the here and now.

Mrs. Reynolds, like so many widows of means, seemed lonely and isolated within herself, as though she lived apart from the rest of the world. It wouldn't have occurred to me then to think that the atmosphere of the house could affect one's personality, but the shifting quality of her moods struck me. I thought that perhaps it was due to her age that she drifted off at times; still, I found her and her stories fascinating. I saw her several times after that, as she seemed to enjoy my visits and my longing to help in the garden amused her. I sensed at times that sharing the tarnished splendor of her surroundings perhaps rekindled some feeling she had lost for them. However, for the most part, she clearly seemed overwhelmed by the rapid deterioration and neglect. I for one found marauding vines and cobwebs charming, and it was comforting to see that over the years nothing ever happened to disturb the tranquil atmosphere of the place. But all that was to change in the spring of 1963.

On the last day I was ever to see Mrs. Reynolds, I found her rummaging around in an abandoned wing of the greenhouse I hadn't seen before. Part of the glass ceiling had been struck by a fallen tree and was now covered with a huge piece of canvas to keep out the rain. The room was piled ceiling high with boxes and broken garden ornaments. Off in a darkened corner I found Mrs. Reynolds hunched over, struggling with an old steamer trunk. I moved towards her and offered to help.

"Clutter, clutter," she mumbled to herself. "I must do something about this clutter. I can't seem to bring myself to throw anything away." She finally forced the trunk lock open. "Some of these things have been here since Woolworth's day. Now the rats are making nests in them," she said, staring down into whatever was inside the box.

"What are they?" I asked.

"Old clothes," she said casually, pulling out an old gown as dust and lint fibers seemed to fall from the disintegrating fabric. "Look, they even have whalebone corsets built into them, for waistlines the size of a mouse. I remember my mother wearing such things. One could barely breathe in these dresses; girls used to faint dead away. They would drop like flies from lack of oxygen." Her hands moved very quickly through the clothes as she talked. "Women paid a high price for beauty in those days, and it sometimes proved fatal. I wonder if one realizes that today."

"Fatal?" I repeated, not sure what she meant.

"Yes, those corsets were deadly, causing all kinds of medical problems that no one ever talked about."

I wanted to hear more, but I was distracted as she began pulling out one breathtaking creation after another. The heady smell of mildew filled the air as frail, decaying silk, lace, and gauze evening gowns came tumbling out of the trunk. The years had mellowed them to faded shades of beige mauve and salmon pink. The bodice of one shimmered with tiny glass beads, satin roses, and clusters of seed pearls. Another had a full skirt of voluminous layers of silk embroidered with flowering tendrils of lace, the ghost of now-rancid perfume still clinging to it. I stood there staring at them in complete rapture. There was about them an evocative beauty that decay could not change—beauty that, despite time, neglect, and ruin, was still alive in those ethereal fibers.

"Such pretty things they must have been," she said finally, tossing them aside.

"You're not going to throw them away?" I asked nervously. She looked up at me, a lock of orange hair falling across her forehead.

"What possible use could they be? They're falling apart," she said firmly.

"Perhaps a museum would take them; they're treasures. We can't duplicate them today—it's a lost art," I said, unable to bear the idea of them being destroyed.

"But they're disintegrating before our very eyes," she insisted. I reached over to touch one of them, feeling its softness as though each silk thread and fiber were alive. Without thinking, I turned and looked her in the eye.

"They can be restored. There's a way. I remember seeing them do it at the Metropolitan Museum of Art in the costume wing. I'll find a way."

"Then they're yours," she said softly.

"Thank you." I said, overjoyed. Just then, one of the workmen pulled up in an old truck filled with dozens of large boxes.

"Mrs. Reynolds, where should I put these?" he yelled out over the sporadic rumbling of the engine. She pulled her thin sweater around her, walked over to him, and peered inside the truck.

"You have more room; collect the orchids, palms, and ferns and take everything over to Slowtide," she said, watching him with apprehension as he pulled the truck around to the back of the greenhouse.

"Are you going away?"

"I'm afraid so. This house has become such a burden, with my husband gone and not enough people to help. . . . I'm just getting too old to keep it up," she said, turning her head in the direction of the house, with a remote, unseeing look in her eyes.

"It's been sold, you know," she said, with an empty resignation. "The new people are going to make it into some kind of school for young ladies. I think that would be a nice change . . . put some new life into the place. Old Woolworth would like that, I should think." She showed no emotion about leaving the house that she and her husband had lived in for over thirty years. She went about the business of sorting, packing, and discarding the multitudinous paraphernalia she had accumulated, as though her possessions had somehow betrayed her. There was about her a hurried impatience I hadn't seen before, as though she wanted to leave as quickly as possible. Then, very suddenly, she stopped working, seeming to remember something that needed to be done elsewhere. Without saying a word, I watched her turn and walk towards the house, her walk revealing her sturdy independent character. I never saw her again, but I was to read some twenty years later that when she passed away she was almost a century old.

I returned sometime later and found the front gate locked. The south gate by the greenhouse was also bound with a chain. Entering in my usual fashion, through the west gate, I ran up the allée of linden trees, then up the marble stairs and found the house deserted. Peering in through the front door, I could see that all the furnishings were still in place just as they had always been, only now everything was covered with white muslin sheets, giving the room a vague aura of sorrow.

On the left wall there hung a large, round gilt rococo mirror, with gold Cupids hovering between a pair of ornate candle brackets that extended out from it. The convex shape of the glass reflected the entire room like some great, bulging panofic eye. In the mirror's reflection of the room, I noticed that one of the heavy Gothic thrones had been moved and was now standing beneath the massive fireplace. The sheet that had covered it looked as though it had been pulled to the floor, where it now lay in a heap. A strange thought entered my mind as I stared at the chair now facing the mantel. It looked as though someone or *something* had resumed his or its position of authority. A week later there was an announcement in the local paper that Winfield would soon become the Grace Downs School for Girls, and that classes would begin in the fall.

It would never be the same again. I felt the queerest sense of despair and utter loss, and in trying to still the sadness, I decided to stay away altogether. I had seen it all too often — what happened to the great manor houses when they were sold, broken up, subdivided, or turned into schools and institutions. The buildings remained, but the magic was gone. Over the next few years I continued to explore what little remained of the Long Island estates; it was during the sixties that some of the grandest country houses went down.

Chapter Two

Rescue Missions

During the fifties and sixties living anywhere on the North Shore of Long Island was like being in a war zone. The land rumbled with the constant sound of the wrecker's ball striking relentlessly at what remained of the Gold Coast mansions. All during the day, six days a week, the steady drone of bulldozers could be heard in the distance. No preservationists fought to save the mansions, no heirs came to reclaim them, and no elegies were given to mark their sudden extinction from this earth.

During those terrible years, I ran about frantically, trying to capture their final moments on film as the estates went down in a spectacular blaze of glory. I stood by helplessly as the destroyers stripped the earth of all trees and exotic shrubs and plowed under the gardens and their ornaments until there was nothing left but a desert of sand.

It is hard to imagine the amount of destruction that took place in such a short period of time, but it is estimated that between 1958 and 1968 around 450 of the original estates went down. Today only about 100 of them remain. The downfall began with the stock market crash of 1929, which was followed by the Great Depression, escalating taxes, and the rising cost of heating fuel. But the Second World War finally brought to an abrupt end the era of grand living. This was due largely to the hundreds of servants required to sustain the estates. Typically, a property with hundreds of acres and vast formal gardens employed seventy-five men to keep it in perfect order. Almost all of the estates maintained enormous stables requiring dozens of grooms, stablehands, and live-in vets. Then there were the farm and dairy workers, chauffeurs, butler, wine stewards, chambermaids, laundresses, cooks, silver and brass polishers, valets, and chimney sweepers.

When the war broke out, most of the men were drafted, and with the possibility of their not returning, the idea of hosting grand parties became unseemly, as did many other pastimes of the rich. Luxury yachts were turned over to the government to help the war effort. Many of the big houses were closed up and abandoned, and they soon became designated ruins.

One of the great losses in all this was Laurelton Hall, the hundred-room Moorish villa designed by Louis Comfort Tiffany. Set on a hill overlooking Oyster Bay Harbor, it housed Tiffany's life's work of stained-glass windows along with unique giant crystal fountains and other priceless examples of his art. During the fifties Tiffany's work had not yet been recognized, nor was it revered as it is today, and with the house left abandoned, vandals set fire to it. The fire burned for a week, turning the skies over the little village black until the winds from the sound blew the smoke away. As flames consumed the house and its treasures, little was done to stop them. There was such an attitude of indifference towards the old Gold Coast way of life that one witness of the fire recalled that even members of the local fire department took delight in throwing beer cans at the doomed forty-foot wall containing the stained-glass mural known as *The Bathers*. In today's money, the destruction of the fabled building and of what was inside it represents a billion-dollar loss. Only the front stone facade, with its mosaic tiled pillars, survived the fire; it is now housed in a wing at the Metropolitan Museum of Art.

Beacon Towers, the Sands Point castle that inspired F. Scott Fitzgerald to write *The Great Gatsby*, was bulldozed because the owners could no longer pay the taxes on it. Some houses stood abandoned for decades with all their furnishings left inside.

Furguson's Castle, a great stone fortress on a cliff overlooking Hunting Harbor, was believed to be haunted. A "For Sale" sign hung on its gate for decades with no offers. When it was finally bulldozed, it went down with millions of dollars worth of imported ancient artwork, including dozens of twelfth-century icons, two Della Robbias, and the famed *Reclining Angel* by Michelangelo.

No one seemed to care or take notice—not the police, the landed gentry, or the local historical societies, who considered the buildings too new to be of any historic value. Land developers were oblivious, indifferent, and often ignorant of what they were destroying. Often no provisions were made to inspect a property to salvage the artwork or investigate its historic origins. Ironically, there were cases where a developer destroyed objects that were worth more than the money he made by developing the land.

One day in spring, one of the largest estates in Lattingtown was about to be leveled. I was there the day demolition began, taking photographs of it going down wing by wing, when I saw something about to happen and could no longer stand still. At the far end of a crystal-and-gold ballroom, there stood an alabaster mantel of such undefinable beauty, it almost made me cry just to look at it. Across its facade there were allegorical scenes of exquisitely carved angels with fairy wings, whose delicate fingers and luminous eyes appeared to beckon and speak of everything divine. It was poetry frozen in marble, and it appeared to glow from within with an ethereal light. I used to visit the site and stare at it for hours, and I had come to the conclusion that if a thing of such beauty could be created by human hands, it had to reflect some eternal truth that was not of this world. Years before, one of the caretakers who had worked on the estate in its heyday had told me that the mantel had once belonged to Catherine the Great.

But on that day I stood helplessly watching the demolition crew attack the building. I became more desperate until something in me snapped. Breaking through the security ropes, I ran up to the man operating the bulldozer and tried in vain to bargain with him. My efforts were ignored as he thundered forward, leaving gaping holes in the marble floor, which splintered and cracked as he passed. The bulldozer slowed down when I got dangerously close, and I offered the man fifty dollars to spare the mantel until I could get help to remove it. He glared down at me as though I were a bug while the devouring machine rumbled in low gear.

"You got two hundred and fifty bucks—it's yours," he growled impatiently.

Frantic now, I offered again to pay him what I had, but even as I pleaded, the sound of the motor revved up, reaching a deafening pitch as he drove the bulldozer through the wall.

"No!" I screamed, charging towards it as the mantel exploded into a thousand pieces. Then, with a perverted glint of mockery in his eye, he turned the iron monster around and headed back through what was left of the shattered wall. I shook with rage as strange and dark thoughts raced through my mind, and I knew that had I a gun in my hand at that moment, I would have shot him, then taken control of the bulldozer and run him over a few times for good measure. But that would have served no useful purpose. Others would have come to finish the job, and there was no one left to rebuild what was being lost.

The floor trembled under my feet as I fled from the site, and ran until exhausted, finding the last refuge of safety at the far end of the property—a stone gazebo that stood alongside a stream. It too would be gone within a matter of days. An orange ribbon tied around one of its pillars marked its fate. I quickly tore off the ribbon in a futile gesture, then threw it into the stream and watched as it floated with the currents and headed out towards the sound.

My world was unraveling around me, and I was burning with rage. Crazy and dangerous thoughts drifted through my mind. I fantasized about blowing up a construction site or two, as it appeared that every bulldozer in the state had moved in on the North Shore of Long Island and was waging a war without any opposition. I stood in the quiet of that secluded sanctuary, listening to the water and feeling the diffusion of light where the veining of blue-and-green vines spread across the ironwork of the domed roof like a peacock's tail. Its lush bowers trailed over the sides all around me like a cocoon, and I began to get control of myself and feel the strange stirrings of spirit in which ideas are born.

There was work to be done, and though puny in stature, I was going to stage a small protest. In that doomed little temple I made a vow that as long as I lived I would never stand by helplessly again, even if it meant taking some revolutionary action. I knew I was powerless to stop the leveling of buildings I did not own, but I could do something about the interiors: the artwork, woodcarvings, and imported details and furnishings that were often left behind. I would find a way to remove every doorknob, stained-glass window, garden ornament.... If they were about to be destroyed, I would find a way to save them. Such an idea would have seemed preposterous to anyone hearing of this plan at the time, but I had two very beautiful and unusual sisters. Carol, who was away at school at the time, would have made a perfect teammate had she been home. The other, Chloe, the youngest of us, had always been a tomboy. She had a wild and daring spirit and possessed the same spark of rebellion just waiting for an outlet.

We had been raised differently from other girls our age. Our dad was a great storyteller, and we would listen to him enraptured for hours. He told tales of daring adventures in faraway places—of princesses held hostage in castle towers and bold missions to free them, and of searches for long-lost buried treasures on secret islands. The seeds of adventure had been planted in our imaginations early on, and never were we told that girls couldn't be pirates. During the summer my parents would rent a small cottage on the bay in East Hampton, where my dad kept a fishing boat. His stories came vividly to life when at the age of ten, he took Chloe and me sailing around Gardeners Island, located several miles offshore. We sailed around the island several times, trying to catch a glimpse of the castle that was said to crown its center. We marveled at the herds of deer and wild turkeys that roamed about freely, but we never dared to go beyond the beach, where "No Trespassing" signs were taken seriously. We had heard that Captain Kidd buried his treasure there centuries ago, but locals had warned us that wild dogs guarded the island and were known to feed off humans, and that if they didn't get you, the ghosts who lurked in the forests would.

Back home, when other girls our age were playing with dolls and tea sets, we were often hunched over a transformer, racing half a dozen Lionel locomotives across the twenty feet of a complex network of railroad tracks that filled an entire room. Our dad had built the train line for us and taught us how to hot-wire all the electrical warning signals and track switches so as to avoid a collision.

When we were older, our dad taught us how to safely use a rifle, climb trees, scale stone walls, and take car engines apart. On the boat he taught us how to tie every kind of nautical knot and trained us in the practical uses of a block and tackle. Though we didn't know it at the time, all of these skills would eventually be put to practical use.

The Gold Coast was made for us, and we were ready to take it on. For weeks after the bulldozing incident, Chloe and I got together after school and plotted. We devised strategies and set the conditions and guide rules that would govern our little underground operation, which we called the Gold Coast Rescue Team. We were determined that between us, one way or another, we were going to rescue or steal what remained salvageable in those doomed mansions. We set up headquarters in the guest cottage in our backyard, where we had played as children. It was a one-room clapboard house with a pull-down staircase that led to a second floor. A charming structure with pink shutters, geranium-filled window boxes, and gingerbread trim, it looked more like the dwelling place of Little Bo Peep than the hideaway of two self-proclaimed revolutionaries.

The cottage was off-limits to our parents, and there was only one key, which we kept hidden under a stone dwarf that overlooked a small goldfish pond. Inside our headquarters we covered one wall with a huge government aerial map of the North Shore area so that we could keep track of the properties that were in danger. Purple flags were the memorial markers for the buildings already lost. Blue flags were for those under surveillance, meaning they were empty, but intact, or protected by guards or dogs, or just waiting to be sold to developers. Red flags were for the hot spots, or "hit jobs" as we called them. They had to have been abandoned for a long time, or to have been targets of repeated attacks by vandals and marked for demolition. The night before our first mission, we raided our father's well-equipped tool shop, located in the basement of our home. We left the following note:

DEAR DAD,
IN CASE YOU ARE LOOKING FOR THE FOLLOWING TOOLS, WE APPROPRIATED THEM FOR A VERY IMPORTANT MISSION. IF YOU HAVE NEED OF THEM, LEAVE A NOTE ON THE PLAYHOUSE DOOR.
one crowbar,
two screwdrivers,
the chainsaw,
a pickax,
two chisels and mallet,
one hacksaw, box of extra blades,
the winch, two hundred feet of cable,
one rope ladder, and the metal box of skeleton keys.
Signed: G.C.R.T.

Months passed before he noticed the note or had need of his tools. In the meantime, we roamed all over the estate properties at dusk, following the bridle trails that gave us easy access to out-of-reach places.

We surveyed endangered buildings and made notes for future operations. After months of research, all the red flags were in place. Then we hit every abandoned manor house from Glen Cove to Huntington. Day or night, rain or shine, in heavy fog and howling blizzards, we persevered, scaling stone walls, climbing gates and fences, even crossing a moat that surrounded a ruined castle overlooking Huntington Bay. We lowered ourselves down elevator shafts, slithered through furnace grates and coal chutes—whatever it took, we got in. All of our rescue missions had code names, and we kept records of all salvaged objects and where they were hidden. Many things were so badly damaged, they could no longer serve any earthly purpose, but we still regarded them as precious mementos, giving them the same importance that an archeologist would give to relics of a lost civilization. There were days when we worked until we were exhausted, but there was just so much you could load onto a horse or stuff in the basket of a bicycle. It was time to write Dad another note:

Dear Dad,
I took the car keys—oh yes, and the car—to serve a noble cause. Will return soon.
G.C.R.T.

I was driving at fifteen, although I was not licensed to do so, but they were short trips, and getaways tend to go fast. No one noticed that one of the cars was missing or that the cottage was soon bulging with strange and curious objects. When we ran out of storage space, we began hiding fragments of carved wood and lighter objects in the loft of the spacious brick garage that was near our playhouse. It was then that my mother noticed something odd was going on.

"Would you kindly remove this junk? You know how I feel about clutter," she said one day, scanning the heaps of rubble and broken objects that were already reaching the ceiling.

"Junk!" I said incredulously. "You call this junk? That moose head once belonged to J. P. Morgan."

"What, might I ask, are you doing with it?" she said, glaring down at us. My sister looked at me, hoping I had an answer.

"Well, Mr. Morgan died, and none of his heirs wanted it cause it had moths," I responded, having long since decided it was okay to give stupid answers to parents. My mother held my gaze for a while, then grumbled.

"Why do I have the awful feeling that I am not raising normal children?" she said, resigned, and she walked away.

We had a problem, and unless we found a safe place where we could store everything, all of our efforts would be in vain. We were getting frantic: mansions were going down faster than we could get to them. Seventeen were destroyed that summer. We decided it had become necessary to share our secret with a kindly caretaker who felt the same way we did, and we traded some garden ornaments for storage space in an unused carriage house in Brookville.

In our first year we rescued forty-two battered antique chairs, seven steamer trunks filled with fabulous turn-of-the-century gowns, and many chintz-covered boxes filled with great frothy hats lush with feathers, flowers, and lace. We removed enough brass and gold-plated doorknobs to replace the hardware on every door in Buckingham Palace. We saved twenty-seven dry-rotted wicker chairs, most of them missing seats or with a broken leg or two—things we knew how to mend in our father's workshop. We discovered a house that had been abandoned for almost thirty years, and there we rescued a half dozen gilt-framed paintings that had been slashed by vandals or were damaged by water from the many leaks in the ceiling. We lost track of all the marble fragments, pediments, capitals, balustrades, stained-glass windows, and fireplace mantels. But there was never to be another mantelpiece like the one lost the year before.

In Old Westbury, a beautiful racing stable was about to come down to make way for a housing project. We went in and removed all kinds of memorabilia of the era's favorite sport. The smell of hay and horses long gone still lingered in the harness room, where we found a huge oak chest filled with red hunting jackets trimmed with the highly prized Meadowbrook Hunt Club buttons. There were mildewed leather boots and broken polo mallets scattered about on the floor. On shelves, in what had once been the groom's study, there was a collection of rare old leather-bound and gold-embossed books on nineteenth-century trotting and racing records. Hundreds of faded trophy ribbons in every color of the rainbow covered the cobwebbed walls.

Chloe and I moved about these deserted places quietly, with intense curiosity and awe, placing what we found in an old horse blanket, to be sorted out later. We were insatiable packrats, but at times we felt as though we were indeed discovering the remains of a lost civilization. It was through those discarded things that we came to know the richness and beauty of the Gold Coast's brief season. Getting around the overgrown roadways leading up to raid sites became easier when at the age of sixteen, my father gave me a white Buick convertible—the kind with flipper fins on the back fender. It was spacious enough to put a concert grand in the backseat had the opportunity presented itself. We named it the Sleuthmobile, and with it our missions became even more daring.

One day, my eye caught sight of a beautiful Victorian gazebo. It was covered with blue lattice and flowering vines and was listing slightly. The wooden steps had already rotted and crumbled, and the entire structure looked as though it might topple over with the next storm. I had to save it.

"Have you lost your mind?" my otherwise-daring sibling screamed when I approached her with the idea. "We've really pushed our luck lately, taken some pretty stupid chances—but stealing an entire building!"

"It's not a building; it's just a gazebo," I responded.

"Are you suggesting we lasso it with a rope and drag it home? Don't you think we might look a little odd walking down Main Street with a hot gazebo in tow?" She set her hands defiantly on her hips.

"It's not a hot gazebo; it's abandoned, and if we don't save it, it will go the way of everything else around here," I said, knowing that without her help it was doomed.

A year passed before we took any action to rescue it. It was the sight of one of those orange ribbons around the site that triggered old furies. This time we recruited the help of our caretaker friend, who had a pickup truck. In the dead of night, using the headlights for illumination, the three of us carefully dismantled the fragile structure, using crowbars and a winch. Then we loaded the pieces into the truck. Some time later, we got permission to temporarily reassemble it on the edge of a golf course in Brookville, where people riding by on golf carts could enjoy it. Later Chloe and I toppled a 150-pound gargoyle from the top of a gatepost going down and left it on the doorstep of the caretaker who had helped us.

It was often the faithful servants and groundskeepers who were left grieving in the wake of all the destruction. For many of them, the ways of the manor had been the only life they had ever known. In many cases the estate owners had left provisions in their wills that these devoted caretakers be provided for; former staff were to remain in their cottages and guest houses for as long as they lived. It was a noble gesture, but the cold reality was that once a property was sold to a developer, everything on it was leveled as quickly as possible. The former workers were forced from their homes, and, unable to adjust to any other way of life, they often went into an emotional decline and died soon after.

During those tragic and wasteful years, we worked at times to the point of exhaustion, regarding our efforts as noble deeds but never feeling we were doing enough. I ached with a sense of loss and hopelessness, knowing that our feeble efforts would never change the fact that Long Island was losing something of awesome proportions—something that it could never recapture.

All the estates at one time had magnificent gardens, lush with rare flowers and exotic plantings and shrubs. When things got slow, we dug up and relocated as much of the flora and fauna as possible, dispensing them freely to people we knew who liked to garden. But these gardens were soon discovered by local folk riding through on horseback, and it was not uncommon to find the more adventurous members of local garden clubs digging amid the derelict greenhouses and untended cutting gardens.

In time, we had several close calls with the police, who were unaware of what we were doing. We were breaking all the rules, and while we didn't agree with those rules, the law is the law. It became obvious that if we kept up our activities, sooner or later we were going to be caught. With dozens of these buildings going down in short order, what followed was the rapid building of development houses that sprouted up like mushrooms almost overnight. With them, the chances of our being seen increased. We went back to the planning board and discussed the problem, with no solution in sight, outside of working at night, which was foolish and dangerous.

One day, while we were going through the attic of our house, an idea came to me. As descendents of a long line of terminal packrats, the attic of our family's home was a curious place, defying description. Amid the clutter of old sewing machines and dress forms was a long pole that stretched from one end of the timbered ceiling to the other. On it were hundreds of costumes stuffed in chockablock fashion. I was never sure if my mother harbored a secret wish to run off and join the theater, but it seemed that as far back as I could remember, she spent most of her spare time sewing the most extraordinary costumes. These we wore to numerous parties, and to shows that we performed in while at school.

One year she made my sister and I matching black poodle costumes for a duet we sang at a high school play. Once worn, the outfits found their way up into the attic to gather dust along with all the others. I pulled one of them off the rack, studied it for a moment, and saw its unrealized potential. The costumes were designed as tight-fitting knit jumpsuits, with a furry tail and ears. Black masks complete with whiskers covered the face. Except for the wired tail, they were comfortable and perfect for slithering about, and ideal for scaling walls.

Excited by my discovery in the attic, I ran to my sister with the idea. We tried the outfits on and looked at ourselves in the mirror and realized we had solved our problem. We could blatantly carry on our missions in broad daylight in full view of anyone who might happen by, but so disguised, no one could identify us. We felt silly, of course, but the guise worked like a charm, and within a few weeks we had salvaged enough Gold Coast treasures to fill another barn. But people in the area were starting to talk.

Our days as the Poodle Banditos were short-lived; our cover was blown one day after I ran a stop sign on Woolver Hollow Road, following an otherwise-uneventful rescue raid. The Brookville Police, used to people coming and going from one costume party to another, took no notice of our peculiar attire, nor of the eight-foot armoire rising up like a monolith out of the backseat of the convertible. We were let off with a warning regarding the stop sign, but we decided to lay low for a while.

Looking back, it was perhaps the narrow escapes that kept us addicted to the excitement and adventure of what we were doing. To us there was nothing in all God's creation more stimulating than a successful salvage mission. I never felt more alive or committed to a cause. There was, of course, the sheer terror of it: the imminent danger of sweet peril—and glorious rapture of leading a secret life. During those raids we laughed and giggled uncontrollably, tears streaming down our faces, causing us to make wrong turns in the woods and on one occasion to crash the car into a tree. It was perhaps the impossibility of some of the challenges we took on, knowing they exceeded all reason, our abilities, and our strength, that drove us.

Our most daring mission was to be our last.

There was an estate on the water's edge in Glen Cove that had a Tiffany lantern or globe hanging from a chain at the far end of a thirty-foot-high palm conservatory. The building had been empty since the thirties, and the only reason it had survived attacks from vandals were that it was protected by an eight-foot wall and that the gate was always locked. The only way to reach the property was by boat. When word got out that the building was coming down, I went to our map, took off the blue flag that marked its location, and replaced it with a red flag. Then together my sister and I came up with a plan to save the lantern.

The next morning, we got up at four, drove to a nearby dock, untied a small wooden rowboat that a friend kept moored there, and headed out for the cove. We followed the shoreline for a short distance, fighting the incoming tide. When we reached the estate, we tied the boat in a thicket of low-hanging trees along the water's edge. As we walked up the beach, we saw that the eighty-room manor was already half-gone. Three bulldozers stood ominously in the drive. Our boots sank in the soft, overturned earth as we walked, and we had to be careful of the broken glass that was everywhere. Part of the glass conservatory had been leveled. My heart sank when I saw that we had gotten there too late to save the carved wooden pillars that had surrounded the indoor garden, and that most of the palm trees were already crushed and lay flattened on the ground. But as the sun began to rise slowly from the East, I could make out part of the steel-and-glass conservatory, where the Tiffany globe hung precariously from a half-twisted girder. With no time to spare, we ran into the servants' wing of the half-demolished house and dragged several mildewed mattresses back to the site, placing them under the glass globe. Then I carefully unwrapped my father's hunting rifle, which was concealed in an old woolen blanket, steadied the barrel on the rim of a broken marble urn, took careful aim, and fired. The blast shattered the glass in a four-foot area of the north wall but missed hitting the chain. Dozens of blackbirds who had been roosting in the rafters exploded into flight and headed in all directions at once.

"Everyone within fifty miles had to have heard that!" Chloe cried out nervously.

"You're breaking my concentration," I snapped, and I prepared to try again.

"The police are going to break your concentration if you we don't get out of here," she hissed, inching her way towards what had been the door but was now a pile of splintered wood, brick, and rubble. The rising sun glinted off the shards of broken glass, reflecting in mirrorlike images the horror of destruction surrounding the site.

I looked back up at the Tiffany prize and marveled at the beauty of its blue-green prisms and the lavender opalescent butterfly at its center and was unable to comprehend the mystery of how it was made. No bulldozer was going to get its jaws on that work of art—not that day. I took a deep breath and kept my eye on the target, the quarter-inch brass chain that was one link away from setting the globe free. I steadied the gun and fired again. In that instant the globe fell twenty feet, landing with a thud on the mattresses below. I heard my sister squeal with delight, and we quickly wrapped the lamp in a blanket, tied it with some cord, and rolled it down the hill to the beach, making it into the rowboat and out of sight only seconds before the police arrived.

Rifle blasts have a way of attracting attention, but nothing would have stopped us—nothing except for the cold reality that finally hit us one day: we had lost the battle, and there was nothing left to save. By 1968, the Gold Coast Rescue Team was no more. Most of the great manor houses were gone, and Long Island had lost its chance to become what Newport, Rhode Island, is today. Even more ironic, it lost its chance to be the setting of the 1974 film version of Fitzgerald's *The Great Gatsby*. The original Gatsby manor, whose real name was Beacon Towers, the foremost symbol of the Gold Coast era, had been leveled during the forties. In the end the filming took place at Rosecliff, a marble palace in Newport that bore little resemblance to the Long Island original as Fitzgerald described it.

Our childhood playhouse has remained unchanged and is still in our parents' backyard. The aerial maps, though faded, still cover the walls, with over five hundred purple flags to mark the places that are no more. Somewhere off in the section that covers the village of Glen Cove, a tiny blue flag still identifies Winfield on the map.

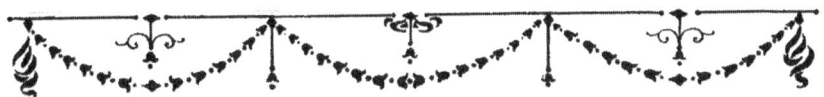

Chapter Three

The Playhouse

In 1965 I took a year off from college to live in Paris and study art while working as a fashion model for designer Pierre Balmain. When I returned to Long Island, a series of coincidences put me in contact with yet another Woolworth property in Oyster Bay. One day while photographing ruined gardens in the area, I ran into an elderly caretaker who informed me that The Playhouse, an estate originally built by F. W. Woolworth's daughter Helena Woolworth McCann, had just been sold. Word was out that the new owners were looking to rent out part of the house and—if they were lucky—find someone who could also help with its much-needed restoration.

During the sixties, renting a guest cottage or living space in the main house was often the only way that large manor houses, with their costly upkeep, could survive. The landed gentry were often hanging on by a thread, but they were not always willing to part with their ancestral homes despite the impossibility of keeping them up. Ironically, in the quiet village of Oyster Bay Cove, there was a local zoning ordinance that forbade owners to rent any part of their property to anyone who was not a family member. When the era began its decline, the village lawmakers quickly put restraints on renting to outsiders, fearing that if this were allowed, the exclusivity of the area would be compromised and the estate community would turn into another Queens.

Anyone with a skill, talent, or genuine love for gardening could often trade his or her much-needed abilities for a room or part of an unused wing in the spacious houses that were often built to house twenty servants. It was illegal for owners to advertise their willingness to rent or trade available space in the local newspapers, though many took the risk and posted notices at the local supermarkets and shops. These were ideal situations and very much in demand, but it was often a case of being in the right place at the right time.

Hearing of this rare opportunity, I immediately drove over to Berry Hill Road, turning into the ivy-covered gate and on up the mile-long drive, which had borders of mountain laurel and ended in a massive cobblestone courtyard. I arrived just as the new owners were moving in. Two moving trucks stood outside the front door as men unloaded handsome furnishings and Persian rugs into the house.

Realizing I'd come at a bad time, I turned the car around and was about to leave when an attractive woman in a bright floral dress approached me, thinking I was one of the decorators she'd been expecting. I told her I wasn't a decorator and offered to come back after they'd settled in, but she said she was exhausted and eager to take a break. She introduced her husband and herself as Mr. and Mrs. Frank and Florence Norris. They were a handsome couple in their forties, and both seemed gracious and already at home in their opulent, though somewhat run-down, surroundings.

I took to them immediately and hoped the feeling was mutual. They spoke with a sense of adventure about their new house and all the work they planned to do on it. As we stood talking in the enormous courtyard, they were quick to point out that the cobblestones we were standing on had been shipped over from Fatheringhay Castle by the Woolworths, and that they were the same stones on which Mary Queen of Scots was beheaded back in the sixteenth century.

The Norrises did not mention a more recent beheading, and it would be weeks before I found out about it. But artifacts with a morbid history were all the rage during Long Island's building frenzy. So many of them were bought up by the estate builders that it's surprising that anything of any note remains in Europe. One property owner had an entire dungeon installed in his basement and filled it with medieval torture devices. Stanford White had his Long Island drive lined with ancient sarcophaguses, and at Ferguson Castle, a pair of giant granite sphinxes brought from Europe set off the great hall.

The Norrises watched as the last of their possessions were unloaded from the truck. They mentioned that the house had been empty for years and that vandals had broken some of the imported stained-glass windows and toppled the statues in the formal garden. They both seemed to know a great deal about the history of the place as they showed me about the grounds, which were laid out in a similar pattern to those at Versailles. Hundred-foot stretches of lavishly designed teakwood trellises were painted in crusting layers of faded blues and greens. Through a glade of clipped pine trees, I could make out several high-pitched gables and the turrets of what looked like an English castle looming in the distance.

"Our neighbor is a Woolworth, I'm told," Florence Norris mentioned matter-of-factly, pointing towards the obscured building in the woods. Then she turned her attention back to the overgrown garden, where climbing roses and weeds had overtaken everything. She shook her head at the monumental job they had ahead of them. I thought the garden was one of the most beautiful I'd ever seen, was so taken by it, I boldly asked if I could come back and paint it in the morning light. The Norrises looked at each other, seemingly pleased with my suggestion, together they asked, "You like to paint?"

Apparently, without knowing it, I had said the magic words, and without knowing a single other thing about me, they asked if I'd like to come and live there. I was never really sure if they took my suggestion as an offer to paint the trellises literally, or whether they understood that I meant to paint them romantically on canvas. Whatever they were thinking, I could only attribute this stroke of good fortune to a general attitude that seemed to prevail where painters, artists, and poets were tolerated like the horses galloping along a private beach at sunset. They were all part of the dream canvas that the Gold Coast, though fading silently, kept alive.

Within a week I had moved in, renting the entire second floor, which included a fifty-foot garden terrace for private entertaining. Because of the local zoning ordinance that made it illegal to rent to non–family members, at their insistence I had to pretend that I was their niece and refer to Florence as my aunt in public. We both enjoyed the ruse and laughed about it whenever one of us slipped in social situations.

Florence, known as Sis to her friends, was the heiress to the Bullwinkle jewelry fortune, but she never adorned herself with anything more than a single long strand of pearls. She and her husband Frank were social creatures and knew all the right people. Weekends became a whirlwind of cocktail and dinner parties, tennis games, dances at the Creek, and Piping-Rock Clubs. Then there was the sticky matter of getting listed in the social register—a must, I was told, if one was going to hobnob with the old guard. We had gathered up the five required letters of recommendation, but the idea was dropped after we learned that one noted grande dame in the area had managed to get her French poodle listed, claiming he was her son. She listed his doggy-obedience training classes as time spent at a posh private prep school. After word leaked out, the thick black-and-orange snooty directory lost a bit of its luster, and some of the best people dropped out, including the Whitneys.

It was only after I had settled in that I learned that the Playhouse had been the scene of a brutal shooting death that made headlines in 1955. On the eve of Halloween, Ann Woodward, a former showgirl, then the wife of millionaire sportsman William Woodward, fired two fatal shots at her husband at close range, completely decapitating him. She claimed she had mistaken him for a prowler. There were at least a dozen versions of what really happened that night, none of which had anything to do with what the final records showed. Ann Woodward, unable to continue living in the area closed up the house, and it had been empty ever since.

The William Woodwards (no relation to Woolworth) had bought the Long Island showplace from F. W. Woolworth's descendants during the mid-forties, where little had changed until the shooting. Ann Woodward, though acquitted of any wrongdoing, was treated as guilty by her husband's social circle. She eventually took her own life after confiding in writer Truman Capote what really happened on that ill-fated night. He betrayed her by publishing her account in *Esquire* magazine. The Playhouse had been on the market since the shooting, but due to the notoriety and the increasing rumors that the house was haunted by the headless ghost of Billy Woodward, there were no offers until the Norrises discovered the house and fell in love with it.

During the six years that I lived there, I never once saw or heard any ghosts, and it was probably during that time that I built up a disregard for what others claimed were haunted houses. I had no belief in the theory that scenes of brutal acts had the power to affect those who came to live there afterward. Whatever had happened at the Playhouse in the past, I found it to be a magical and inspiring place to live. I turned one of the guest rooms into a studio, and it was soon filled with dozens of canvases of dreamlike landscapes, forest glades, and overgrown outbuildings.

The main house was surrounded by hundreds of acres of meadows and fields of buttercups where peacocks, sheep, and horses grazed around a pond surrounded by weeping willow trees. The horses, sheep, and peacocks belonged to a neighboring estate, but there were no fences or boundaries, and the bucolic animals chose to spend most of their time on our property because of the pond. We were happy to have them as part of the view. Just beyond the trellised gardens there was an allée of cherry trees in perfect rows that stretched to the south as far as the eye could see. In the spring the slightest breeze would cause the blossoms to flutter about like a blizzard of pink snow. At the end of the path stood a small Greek temple with a fountain in the center.

The Playhouse itself was simple in design, a sandstone-colored, sprawling stucco villa covered with ivy. Ivy vines all but engulfed the indoor tennis court, which dominated the north side of the house. The indoor tennis court was an architectural feat of engineering that took on the appearance of a giant green house, with its glass ceiling that rose up sixty-two feet.

During the fifties, the Woodwards, who were more into horses than tennis, rented the court to a movie company, and it was there that the innovative screening process Cinerama was developed. The very first screening of *This Is Cinerama* was projected onto a sixty-foot screen at the Playhouse, and all of the locals and Hollywood bigwigs were invited to experience what would become the new craze in America. On the night of the shooting, it was one of the Cinerama guards, who lived in the attached guest cottage, who heard the shots and called the police.

When the Norrises bought the property, the court had not been used since the movie screening, and it had fallen into a state of disrepair. Ivy tendrils crept up the stucco walls and worked their way into the tall glass doors and along the steel girders that supported the glass ceiling. By then the entire room was nearly engulfed in vegetation. Over the years, storms had broken several of the large glass panels. Each day dozens of black starlings managed to find their way through the jagged openings. They would panic and were often unable to find their way back out. At night, you could hear the birds' frantic cries as they darted about, shrieking from one end of the room to the other until, exhausted, they would fall to their deaths on the clay floor below. It was the caretaker's somber job to collect the dead birds each morning, load them into a rusting wheelbarrow that squeaked disturbingly, and carry them off into the woods. For years, the Norrises tried to get the ceiling fixed, but finding a construction company to come and repair the broken glass was close to impossible. Local workers were terrified of the height. It was just as difficult to get anyone to come and service the huge furnace when it broke down. I was alone at the house one winter when the heating system failed. When I called for help, the fuel company operator responded with: "Hell, I ain't going over to Woodwards' old place. Everyone knows the house is haunted."

During the first year that I lived there, we fought a never-ending battle against leaks, burst pipes, electrical outages, animal invasions, and falling ceilings. By spring, all efforts were focused on the gardens, and the statues were cemented back on their pedestals, the lawns were cut, and the two reflecting pools were filled with water lilies and fan-tailed goldfish.

Our closest neighbor was Mrs. Connie McMullen, F. W. Woolworth's granddaughter and first cousin to Barbara Hutton. She remained on the property after her mother, Helena Woolworth McCann, passed away in 1937. Mrs. McMullen lived with her husband, Joe, in a rambling French Normandy-style manor called Beaupré, which looked as though it had been uprooted from some European countryside. It was shielded from the world by acres of towering pine trees and separated from our property by a hedge grove of clipped hemlocks and a series of fanciful topiary trees cut in the shapes of swans and peacocks and in tall spiraling conicals. On days when the wind was blowing in the right direction, we could hear the gardeners on her property clipping away in her rose garden. Shortly after the Norrises bought the Playhouse, Mrs. McMullen wandered over to our property with a basket of her fine prize-winning roses and introduced herself.

An elegant and gracious woman in her sixties, with a bright, pleasing smile, she wore her gray hair combed back, with soft waves around her well-proportioned oval face. Her manner was even and low-key, and her taste in all things was impeccable. Her husband, Joe, was a world-renowned expert on the subject of fine Oriental rugs. They entertained weekly with the help of their ancient English butler, Dudley, who served cocktails on a gleaming silver tray. The butler was also a fine artist, and on his day off he was often seen in the garden, painting landscapes.

One afternoon, Dudley walked across the lawn in his livery uniform, rang the bell, and handed Mrs. Norris a cream-colored card inviting all of us for dinner the following weekend. I overheard Mrs. Norris graciously accept, and she was told it would be a small gathering of about ten guests. When we arrived at her house a few days later, Mrs. McMullen greeted us in her fruitwood-paneled drawing room, wearing a simple almond-colored velvet Mainbocher gown with a single strand of pearls around her delicate neck. She introduced us to her guests, some of whom I recognized, having passed them while riding the familiar trails in the area on horseback. The women wore stylish, unadorned gowns and very few jewels, but the men seemed more imposing in their navy blazers with the gold Harvard and Yale insignias that gave them an air of subdued nobility. I was so nervous I could hardly speak, but Mrs. McMullen, who insisted that I call her Connie, had the ability to put anyone at ease. But, uncomfortable with the old guard, I found myself talking about art with the butler every chance I had, which was a breech of form.

In a misguided effort to look as though I belonged in this elite circle, I chose to wear one of the Paris gowns that I had rescued from Farnsworth just before it was bulldozed. But I was mistaken, as the wearing of vintage clothing was not considered fashionable as yet, and the long silk 1920s frock began disintegrating around me, and the tiny brass beads became undone and began falling to the floor. I saw Dudley picking them up whenever he could, but I was mortified.

The cocktail hour seemed to dominate the evening as drink after drink was circulated around the handsomely appointed room. The guests were all refined, well educated, sedate, and indolent until they were on their fifth gin and tonic, and then they became very interesting.

Almost ten years had passed since the Woodward shooting next door, but the landed gentry still spoke of it. They reveled in sharing every little juicy detail one or another of them might have picked up from anywhere, or anyone, along the way.

"It wasn't the first time she shot him, you know," I overheard one guest say to another.

"Indeed," another responded casually.

"Several years before she finally killed Billy, they were on safari, they argued, and she shot him in the leg. That time she claimed she mistook him for a water buffalo."

"Oh dear, I hadn't heard about that," another guest responded.

"It's true. I'm told he was buried with a fragment of the bullet still in his leg from that first shooting incident. One of the police told me it was in the autopsy report. Of course, it never came out at the inquest," the informed guest added.

"Well, I think they handled the whole unpleasant affair rather well," one of the women commented. More drinks were ordered and passed around the room.

"Thank God she didn't shoot the horse," a gentleman named Bronson added jovially, while flicking the ashes from his cigar into a silver tray. The horse in question was Nashua, the top-ranking thoroughbred of the year, who had won just about every horse race in the country the year before. He was a virtual gold mine and the prized possession of the William Woodwards.

"I know for a fact that he behaved rather unseemly toward Ann, always putting her down, never wasting an opportunity to remind her of where she came from," one of the few women there said in defense of Mrs. Woodward, who was now treated as a leper by society. Another woman in the group got up and walked across the room to take a closer look at one of the hunt prints on the wall.

"I saw Ann in town just before the tragedy. Her eye was swollen, and she was hiding behind dark glasses," she said with a nonchalant air. There was a long pause. The butler, who stood by the door, was the picture of robotic decorum in his dark livery and stiff striped vest. His face, though stoic and unmoving, was beginning to show signs of unraveling as his gray bushy eyebrows began to twitch slightly revealing an undercurrent of inner anxieties.

"She had hot pants," one of the male guests blurted out over the din of conversation, and the butler sprang from his post, ran over to the man, and refilled his glass with gin, distracting him just enough to keep him from going on. Mrs. McMullen, always the lady, gave him a signal, and he quickly picked up a silver bell from a side table and rang it to let everyone know that dinner was served.

Slowly everyone rose from their comfortable seats with labored, languorous movements and followed one another into the spacious dining room, lit with candles and fragrant with fresh roses from the garden. Guests quietly found their cream-colored handwritten place cards, took their seats, and enjoyed a meal of Cornish hens, endive salad, creamed pearl onions, and a variety of vegetable dishes referred to as legumes. Mrs. McMullen was a gracious and intuitive hostess, letting her husband, Joe, do most of the talking, and while at the table the conversation centered around art, history, music, and, of course, the collecting of rare Oriental rugs.

After dinner, because I was new, Connie McMullen offered to give me a tour of the house. Mrs. Norris chose to stay with her husband and joined the others in the drawing room for cordials.

With my vintage gown still shedding in bits and pieces, I followed my hostess as she moved from room to room. Our footsteps were muffled by the rich profusion of carpets that had been brought over from various castles all over Europe. The rooms were elegantly appointed, but had a relaxed country feel to them. There were fine landscape paintings on the walls and built-in shelves to display a priceless collection of English and Sévres porcelain. Mrs. McMullen never spoke about the Woolworths or her relation to them. Had I not been told about her background beforehand, I would never have guessed it. There was none of the ostentatious display of wealth that you found at Winfield or at the Playhouse next door.

My curiosity about her grandfather's palace, and what she might remember of it from when she was young, began to get the better of me. Then I spotted a table in the corner of her library that was filled with family photos, and I seized the chance to bring the subject up. Amid the dozens of portraits, one stood out. There was a small, ornate gold frame with the Napoleonic seal on top. I thought I recognized the intense, steely eyes from those carved into the marble coat of arms over the mantel at Winfield.

"Is that your grandfather?" I asked, leaning forward, but not daring to touch anything in the room.

"Yes. How did you know?" she asked, looking somewhat surprised.

"From the Empire frame," I said. Then I told her about my meeting with Mrs. Reynolds years ago and about having seen the Napoleon room.

"Yes, he was rather taken by Napoleon and loved the art and history of that era," she said, revealing nothing more. Then she picked up a silver frame studded with tiny jade stones. "That's my mother, Helena. She built the house you're living in now. Those are my two aunts next to her, Edna and Jessie, who was the youngest," she said softly. Then she put the frame back in its place.

"They're all very beautiful," I said, noting their white lace dresses and high neck collars, but their somber expressions made them seem as though they were carved out of alabaster.

"What was Edna like?" I asked, curious about what I'd already heard.

"Well, I was just a young girl when she died, but she had an accomplished operatic voice and longed for the concert stage. But such a thing was unthinkable for a girl in her position."

"How did she die?" I asked.

"Poor dear—she fell out of a window at the Plaza Hotel. . . . Oh, wait, that was someone else. No, I believe she drank something disagreeable, which proved fatal. It was a terrible thing. Her daughter, little Barbara Hutton, found the body. She was only four. She was such a beautiful, sad child," she said sadly.

"Mrs. Reynolds thinks Winfield is haunted by Edna's ghost," I said.

"People think the Playhouse is haunted by Billy Woodward's ghost, but you must know by now, that's all rubbish. I wish we'd never sold that house to the Woodwards, but they fell in love with it and with those beautiful gardens that my mother created. Then they made a mess of things, first with those movie people traipsing around—Cinerama, they called it. Now it's a tourist trap, with strange people coming up the drive at all hours, wanting to see where IT happened," she said edgily.

"I love living there. Everything has been so peaceful," I said.

"Give it time. The morbid season begins in the fall. By Halloween the place becomes a circus," she said, moving to another part of the room. "There's something I'd like to show you, if I can find it. There . . . it's up there. You're taller than me; perhaps you can reach it—the big leather book."

I did as she asked but moved too quickly. Then I heard several more brass beads slip off the rotting thread of my gown and roll onto the carpet. I tried to focus on retrieving the oversized book hoping she hadn't noticed my dress. I pulled down an old, dark green-leather photo album with the name *Sunken Orchard* emblazoned in gold on the cover.

"These were taken when my mother first built the estate—Sunken Orchard was its original name. It became the Playhouse after we sold off part of the property to the Woodwards back in the forties. As you can see from these photos, it was quite different then. My mother had twenty-four gardeners tending to the rose gardens, and there were barns and greenhouses that are no longer there."

I watched her as she turned several more of the thick pages of photographs; the gardens appeared to be frozen in time. Every movement of her hand was graceful and sure. Then she stopped at a page that was only vaguely recognizable.

"Here it is. This was the great hall," she said, pointing to a page that did not seem of this world.

"The hall had once been part of a cathedral that my mother had brought over from Essex, England. The entire house was built around that room, which measured ninety-six feet in length and rose up forty feet to the ancient beamed ceiling," she said in an apathetic tone.

I noted the exquisite Renaissance furnishings and what looked like a Rembrandt on the wall. Hanging from the high ceiling were enormous flags and armorials, and a twenty-foot tapestry hung from a balcony that concealed the pipe organ. Shafts of light filtered into the room from imported sixteenth-century stained-glass windows. I had never seen anything quite like it before, not even on the Gold Coast.

"You may borrow this if you like; you can return it to Dudley if I'm not here," she said graciously.

"I couldn't think of taking it."

"It's alright; it's just gathering dust here; I'd forgotten I had it," she responded just as someone called out her name. She turned and left the room to join the others.

I sat there alone in her room a while longer and continued studying the age-tinted photos. The Great Hall had been empty for years now, and bats had taken to roosting in the rafters, alongside the carved faces of gargoyles. Days before, Mrs. Norris and I had found a dead bat lying on top of the wire strings inside the open concert grand piano that stood in the alcove.

Mrs. McMullen's warning about the invading masses proved true. As the summer wore on, people began ringing our doorbell at all hours of the day and night, wanting to see the scene of the shooting. They asked if there were bullet holes in the wall and bloodstains on the floor (there were). Mostly the inquirers were harmless—just curious local folk from the village—but one party had come halfway across the country. Almost all brought cameras; one had brought his entire family. We were tolerant at first, but then we took to telling strangers they had the wrong house and sending them down the road in the direction of the swamp marshes on the edge of the bay.

Within a week I had made photocopies of Mrs. McMullen's leather album and returned it, bringing her a large bouquet of white lilacs from our garden. She was always friendly, engaging, and willing to share her experience and knowledge on gardening, and on several occasions she even sent her gardeners over to give us a hand.

Meanwhile, at the Playhouse, Florence and I worked together in trying to restore what had once been one of the most unique and beautifully landscaped gardens on Long Island.

With the old photos to guide us, it was mostly a matter of finding the old paths, cutting back the overgrowth, and retraining the roses that had overtaken the vast trellises. By the end of the summer, our efforts paid off, and I took new photographs and started showing them to advertising agencies and magazines in New York. At the time I was still modeling in the city, and I knew there was a great demand for beautiful settings to use as backgrounds. Many of the big fashion magazines were flying their crews and models to Europe to get an old-world look that they were not aware could be found in their own backyard. That first year, we did several photo shoots at the Playhouse, and the demand for other locations like it gave me the incentive to enlist other estates and gardens nearby. Soon I had more calls for mansions and castles located within forty minutes of New York than I had for modeling jobs, and a new business venture was beginning to take off.

When a call came in from *Vogue* magazine asking for a palace with gilded interiors, I drove over to Glen Cove to see if Winfield was still standing.

Chapter Four

The Girls'-School Years

In the heat of the summer, the coolest route to Glen Cove was Lattingtown Road. It hadn't changed in over a hundred years and was still lush with ancient trees and plantation-style mansions partly hidden by old iron gates. The picturesque road ran parallel to Long Island Sound, and it ended in a fork. To the right was J. P. Morgan's private island; to the left Dasoris Lane, which was made famous by the fifties movie *Sabrina,* starring Audrey Hepburn.

As I wound around the quiet little street to Crescent Beach Road, that old anxiety came over me: I didn't know which was worse, having a favored place bulldozed into oblivion, or seeing it turned into an institution. But a charm school — now that was something different.

I pulled into the open gates of the former Woolworth mansion and up the gravel drive. All the fountains were turned on, and flowers surrounded the house and reflecting pool outside the entrance. As I was walking towards the front door, a gust of wind shifted direction and I was hit by a spray of water. My dress and hair got wet, but I was glad to be there, and relieved to find that it hadn't changed at all. The front door was wide open; a pair of terra-cotta urns filled with bright yellow pansies stood on each side as if to welcome anyone who came by. Then I spotted it: the first jarring sign of new ownership. Above the door, the name "Glamor Manor" was painted in garish pink-and-gold letters on a wide banner along the glass-enclosed archway. *Good God,* I thought, *some-*

one has a sense of humor. Inside the main hall, the oversized gilt furnishings stood unmoved in their original places.

To the left, there was a large receptionist's desk where an attractive young woman was busy typing and taking calls at the same time. I was about to speak to her when the loud drone of a power mower passed just outside the open door. I recognized the gardener from when Mrs. Reynolds lived there. "Angelo," I called out, and he looked up, nodded, and tipped his familiar hat without breaking stride. Then he headed across the lawn, grass clippings swirling all around him. When the receptionist saw me, she smiled and continued plucking away on what looked like an antique typewriter. She was heavily made-up and wore her hair in a teased beehive.

"Hi, I'm Bunny. What can I do for you?" she said brightly while vigorously chewing gum.

"I was wondering if I could speak to whoever is in charge."

"Are you interested in registering for one of our charm classes?" she asked, her hands moving towards a pile of application forms.

"No. It's about the house."

"Follow me," she said, standing up from her desk. As she walked, her bright pink stiletto heels clicked noisily on the hard marble floor. Halfway down the hall, she stopped and paused a moment in front of an ornate mirror, adjusted a strand of her hair, then removed a large wad of gum from her mouth and pressed it under the rim of a gilt baroque side table. The ancient piece looked worn and fragile, as if bubblegum were the only thing holding it together. The girl turned and continued down the hall and through the dining room, where a massive oak table was neatly set for about thirty people. A crystal vase filled with multicolored roses stood at the center of a cream-colored lace tablecloth. A pleasant odor of apples and cinnamon drifted in from the kitchen. Finally, we stopped in front of a mahogany door with "Mrs. Borges" engraved on a brass plaque. I was asked to wait. As I stood there, I heard the sudden crash of what sounded like broken glass coming from the kitchen; then a large unkept golden retriever bolted from a swinging door, ran across the room, and headed out the front door.

"It's okay. Mrs. Borges will see you now," the girl said. She placed a fresh wad of gum in her mouth as she passed me and headed back to her desk.

As I entered Woolworth's old billiard room, I noted signs of change.

The stuffed animal heads had been replaced with wall-to-wall rows of gold-framed graduation photos of former students. They all held the same pose and faced the same direction, and their hair and makeup were identical. Seated behind an enormous Empire desk cluttered with papers and gold statuettes of little goddesses and ballroom dancers was an attractive woman in her forties with short auburn hair and bright welcoming eyes. The rich dark paneling of the room gave her a certain dignity as she rose to greet me.

"How can I help you?" she asked pleasantly, looking me over quickly as though I might be a candidate for enrollment in her school. She was the perfect embodiment of the gracious hostess, and with her sweet and buttery voice, she could have charmed the birds from the trees. She offered me a seat, and I told her about the film studio that was in search of a mansion such as hers to use as a background in one of their commercials. I pointed out that the income might help with the upkeep of such an enormous place. Mrs. Borges was very enthusiastic about the idea, and she was quick to mention that the gardens had been improved since they'd taken over the estate from Mrs. Reynolds.

She was about to say something else, but the noise from the sputtering mower outside made it impossible to hear her. She mumbled something under her breath, turned, then hurried from the room and headed towards the rear terrace. I followed her to the Italian gardens, where a fountain was hurling water twelve feet into the air. The gardener had worked his way to the back lawn and was hunched over the mower, fanning black puffs of smoke with his straw hat. When he caught sight of his boss watching him, he began screaming in broken English.

"It-a-no-work! Non posso . . ." Then he threw his old hat on the ground in mock disgust, turned, and walked away, leaving the mower gyrating in place as the grass around it began to turn black.

"He came with the house," she said, throwing her hands up in frustration. I was quick to share that Mrs. Reynolds had told me he was there in Woolworth's day and was probably pushing ninety.

"Ninety," she repeated, rolling her eyes. "He makes me crazy. That's the third machine he's destroyed. He thinks it's a bulldozer; he mows everything with it—the boxwoods, the rosebushes, rocks!" she said, shaking her head. "This place is far more work than we bargained for. Maybe your studio people can buy us a new lawnmower." she said cheerfully.

"The gardens look wonderful. You've really done a fine job keeping them up. The place seems more alive than the first time I saw it. The only things missing are the moose heads. . . ." I said, pointing towards her office.

"Moose heads?" she repeated, looking puzzled.

"The stuffed animals that were in the billiard room."

"Oh, those ghastly things from the dinosaur age? Can you imagine anyone wanting those old mothy heads hanging in their home?" she said, turning to go back to her office, then stopping to pull a dead flower from one of the huge vases in the main hall. "All of our classes are held in the old carriage house. We partitioned off the garage and servants' quarters to make classrooms for our students. The only drastic thing we had to do was dismantle those creepy rooms upstairs. They're the girls' dormitories now. They just love living here in an old Gold Coast mansion," she said proudly.

There was a long awkward silence, and I could feel my mouth tighten.

"I'd never seen anything like those rooms," I said, trying to keep my voice even.

"We hated to do it . . . but this is a school now, not a museum. We saved everything, though; it's all packed away out in the greenhouse." she said looking down at the floor. Then she was distracted by the sound of her phone ringing back in her room. "You'll have to excuse me. . . . Oh, feel free to wander around; take all the photos you need," she said as she ran down the hall. As soon as she was out of sight, I rushed down to the greenhouse and burst into tears. The shock of seeing Woolworth's collection of treasures tossed about in the leaky greenhouse, where half the glass was missing, left me shaken and angry, but there was nothing I could do about it at that moment. I was not in a position to say anything, or even to show any emotion. My mind was reeling, and I knew I had to find a way to save the treasures, but this time it would have to be legitimate and aboveboard. It didn't take me long to come up with a plan.

Within two weeks the first commercial was filmed at Winfield. The students were delighted with the attention their school was getting, and with the chance to talk firsthand with the crew and actors on the set. On the practical side, Mrs. Borges got her new lawn mower and enough money to make some major repairs to the garden and fountains. After that, I made a special effort to get the house booked as often as possible, and I simply discontinued showing the other properties in the area. Winfield had it all. From an architectural and esthetic standpoint, it personified romance and magic and was the ideal setting for selling everything from elegant evening gowns to expensive automobiles. There was no need to go anywhere else.

In the business of finding locations for films, it was the general rule to charge a percentage of the fee being paid to the owners for the use of their home. When Mrs. Borges finally asked what sort of fee she might owe me for my efforts, I was quick to answer.

"Money does not feed the soul." It came out sounding pompous, but I meant it nonetheless. Everything I cared about was moldering away in some greenhouse or attic or being swept away into oblivion, and no amount of money could stop it.

"I see," Mrs. Borges responded, looking at me blankly.

"Let's make a trade instead. Every time the house gets booked, I'll take some of that junk off your hands."

"What junk?" she asked.

"All that stuff rotting away in the greenhouse," I said, trying to be nonchalant and not sound too slippery; I had no idea if she realized what was really out there. Had she known the history of those priceless things, they would not have been tossed about in that rain-sodden building in the first place.

She gave me a quizzical look, but she was only too happy to accept the offer.

I was nearly delirious with joy, and again I had to wait until she was out of sight before doing several vigorous cartwheels across the lawn, working my way towards the crumbling glass building. I had to admit that doing things legitimately didn't have the same zing as a midnight raid, but the challenge to rescue and save little bits of history was still there.

By now the greenhouse was a sorry sight. Removed from their historic rooms, Woolworth's once-prized possessions did not show to their advantage. Now faded and shabby, they had lost their aura of magic. Everywhere I looked, chairs were missing legs, tables were scratched, mirrors were cracked. Rusted springs poked out of the straw stuffing of a Victorian settee; bits of gold leaf and gesso had fallen from a begrimed statue of a woman whose crumbling arms supported what looked like a Tiffany lampshade. Dozens of lamps were tossed about in a corner like fallen bowling pins.

Angelo had been assigned to the task of escorting me down to the greenhouse. I'd pick something out, and he'd look at me and shake his head, and we'd have a conversation about the piece in question.

"This-a-no-good," he'd say. "It-a-got-bugs—you-no-put-in-your-house—they-eat-your-house."

"It's okay—I'll spray it," I'd respond, or, "This has potential; it can be mended, reglued, regilded, or recovered—whatever it takes; things can be restored." Then he'd help me load it into the now-aging Sleuthmobile. Before long I'd worked my way through the Empress Josephine room and the Marie Antoinette room. I was halfway through the Edwardian room when I realized that Napoleon's things from the Empire room were nowhere in sight, except for one vital item that had been left behind, but I was going to save that for last.

One day, while going through one of the glass bookcases that came from Woolworth's old study, I came across an old leather book written by James Frazier. The pages fell open to a passage that struck me:

"Things that have once been in contact with each other continue to act upon one another at a distance after physical contact has been severed—and like produces like and the effect resembles its cause."

I didn't fully understand the meaning of those words at the time, but something strange was beginning to happen.

By the following year, the mansion was making almost as much money as a film-location site as the school itself, but with the coming of art directors and film and TV crews, the character of Winfield began to change. There was a feeling of subtle unrest about the place, almost as if the house didn't like being in the spotlight.

Aside from myself, no one felt this sense of unrest more strongly than Sunny, the cook, who lived in a small stone cottage in the woods near the west gate. She doubled as den mother and worked tirelessly seven days a week cooking three meals a day for some thirty-five boarding students. Meals were served in the dining hall, which remained largely unchanged from the days when Woolworth entertained his guests at its thirty-foot carved oak table. A graceful black-marble fireplace dominated the room; only now, a somber portrait of the school's founder, Grace Downs, hung over the mantel.

Sunny, a robust matronly woman in her fifties, seemed indifferent to the grandeur that surrounded her. She dressed in sturdy, but outdated, clothes and wore her steel gray hair clipped short. She took on so many roles at one time that she seemed to be the very pulse of the house. A deep, complex, and compelling personality, she had a way of staring at people that was often unnerving, but in time everyone came to know that she had his or her best interests at heart. She didn't speak to me the first time we met, as she passed hurriedly from the kitchen. She looked up, held my gaze for a moment, then went back to her work.

Sunny was originally from South Carolina, and the girls were fascinated by her sullen and evocative accent. Because of it, they granted her the romantic status of a character out of *Gone with the Wind*. She shifted back and forth from being cynical to being dreamily illuminating. After dinner, when her chores were finally done, the students would gather around her at the table and ask her questions nonstop. She was a natural storyteller, a kind of in-house Barbara Cartland, and she held the girls' attention by creating tales in which the good and virtuous triumph. When she grew weary, she would stand up, and say, "Enough," then retreat to her stone sanctuary in the woods.

Animals seemed to follow her around, and aside from her many other duties, she doubled as an amateur veterinarian. Living with her in the cottage were several infirm dogs and a three-legged cat. At the big house, the kitchen was her domain and off-limits to students; unlike the rest of the building, it was warm and cheerful, with plants and herbs cluttering up the windowsills. Sunny spent her days bustling around a massive antique wood stove, checking the lids of steaming pots, her hair hanging down in strands around her pale oval face. When she was hard at work, she had the absent air that weariness brings; she rarely had a moment to rest. One night I had a photo shoot at the house that was running late, and I found Sunny in the kitchen after everyone else had gone up to their rooms. She was hovering over the huge porcelain sink in the pantry, giving a flea bath to a baby raccoon. I had caught her off guard, and she looked up at me sheepishly and said, "I trust you won't mention this to anyone; they'd give me my walking papers for sure."

"Mum's the word," I said as I watched her scrubbing bubbles of frothy soap from the little animal's face. The creature chortled contentedly in her knowing hands. "Where did you find him?"

"He was stuck in one of the chimneys. I think the mother took off with the rest of her brood and forgot this little fella," she said, wrapping him up in a warm towel she had left hanging near the stove. "They make great pets at this age, but eventually they turn on you, and you have to set them free." She reached over for a tiny baby bottle she had already filled with warm milk. It was her loving way with animals that really endeared her to me, but not long after that I discovered she was also psychic. Whenever she looked at you, you had the feeling she not only knew all about you but saw your past and future as well. She was unlike anyone I had ever known before, and like the girls at the school, I felt drawn to her and sought her company as often as I could without disrupting her routine. Sunny had her good days when she seemed content with the responsibilities that her job brought, but then some days those burdens seemed to break her spirit, and her eyes would register an unspoken disapproval. She could be tough as nails and quick to speak her mind when a student broke the rules. But as the summer wore on, it seemed that she was not only taking on the problems of running the school but something else as well. She seemed to project a kind of hypervision that centered on the very house itself, as if she watched over it and some inner cycle that needed tending to.

"The natives are restless today," she said one day while stirring a bowl filled with batter for a birthday cake she was making for one of the girls.

"Maybe they're just excited about the film shoot tomorrow," I said.

"I'm not talking about the living," she snapped in a husky, grave voice that did not seem like her own. "They play tricks on us fools just to let us know who's really in charge. . . . They're all here, you know—every last one of those Woolworths," she said in a disquieting tone as she popped the cake pan into the oven.

"You don't really believe that."

"I don't believe it. . . . I know." Her eyes flashed back at me. She seemed to be delivering a darker message.

"The last owner, Mrs. Reynolds, said she saw a ghost in the garden," I said to get her reaction.

"She's still there," she said matter-of-factly.

"You've seen her?"

"Many times," she responded casually. "She comes back on warm summer evenings, like she's waiting for someone. She's come back year after year for as long as I've been here, and she'll keep coming back long after I'm gone," she said, leaning against the sink and taking a deep breath.

"Sunny, I live in a house that was also built by the Woolworths, and something really horrible happened there, though long after the Woolworths were gone. Everyone said the place was haunted, but I've never seen anything unusual. . . . I've heard strange sounds now and then, a random note or two coming from the pipe organ, but nothing that couldn't be explained logically."

"You don't have to see or hear anything to be affected. It's very subtle, very, very subtle. The energy is all around you. It controls people in ways they're not aware—that's the danger," she said in a grimly resolute tone. "You don't know what goes on around here. There's something about this house that affects people. When the girls first arrive here, they seem perfectly normal—just average teenagers—but after a time something seems to shift, something goes sour in them. At first they all get along, but before long they're at each other's throats. The other night I caught a group of them holding a séance in their room as if it were some form of entertainment. Damn fools, they don't know what kind of mischief they're stirring up. It fans the flames. They're poking into things that shouldn't be messed with. Some of the girls have seen things they wish they hadn't—damned near frightened one of them to death. This house was never a happy place," she said, unaware that she was repeating Mrs. Reynolds's words from years ago.

"Is that room upstairs still locked?" I asked.

"Yes, we keep it locked," she answered wearily, bending down to pull the steaming cake out of the oven. It filled the room with the fragrant aroma of vanilla.

"Why?"

"It's not a room for the living," she said in a way that choked off all further conversation as she filled a pitcher with water and hastily watered some herb plants that flourished in terra-cotta pots on the wide window ledge. She cleared her throat as though she were about to say something more, but she remained silent. I walked over to the window and glanced out absently. Everything was perfectly still. There were no breezes moving in off the sound, no sounds of birds.

"What does she look like?" I asked. Then I turned around, but Sunny had vanished from the room.

I gave little thought to the conversation, and she never brought the matter up again, but several weeks later, on a very hot night when I couldn't sleep, I drove over to Glen Cove on impulse and found myself parked outside the gate at Winfield. I left the car there and walked the short distance to the rear gardens to satisfy my curiosity. There were no lights on in the house. The wind was strong and lifted the branches of the trees. The moon was full and cast eerie shadows on the marble statues, but no ghost appeared in the garden.

During that summer there had been a flurry of commercial and photographic shootings at the house. I had also put a color portfolio together and sent it out to the big movie studios, hoping they would jump at the chance to use Winfield and some of the other places in the area that were so near the city. But, try as I did to interest them, no one ever called back. I was told that with the movies, it was a case of who you knew, and I had no connections with the Hollywood set. Not yet, anyway.

I wasn't about to give up, so I took a folder of photos of the old estates up to the *New York Post,* and they ran a feature story on the Gold Coast in their Sunday magazine section. This proved to be a turning point; people, including movie folk, suddenly became aware of this lost world. There was talk in the industry of a remake of Fitzgerald's *The Great Gatsby,* but it would be a few years before the plan got off the ground. I prayed that there would be a Gatsby mansion left standing by the time they got the backing.

In the meantime I was happy to have the small photo shoots going on at Winfield. *Modern Bride,* one of the clients I had modeled for years before, not only had fallen in love with the gardens but asked if I would pose as one of the brides in a layout. On the day of the shoot, we used the Gothic library as a dressing room, and as I emerged from the room all in white, I spotted Sunny heading up the stairs. She was being followed by one of her newest strays, a shaggy-haired beast whose head hung so low it almost touched the floor.

"Sunny," I called out to her, wanting to show off my dress. She did a double take when she saw me dressed as a bride.

"We're all getting married in the garden today," I said cheerfully. But she looked sad and preoccupied.

"There were no happy marriages in this house," she said, her voice sounding like hedge clippers. I gathered it was one of her bad days.

"Sunny, this is only make-believe; it's more fun that way," I said, trying to make light of her reaction. She gave me a baffled glare and ran her hand across her brow in a gesture of weariness and despair. Then out of the blue she turned to face me and said, "You're going on a trip across the sea, and soon."

"No. I'm not planning to go anywhere." I responded.

"But you're going all the same, and soon," she insisted, then stooped down to attend to the rag mop of a dog as he was about to tumble down the stairs. With more strength than I thought she possessed, she gathered him into her plump arms and carried him up to the second floor.

The following week my agency in New York called to say they had arranged for me to fly to Switzerland on a modeling assignment for the Whitestag sportswear firm. I didn't really want to leave Long Island, but at age twenty-five I was already considered over-the-hill, and I thought this might be my last chance to see that beautiful country. My usual fear of flying was abated by my belief that if the plane was going to crash, Sunny would have warned me not to go. Climbing Mount Jungfrau's frozen glaziers proved far more dangerous than flying—the photo shoot took place at the top of the fourteen-thousand-foot mountain. I kept fainting from lack of oxygen and was terrified the whole time I was there.

When I returned from Europe, I was told that Sunny's cottage had caught fire and been gutted, leaving only the walls and chimney standing. One of her sickly cats was later found inside, charred to a crisp. The smell of the fire hung in the air for weeks. Sunny seemed to take what had happened in stride, never showing any bitterness over her misfortune. She moved into the main house, bringing her menagerie of animals with her.

Sometime later, there was a message from Mrs. Borges, saying that she wanted to see me. From the tone of her voice, it sounded serious, and I thought perhaps the commercial shootings had proven too much of a disruption for the school. When I went to see her, I found her in her office, pacing back and forth nervously. She seemed agitated about something, but when I entered the room, she looked up and forced a smile and asked me to have a seat.

"Would you consider teaching a class on modeling here at the school?" she asked, taking me completely by surprise.

"But I don't know anything about teaching, or modeling either, for that matter."

"But you manage to do it," she said in an insistent tone.

"I fell into it by accident, and it doesn't require a whole lot of intellect. You just sort of stand around looking anorexic and project an attitude," I said, never having had too much respect for the profession.

"Attitude?"

"Yes. A detached aloofness, like you're not quite connected to your fellow earth humans. It's really not healthy, or natural, if you ask me, but it's what the fashion industry demands."

She gave me a vacant look, then walked back around her desk and sat down. "But you can be of help to my girls in getting them started. You know about the kind of makeup to use for photo sessions, how to approach the agencies. But make it sound glamorous; they need that," she said as she began to rummage around her desk for her calendar. She looked up, then added: "Of course, we would pay you. It would be a good learning experience for you and the girls. I would be so grateful; their minds are not on their work. This town is full of lowlifes just waiting to get on these grounds and . . ." She paused a moment, then added, "It's taking its toll on me and the school, and Sunny is beside herself," she said, snapping a pencil in two.

"Is something wrong?"

"You have to watch those girls every second; it's like they're in heat. Sunny can't control them. The night watchman said they have a way of leaving the building without being seen, and they all cover for each other when one of them doesn't show up at breakfast. I just think a program on how to get started in modeling would give them something else to strive for. Please say you'll at least think about it," she asked in her most persuasive tone.

"I doubt there is anything I can teach them that will curb their raging hormones. But okay, I'll put a class together, but only for six weeks. Oh, and you don't have to pay me; our usual arrangement will be fine. There's something out in the greenhouse that's turning green and moldy and needs to be restored before it's too late," I said, trying to sound humble.

"Like what?" she asked.

"That little round gold thing."

"What gold thing?" she persisted.

"The gold canopy that hung over the bed in the Empire room."

She shook her head and hesitated a minute, and I realized she had no idea what I was talking about.

"If that's all you want, by all means. But can you start next Monday?" she asked, holding her pen in midair, ready to circle the date on her calendar.

"I'd be happy to."

I left her office and headed out the front door, leaping across the lawn.

Then I backed up my car to the greenhouse entrance. It took a while to find Angelo, who was out back pruning a cherry tree with an ancient saw pole. When I pointed out my latest find, he shook his head.

"What is this-a stupid thing you got now?" Then he checked it out for dry rot and bugs but couldn't find any. Together we carried the piece to my car and lifted it into the open backseat. I thanked him, and he went back to his cherry tree.

It would be some time before anyone realized that the class I gave that year was the most expensive ever given at the school. Documents turned up later that proved that the Empire canopy had once hung over one of Napoleon's beds; it was worth its weight in gold.

Teaching a class on how to get started in modeling turned out to be a very interesting experience, and I tried to make it a progressive class and let the girls ask their own questions and move at their own pace. Workshops were held outside in the garden rather than in the gloomy carriage house, but for the most part their minds were on getting dates and what to wear to attract men.

Over the weeks they came to trust and confide in me, and they began to share their own fascination with the house and how they took advantage of the secret passageways and trapdoors and some of them knew about a tunnel that ran from somewhere in the basement out to the teahouse pavilion. This allowed the select few who knew about it to leave the building after their curfew of 10:00 P.M. I was told a number of stories after that, though there is no way for me to know what is true and what was the overactive imaginings of youth. Allegedly there were dozens of sightings of ghosts during the time the building was used as a school.

One of the girls had bragged that, on a dare, she had smuggled her boyfriend into the house without being discovered. Then they spent the night together in the room that had always been kept locked. She claimed there was a secret entrance into the room that the staff didn't know about, but while there, she was awakened during the night and startled by a hazy vision of a young woman in a blue dress, who stood before her crying. The ghost then whispered that the girl would be joining her soon. The young man who was also in the room had apparently slept through the whole thing, and he slipped out of the house before dawn. No one at the school who had heard the story took the incident too seriously. Two months later, not far from the house, the girl was killed in an automobile accident. It happened four days before her graduation, and Sunny took it very hard. She withdrew into herself and refused to discuss the matter with anyone.

A hushed stillness hung in the air, and for a time it seemed everyone spoke in whispers. The semester ended, along with my class, and I had no cause to go back there all winter. The following year there was a similar incident involving one of the school's secretaries, Esther Schwartz. She too had spent the night in that same room. She claimed to have been attacked that night by a swarm of giant bees, then given an ominous message, and two weeks later she died of heart failure.

I waited until the spring before returning. I found Sunny in the garden, bending over a clump of daffodils sprouting among the weeds. They had been planted when the garden was first laid out, and though neglected, they burst forth every spring, cheering those who took the time to notice them. I watched her work for a while as she gathered up the yellow flowers and placed them in a wicker basket. There was a quiet stamina about her, an inner strength that made it seem as though she could weather any storm. She was so much a part of Winfield, and yet she seemed to stand separate from it, radiating her own quiet energy so that the house held no power over her. I stood there for a while longer, then followed the ivy-covered path to greet her. She looked up and smiled pleasantly. "Hello, stranger," she said then continued with what she was doing.

"How lucky you are to live here!" I said, happy to see her and grateful that spring had finally come.

"How lucky you are to still see everything through rose-colored glasses!" she responded, as if to convey a hidden message.

"I think I would give anything to—" I began, but she cut me off, knowing somehow what I was going to say.

"Be careful what you wish for; it might come true," she said, waving a philosophical finger at the air. She struggled to raise herself up from the ground, pressing her hand into her back as though it pained her. Then she added more flowers to the basket.

"Can I help?" I asked, kneeling down in the grass. She nodded but then stopped to rest on a stone bench near the path.

"These are for the kitchen, but I can use some more for the dining room table," she said, looking up to watch the birds.

She was never one for small talk, seeming to save her energies for more important things, but I had missed talking to her and welcomed her odd bits of wisdom and unique perceptions of things no one else talked about. She was silent for a long while, and all you could hear was the squeaky snap of each daffodil as it was torn from its stem. I handed them to her, and she placed them with the others.

"Do you think we come back?" I asked, breaking her reverie. She looked at me but didn't answer, so I tried again. "I don't mean as ghosts. But can a person come back from one life and remember places and things from that life?" I asked hesitantly.

"We all come back. Everything in God's creation comes back—the trees, animals, people. Just look around you; look at the flowers in your hand. It's like those ancient bulbs are the soul. You can't see them in winter, but their force, their energy, remains, and then each spring the flowers bloom, then die, and you don't see them again until it's their time. Nature is a wise teacher, but we just don't make the connection. Most religions make a muddle of things—of truths that are really very simple," she said, taking a long deep breath.

"But our lives are more complicated than flowers and trees. Why would we come back?"

"To learn lessons, to pay our debts for wrongs committed, to balance the scales. No one ever really gets away with anything. It's all recorded in the ether. There are no secrets in the end. . . . There is no hiding from the truth. Those who do wrong, who wrong their fellowmen, keep coming back until they get it right," she said in a resolute tone.

I looked at her uncomprehendingly. What she said was beyond my grasp. Years would pass before I understood what she meant, but she planted a seed in my thoughts that day, and in time I would come to believe that everything she said was true. She sat quietly on the bench for a while, seeming content to just think and dispense answers freely, as though it were somehow part of her job to answer questions. Like the students at the school, I hung on her every word. My curiosity was boundless, and I decided to share something that had puzzled me for some time, but I found myself fumbling for the words.

"Sunny, what does it mean when you dream about things and places that you know are real, but you couldn't possibly know that because you've never been to them. . . ." I stopped, realizing I wasn't making any sense. "I know this sounds crazy, but sometimes I dream about whole events, like the day in the life of another person, and everything is just as it was in the year eighteen-ninety-six, or whenever," I stammered. Then I cleared my throat nervously and struggled on.

"These dreams were different from normal dreams. It's very hard to put into words, but they had a clarity, dimension, smells, sounds; they were just as vivid and real as we are now, standing here in the garden. I dreamt about Winfield a long time ago—at least I think it was Winfield. It must have been when it was new; it looked very different; you could see the beach and water then. . . ." I looked back at Sunny for a moment, and she gave me a look of understanding. Taking comfort from her apparent acceptance, I felt the need to go on and share things with her that I never had revealed to anyone before.

"There were other dreams, just as real: a boating regatta—I'm not sure where it took place, but I was there, surrounded by this indescribable spectacle. There were hundreds of boats, all kinds of boats, all decorated with garlands and swags of flowers and orange blossoms. Some of them had lit paper lanterns strung from the masts. The women wore white-lace gowns and carried ruffled parasols. It wasn't just the beauty of the scene; there was this indescribable energy, this feeling of anticipation that was infectious. What struck me the most were their radiant faces, that look of joy, a shining light in their eyes. They didn't just surround themselves with beautiful things; they turned their lives into art. They were celebrating being alive in that moment on one perfect day. I never see that look of joy in anyone's face—not in the world we live in, anyway. We seem to be sleepwalking through life, never holding on to a moment as though it were precious or worthy of the effort to create something magical out of it. We seem to race about from one frantic activity to the next. Then, exhausted, we numb ourselves in front of a TV set at the end of the day. What did people know a hundred years ago that we don't seem to know today?" I began to shiver, and the flowers I was holding in my hands were beginning to blur in wide smudges of yellow as I struggled to hold back the tears, but I could not. There was a terrible feeling of isolation and confusion that came with those dream memories. I tried to suppress the sudden feeling of panic I was feeling, but I was emotionally undone. My throat tightened, and I just froze. Sunny picked up on it.

"Go on," she said reassuringly as she shifted her weight on the bench.

"One day something happened that shook me even more than the dream itself. I was at the Forty-second Street Library, in the Main Reading Room on the third floor. I spent years there tracing the history of the old Long Island estates, but one day I went to do research on some of the old gowns Mrs. Reynolds had given me when she sold this house. I was just randomly turning the pages of old *Town and Country* magazines, looking at the sepia pictures from around the turn of the century . . . and there it was. The boating regatta, the one I'd been to. . . . I mean, the one in my dream, only it wasn't a dream. It was there, just frozen on the page as if it were taken yesterday. I stared at the photograph until my eyes hurt, then lost track of the time. Finally the library was getting ready to close; they had to practically pull the book out of my hand. . . . You must think I'm mad," I said, putting my hands over my eyes and suddenly feeling drained and exhausted.

"You may have a gift. I was born with the ability, but it takes time to get used to. I think we're all born with psychic abilities; traveling back in time is just one of them, but society, schools, and religion have a way of crushing them out of us before we get a chance to develop them. The old man who built this place was on to this, and he went to a hell of a lot of trouble to try and do what you seem to be able to do at will," she said, holding my gaze.

"I don't understand," I said softly.

"Those rooms upstairs—I saw them before they got torn apart to be turned into the girls' dormitories. There was a lot more to them than just fancy decorating. They served a purpose," she said, her voice assured and even.

"Like what?"

She paused a moment. "I can't speak for him, but it looks to me like he was trying to go back in time. Those objects he collected—they all had a history; they all belonged to very important people. It goes way beyond anything I can know . . . but nothing came into this house by chance," she said. Then she lifted herself up and stood, gathering up the last bunch of flowers I handed her and adding them to her basket, which was now spilling over with yellow blooms. She was about to head back up to the house when she turned to face me.

"Those dreams and images that you have probably help guide you. You must learn to trust what they mean to you. If you're drawn to something, go with it. There's always a purpose to everything."

"I've felt that way about this place ever since I first saw it," I said.

"Yes, I gathered that," she said under her breath. Then she turned away from me.

"You don't seem to approve somehow."

"This house takes hostages. It's very fickle. It brings some people luck for a time, but there's always a price to pay, and you never know what that price might be. It gives with one hand and takes with the other, just like the man who built it—it was his way," she said, looking up as a cloud passed over and threw everything into shadow for a moment.

"It's only a building—" I started to say, but she already had an answer.

"It's not the building; it's the people who are trapped here," she said with an anxious frown. Then she stooped to pick up some of the flowers that had fallen from her basket.

"I've got to be getting back to the kitchen and start supper," she said, heading up the stairs towards the house. I stood watching her as the sun emerged again from behind a cloud, igniting the spring flowers with light. Sunny stopped at the landing, turned, and called out.

"Use those gifts of yours wisely. They come with a big responsibility." She disappeared in the doorway.

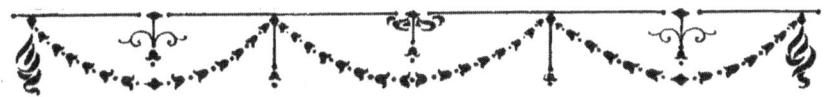

Chapter Five

The Auction

That summer I got the call I'd been waiting for. A representative from producer David Merrick's office called, saying that he had seen the photo story in the *Post* on the Gold Coast mansions, and that Paramount Pictures was about to do a remake of *The Great Gatsby*. In 1949, a black-and-white version of the film had been made, starring Alan Ladd. The new movie was to be a lavish and costly interpretation of Fitzgerald's book, first published in 1925, and It would star Robert Redford and Mia Farrow. The original plan was to film the movie where the story took place, on the northern coast of Long Island.

I was asked to go to the St. James Theater in New York and to bring as many photographs of Gatsby-style mansions as I could carry. If they liked what they saw, work would begin immediately.

When I arrived at Mr. Merrick's office, I was amazed at the opulence. It looked like a Paris bordello. There were red-plush, silk damask walls, red-velvet drapes, ornate Victorian furnishings, gilt candelabras, a red lacquer piano, matching red carpeting, and a huge vase filled with red roses. Mr. Merrick remained silent as one of his coproducers, Hank Moongene, spent an hour going through the hundreds of photos I'd brought. They selected several places to scout in person, and I was thrilled that Winfield was among them. For the next six weeks, we scouted the entire North Shore, first by limousine, then by private plane and chartered yacht. In search of Gatsby's house, we visited every mansion that was still standing. In the end, Jack Clayton, the English director, wanted Pembroke, the Glen Cove estate that borders Winfield. It broke my heart to have to tell him that Pembroke had recently been bulldozed. The Production people toured Winfield and its unique gardens but decided the house was too gloomy. The director wanted a light, airy ballroom with lots of French doors that opened out to a wide veranda with sweeping views of the sea. In the end the perfect Gatsby mansion was finally located by one of their scouts in Newport, Rhode Island, and the lavish party scenes were shot at Rosecliff. Seeing that I was crestfallen, they gave me a part, and I took Charleston lessons to become one of the many dancers in the film. Some of my twenties costumes, which had been rescued from the fallen mansions years before, also made their way into the movie.

The long-awaited film generated a lot of publicity for the Gold Coast and its lost way of life, and while none of it ended up being filmed on Long Island, everyone assumed that it was. It turned out to be a perfect public-relations campaign for Long Island and its fabled history. I started getting other calls for big country estates, and the next feature I worked on, *The Fortune,* with Jack Nicholson and Warren Beatty, was shot at an old Georgian manor in Sands Point. That same year, *The Godfather I* filmed a famous horse scene at the former Guggenheim estate's polo stables.

Many films followed, but there would never be another like *The Great Gatsby,* which brought the whole twenties era so vividly back to life. During the early seventies there was so much filming going on in the area that I was too busy to notice any problems at Winfield. But in 1975, the girls' school ended a run of bad luck and closed its doors forever. The news of the closing was announced in the *New York Times,* along with the upcoming sale of the house and its contents. The public auction would take place on the grounds on November 29, 1975. I felt a sickening sense of sadness and thought all was lost. Once the house was empty, it was only a matter of time before it would be attacked by vandals and then go the way of all the others.

I called an old friend of mine, William Niven, a successful stockbroker who was in the market to buy a large country house, and together we attended the sale. Mr. Niven had once told me that he would not consider anything with less than forty rooms. Winfield qualified, and I was determined to do everything I could to convince him that this was the house of his dreams.

On the day of the auction, it was impossible to get within a mile of the place. Hundreds of people surrounded the building and grounds as cars clogged up the narrow roads that lead to the estate. Every inch of lawn was taken up by cars and trucks, and the several guards, unable to deal with the chaos, shouted instructions using bullhorns to the disgruntled masses. The turnout was largely due to the Woolworth name. They came mostly out of curiosity and the lure of Gilded Age wealth. Outsiders outnumbered the local residents as they wandered about the house and grounds, glassy eyed, stone faced, all vying to take home some of the luster of the past. Some of the people seemed confused and disenchanted as they gazed at objects with studied indifference, resigned to the fact that there was not one piece of furniture that would fit comfortably in a normal home. Everything was faded and shabby, and they seemed overscaled, almost grotesque, once removed from the rooms designed to glorify them.

I overheard some strange conversations that afternoon. A man wearing a fringed leather jacket turned to the woman next to him. "What is it?" he asked about a Louis XVI throne that was designed to fit over a toilet.

His partner lifted the caned lid of the commode. "I don't know. I guess you hid your jewels in it," she responded. Then walked away.

"This is class," said a supercilious woman in rhinestone-rimmed sunglasses as she fondled a sterling-silver ice bucket shaped like a Grecian urn.

A young couple with three kids in tow eyed an ornately carved sideboard covered with snarling gargoyles and serpents with dragonlike clawed feet. "This would be great for Halloween, with a pumpkin on top," the wife said.

"It's too creepy," the man responded, and he moved his brood on.

Then a man walked up to the podium and fumbled with the microphone, which pierced the air with several shrill shrieks, and announced that the sale was about to begin. Everyone scrambled for the seats that covered the entire front lawn. There were some familiar faces in the crowd, Mrs. Borges's among them. She sat in the front row, studying a list of items that were to be sold. I waved to her, and she nodded solemnly, but her face was ashen and seemed resigned to the loss of what had been her whole life. I looked around for Sunny, but she was not there, and I wondered if I would ever see her again. I learned later that day that she had returned to the South to be with her family.

There was a strange tension in the air, a feeling of unrest, and people stopped talking.

The auctioneer stood on a wooden platform set up to the right of the entrance to the house and studied the prodigious crowd. He was tall, with a wild mane of salt-and-pepper hair, and he gave the appearance of having been dragged away from a carnival. He watched dispassionately as the first piece of furniture was carried out the front door and placed at the top of the landing. It was an oak cabinet from the billiard room. He gave a brief description of it. Then his voice lifted, and it became louder as he called out, "Do I hear five thousand dollars?" There was no response. His eyes became animated, and he began to work the audience with the skill of a showman. He began with a story conjured up on the spot; some of it was amusing, and occasionally a wave of laughter rippled through the audience. The cabinet sold for $250 and was quickly moved off to the side of the driveway.

"Ladeez 'n' gentlemen," he droned on in a stentorian barker's tone as the next item was carried out. "Here we have a fine gold-leaf throne; originally it graced a castle belonging to Catherine the Great."

A woman behind me with teased blond hair giggled and said to her partner, "Wasn't she the one who died screwing her horse?"

"No, stupid—that was Mary Queen of Scots," her partner responded. In a rare moment of brashness, I turned to face them.

"Excuse me, but Mary Queen of Scots was beheaded on the cobblestones that are now in our driveway," I said, unable to resist the opportunity to play historian. Mr. Niven jabbed me in the arm.

"Behave yourself," he said under his breath.

"Well, it's true," I squeaked, slinking down into my chair.

Catherine the Great's throne went for $60. A French writing desk followed and was hyped to the hilt.

"You can imagine all the illustrious men who have probably sat at this desk. Why, Jay Gatsby himself may have taken his morning coffee at this piece of fine furniture, and J. P. Morgan, who lived next door, was a frequent guest, not to mention the Prince of Wales and the like."

As the house was being emptied of its precious contents, the auctioneer was in high gear. His mood grew effervescent, and the adrenaline seemed to pour through his veins. He held center stage at what may have been for him the sale of a lifetime. Then a dozen men struggled as they walked out the front door carrying the fifty-foot Aubusson rug that had graced the ballroom floor for over sixty years. The audience listened intently as they heard that Greta Garbo, Rudolph Valentino, and Diamond Jim Brady might very well have danced on it. The rug sold for a mere $360—a fraction of what it was worth.

Next on the block was an eighteenth-century Chippendale dining room set that Woolworth had supposedly brought over from a castle in Scotland. Again the bids were very low. The sale was not going well. The auctioneer, though making a gallant effort, was running out of stories, and soon things were being sold in lots. The entire Chippendale dining set went for $1,600, though worth at least twenty times that. The red-velvet and tapestry chairs that had lined the walls of the main hall were well worn and shabby looking after years of abuse, and now looked like props from a Coney Island wax museum. Dozens of other chairs from storage sold for $5 each.

Next on the block was the greenhouse. It appeared that no one there had actually seen it, as it was hidden from view and engulfed in wisteria vines. The entire contents of the derelict building were sold, sight unseen, to a local estate owner for $500. At that point, whatever was left inside it was so waterlogged and rotted, it could scarcely survive being moved off the premises.

None of the artifacts that had once belonged to Napoleon were part of the sale that day. They were auctioned off at a later date through a more prestigious gallery in New York, most likely Sotheby's.

Halfway through the sale, a CBS mobile unit pulled up on the lawn, adding to the confusion as it disgorged newscasters and crew with cameras and cable, who then wove their way through the audience. Newscaster Carol Martin spoke nostalgically about the tragic passing of yet another of Long Island's Gold Coast mansions, then moved inside the house and shot footage of the ballroom to air on the six o'clock news that night. They filmed the furnishings that had already been sold and that were quickly being stacked up in melancholy lines along the driveway, waiting to be claimed by their new owners.

During a brief intermission, I noticed a tall man with piercing eyes standing beside a huge armoire that was about to be loaded into a truck. There was an intensity about him as he stood looking up at the house like a child mesmerized before a candy-store window. Then another man, who bore a striking resemblance to Gov. Hugh Carey, stepped to his side. He tapped the tall man on the shoulder and was greeted with a welcoming smile. Something distracted me, I looked away, and when I turned back, both men had gone.

After the house had been stripped clean of all the rugs, paintings, and furniture, the auctioneer announced that bidding on the house would begin at $400,000. A lengthy silence ensued as he gazed out at the sedate and very silent audience. He stretched out both arms and grasped the sides of the podium, took a deep breath, then stated that the original cost of the mansion was $9 million, making it in its day perhaps the most costly house ever built. At this time, the taxes were $62,000 a year, and very few people were willing or could afford to take on such a burden. There was no movement anywhere as the audience remained in their seats, some clutching their smaller purchases, waiting as the tension mounted. You could hear a pin drop as the audience sat waiting to see who would bid on the white elephant. The auctioneer was patient, determined to sell what was the main attraction of the sale. He began with the building's finer points: the solid construction; how ten Woolworth fortunes couldn't build a house like it today. He mentioned the solid gold doorknobs, the sixteen marble bathtubs, the seven-foot crystal chandelier, but only silence followed. I turned to my friend William, who had sat intently throughout the sale, and whispered, "What do you think?"

"It's too gloomy," he responded dryly. I leaned towards him.

"You can cheer it up—some organdy curtains, a few flowerpots on the windowsills, maybe a goldfish bowl in the hall, some pink plastic flamingoes on the lawn," I said, teasing.

William looked at me, then smiled. "It's the gloomiest house I've ever seen," he repeated. In that moment I could think of nothing to say.

The auctioneer searched the crowd with his eyes as a chill wind blew back a lock of his graying hair; then he boomed:

"Think about it folks: the buy of a lifetime, the house of every red-blooded American's dreams. . . .

"You'll be the envy of your friends."

The silence stretched on, and finally he threw up his hands and slinked down from the podium. The crowd began to scatter in all directions. The front door to the house stood open as the sound of workmen's voices echoed strangely from inside the now-empty building.

The towering fortress glared down mockingly. The sale had ended.

Chapter Six

André Von Brunner

Several months after the auction, the local newspapers ran a human-interest story on two men who had met at the sale and discovered that they shared a love for the house. Together they pooled their resources and came up with the purchase price. That spring, when buds were beginning to sprout and the lawns were awash with fresh green color, I drove over to the estate in hopes of meeting the new owners. As I pulled into the gate, I saw a tall man moving about in the tennis court off to the right. At first glance, he appeared to be playing a game of tennis with his dog. Nearing the court, I recognized the man I'd noticed at the auction and was again struck by the brilliance of his eyes.

I waved to him and quickly walked towards the court.

"Greetings," he called out with a friendly smile. It was then that I realized that the animal with him was not a dog but something else.

"Are you the new owner?"

"I am," he answered. He flung something in the direction of the strange-looking animal, then walked over to me and extended his hand warmly. "André Von Brunner here — and you are?" he asked, cocking his head to one side. I introduced myself, and, perhaps out of nervousness, I started to babble the entire history of the house such as I knew it, but I couldn't take my eyes off the pile of fur that was moving towards us. Finally the creature sidled up to his master as if to protect him from me.

"What is that?" I asked, backing away.

"This here is Wooley, our attack sheep . . . and my tennis partner," he said with what sounded like a slight German accent.

"A sheep," I repeated, thinking it did not look anything like a sheep, but like something more exotic, even prehistoric. It was huge, and its fur was matted and resembled mildewed grass clippings.

"Does he really play tennis?" I asked, watching the man's eyes, which seemed to sparkle with childish glee.

"Watch." He took something out of his pocket, then snapped his fingers, and the sheep leaped over the tennis net, landing like a rag mop on all fours, puffs of dust billowing out from his long, matted fleece. The strange animal stood there a moment, sniffing the air. Then he waddled over to his master and was rewarded with a Mallomar cookie, which he devoured while making strange gurgling noises. When he finished, his master snapped his fingers again, and the animal did another leap and then another.

"How long will he go on leaping?" I asked as he continued to jump back and forth over the net, huffing and puffing and fast running out of breath.

"Take five, Wooley," Mr. Von Brunner shouted, seeming pleased to have an audience that afternoon. The animal stopped, but this time he didn't move to claim his reward but collapsed in a heap on the court. As he lay there breathing heavily, I could not tell his front end from his rear. "What an unusual pet," I said, trying to be polite.

"I taught him everything he knows," he said, tossing him another cookie, but it went unclaimed.

"Are you planning to make this your new home?" I asked, just to make conversation.

"More or less. I move around a lot, travel abroad, and my partner, Martin Carey—he's more of a silent partner—doesn't come around much. He's got four other houses to live in. It was Carey who rescued Wooley after he was found wandering the streets in New York. My partner has a soft spot for critters and would turn this whole place into a zoo if he could, but Wooley is an asset, he scares everyone away." He said as he reached up and latched the gate on the enclosed tennis court. I followed as he began walking across the dandelion-covered lawn.

"Will he be alright?" I asked, looking back at the resting mass of fur.

"Oh, he's fine—got plenty of water and bugs to eat," he said, joking.

"I remember seeing you at the auction. When no one bid on this property, I thought that it was doomed—that developers would grab it for back taxes and tear it down. I'm glad that you and your friend came along."

"Yes, I was surprised no one else was interested in bidding on it—lucky for us. We got it for a song," he said, gazing up at the house, which stood majestically in the distance. "Looks like the White House from here, doesn't it?" he said proudly as he continued to stare at his prize with a far-off expression. He moved with an air of controlled assurance, but he held his body stiffly as though it were a fortress. He was gregarious and enigmatic, but there was something untouchable about him. André Von Brunner was not what you would call handsome, but he possessed an incredible energy and enthusiasm that were infectious. He expressed himself with sweeping flourishes and waves of his hand, as though words were not enough. He had strong features, including a long Roman nose, and his Edwardian-style sideburns gave him the appearance of Basil Rathbone's Sherlock Holmes. He continued to walk across the lawn with a jaunty swagger, his eyes sweeping the vast acreage around him in a way that betrayed perhaps that wealth was something new to him. He spoke very quickly of his help, his staff, his team, in a way that old money never does. It made me all the more curious to learn about how he came to be there.

"What are you going to do with it?" I asked finally. He paused for a moment, straightening up to his full height and folding his hands against his brown tweed jacket in an attitude of polite attention.

"Hold on to it until they legalize gambling in New York State. I've been assured from the highest of places that it will go through sometime soon," he stated with a hint of arrogance. "It would make a great casino, don't you think?" I was taken aback.

"Gambling in Glen Cove—you've got to be kidding!" I said in a bemused tone.

"Why do you say that?" he asked, glaring down at me as though I'd said something blasphemous.

"This is a very conservative community—a lot of very old families. They'll fight you."

"They're dinosaurs, a dying breed, and they have little control over what's really going on," he responded almost angrily.

"What will you do in the meantime?" I asked to change the subject. He walked with his head down for a while, not saying anything.

"To tell you the truth, I've been a little overwhelmed by the place. It's one thing to buy your dream house; it's another thing to furnish it. The only thing I've bought so far is a bedroom set for myself that was on sale at Bloomingdale's. Other than that, the house is just as empty as the day I bought it," he said, stooping down to pick a dandelion from the lawn.

"You didn't bid on any of the furnishings on the day of the auction. They were practically giving them away."

"I know. I regret it now, but everything looked so shabby, so big, and kind of alien to me. It wasn't until after they sold everything that I met Martin and realized that together we could actually buy the place." I was about to tell him that I owned several rooms of the original pieces, but I stopped myself, fearing he might offer to buy them, and I wasn't willing to part with any relics that came from that house.

"You had to see it in its day," I said wearily.

"Oh, were you around then?" he said, half-bemused.

"Of course not, but I knew Mrs. Reynolds. She kept the place as a kind of shrine. Nothing had changed from the time she bought it from the Woolworth heirs in twenty-nine." I looked up at him and got the feeling that my comment was inconsequential to him, that he was not the least bit interested in the property's history. Unable to think of any other way to justify my intrusion that day, I naively tried to interest him in a deeper appreciation of that immense and ponderous pile of architecture whose deed he had so recently signed.

"I have some old photographs of the original interiors. You might find them helpful if you're going to make the place livable again. I can make you a set of copies if you like."

"Yes, I'd like that very much," he said in an atonal voice. Then he handed me the dandelion. The light shifted as some clouds passed over the sun for a moment, and as it did, his eyes caught the light of the emerald green lawn and seemed to change from dark green to hazel.

"What made you drive up here this fine day?" he asked finally.

"Oh, I'm sorry, I almost forgot why I came. Of course, I was hoping to meet you or your partner. Would have stopped by sooner, but I assumed you needed time to settle in." At that point I handed him the large leather folder that I'd brought with all the *Vogue* magazine ads and the bridal gown layouts we had shot there during the last few years. "The magazines pay very handsome fees, even for a one-day session—thought it might help with getting the place furnished again."

He stared at the tear sheets in their plastic cases for a long while, and I could not tell if it was the house that held his attention or the models posing provocatively in the foreground. He leafed through the pages again, smiled, and said, "People really get paid for this sort of thing? Maybe they'll furnish the house for me."

"Sometimes they do dress a room or two for a TV shoot, but then it all comes down when they wrap. Of course, it's only fair to tell you, having a film crew in your house can be very disruptive if you prefer peace and quiet," I added as he handed me back the folder.

"I find peace and quiet unsettling; I can use a little excitement around here. When can we start?" he asked enthusiastically.

"I'll put the word out. How can I get in touch with you?"

He reached into his jacket for a pen, then put the pen into his mouth for a second as though it were a cigar. With an enthusiastic movement he scribbled his number in a large, bold hand on the folder I was holding.

"There's only one phone up at the house, so it's hard to hear. If you have any trouble getting me, you can always stop by and leave word with my caretaker or one of the gardeners. One of them is always about," he said, turning to follow me back to my car. "Will I get to meet any Hollywood movie stars on those film shoots?" he asked, leaning down against the open car window.

"You never know," I said, realizing he might have some misconceptions about what a film shoot at your home was really about. I thanked him for his time and glanced back at the tennis court and noticed that his strange pet was now standing with his nose pressed up against the gate. I drove down the long driveway feeling pleased with myself for having made the contact and glad that a new chapter in Winfield's history was about to begin. The following week I sent him the photocopies I'd promised and included some of the old magazine ads as well, but I was unable to reach him by phone a short time later when a filming opportunity came up. One day I drove up to the house, and a caretaker informed me that Mr. Von Brunner was abroad on business for several months.

I didn't hear from him until the following year, in the spring of seventy-seven. He called one day to say that he was back, and that he had been approached by a fund-raising organization to do a designer's showcase at Winfield. Showcases were just starting to become popular in the area. Each spring one of the big manor houses that might otherwise have fallen to ruin was restored and decorated according to the whims of an army of up-and-coming interior decorators. The shows served both to bring recognition to the designers and at the same time to raise large sums of money for local worthy causes. Mr. Von Brunner seemed excited about the idea of having the house furnished, even if it was only for a month. The upcoming event and opening ball promised to be among the most glamorous affairs to take place at the house since Woolworth's day. I was invited to stop by anytime.

Naturally curious, I drove over the next day and discovered the house looked very much like a movie set being dressed up for a film. Throngs of technicians and crew members milled about as landscape people ran from one end of the property to the next, planting flowers and new shrubs in the garden and filling the huge marble urns with palms and geraniums. A team of masons was on the terrace, resetting loose tiles, while gardeners were trimming back the overgrown trees and vines. Inside the house, the oak paneling was being oiled, and lighting fixtures were polished until they sparkled.

As I entered the hall, I spotted Mr. Von Brunner hanging from the chandelier in the adjoining room. From where I was standing, he just appeared to be hanging suspended. As I moved into the room, I could see one of his feet was balancing on a sixteen-foot ladder while his hand gripped the chandelier cable. He had a large paintbrush in his mouth and just grunted through his teeth when he saw me, while paint dripped from the brush on his workshirt. His eyes twinkled as he climbed down the ladder with the speed of a monkey, then dropped the brush back into a pail of paint. He smiled and rushed across the room towards me and extended his wet hand in a brisk handshake.

"Oh," I said, looking down at the paint that was smeared all over my hand.

"You don't like the color?" he said innocently.

"Purple . . . is a nice color," I said, gritting my teeth.

"Oh, excuse, excuse. I'll get a rag," he said, noticing my hand. He then left the room. "So what do you think of the ceiling? I painted it myself," he said, returning a moment later and handing me a cloth from the kitchen.

"It's purple—you painted the ceiling purple . . . how festive," I said, trying to conceal my horror.

"Let me show you what we've been doing around here. They ripped down all the walls on the third floor. Those tiny little rooms were so cold and useless. We're going to put a bowling alley in part of it," he said excitedly.

"Those rooms once housed twenty or so domestic servants, I was told."

"They looked like prison cells to me."

"To be sold into service was like being in prison in those days."

"Well, there'll be no more prison cells in this house," he said piously. "Those wacko decorators are transforming them into futuristic space stations, like the ones in the movie *2001: A Space Odyssey*." I swallowed hard and must have turned a pale shade of gray. Then he turned to me and said, "Don't worry, it's only for the show, and then everything goes back the way it was."

"The walls too?" I asked skeptically. He didn't answer but waved to some men who were passing through the hall, carrying two cans of paint in each hand.

"They've gone through a hundred cans so far and haven't even started painting the second floor," he said, stopping to pause at the base of the third-floor staircase.

"We've been finding all kinds of wall safes and passageways hidden in places you wouldn't expect," he said, with eyes that sparkled like those of a kid on a treasure hunt.

"When this was a school, the girls made good use of those passageways, I think mostly to escape the building at night. Some of the students thought the place was haunted. Do you believe in such things?"

He gazed upwards for a while but hadn't yet taken a step.

"This is a very strange house, like something out of the 'House of Usher.' There've been nights when I've stayed here alone and . . ." His eyes narrowed as he shrugged, turned away from me, and started up the stairs.

"What happened?" I persisted. He laughed self-consciously.

"There's a kind of echo in the walls. I can't really describe it."

"Like voices?" I asked.

"I don't know what it is—just a disturbing echo," he repeated.

"Old houses are funny sometimes—they don't like to be changed or violated," I said, repeating something Sunny had told me years before. He turned and gave me a funny look, but he was quickly distracted by two workmen who came running up the main staircase to get his attention.

"Mr. Von Brunner, they're here," one of them said, and he hurried to follow them back down to the main floor, where he flung open the front door. A half-dozen uniformed men began racing into the hall, carrying huge potted palms, rolls of sod, wrought-iron garden furniture, and life-size statues of forest animals and wood sprites.

"This was my idea. We're putting in penthouse gardens on all the terraces upstairs." My host beamed while navigating his way around the growing forest of palm trees.

"When is the big day?" I asked.

"The opening ball is May eighth. . . . Have you got a date?" he blurted out, turning to face me.

"Well, no . . . actually I wasn't planning to attend," I stammered.

"Would you consider doing me the honor of going with me?" he asked, catching me completely by surprise. I took a deep breath.

"I'd like that very much," I said, noting he seemed to breathe a sigh of relief, but he clearly was in a hyper state and eager to get on with the arranging of his terrace gardens.

In the time that stretched between that afternoon and the actual event, I spoke to André Von Brunner only once. I was excited about the party, and while this was not a cotillion ball for the landed gentry, going to such an event satisfied my longing to see the house reclaim the glamor it once knew. But I was even more curious to learn more about this very strange and compelling man.

The theme of the ball was the turn of the century, so I decided to restore one of the vintage gowns Mrs. Reynolds had given to me years before. It was a great phantom of a ball gown of cream-colored Belgian lace embroidered with gold-and-silver thread on silk tulle, with layers of silk petticoats. It had a long train that gave it a dreamlike effect but made it difficult to walk or dance in.

The Winfield Ball in seventy-seven was a dazzling spectacle of light and color. The entire house glittered with mirrors, candles, flowers, and hundreds of elegantly dressed guests, and for the first time in half a century, the sounds of music filled the rooms and floated out across the lawns and into the far corners of the garden. The mysterious Mr. Von

Brunner stood in the entrance hall, looking stately in his new tuxedo as he acknowledged each arriving guest with an introductory bow. He seemed to glow with a joyful exhaustion, as if he'd prepared all of his life for that moment. As the gracious host, he took delight in the praise of Winfield's transformation and gallantly kissed all of the ladies' hands as they entered the massive candlelit hall. He possessed an incredible charm, and people seemed to take to him in delighted fascination. I stood dutifully by his side, trying to maneuver the voluminous layers of silk from my gown away from the flow of spectators.

Though caught up in the moment, I grew restless, and at the first opportunity I slipped away into the house to see what the overzealous decorators had done to it. The ballroom was decorated in pink-and-azure-blue satin, with a six-foot gold sculpture depicting the theatrical faces of comedy and tragedy setting off the south wall. A gleaming, white-lacquered piano stood in the far corner, and several guests gathered around it, taking turns running their fingers over the keyboard. One heavyset man began to vocalize, then burst out in a florid rendering of an aria form Strauss's *Rosenkavalier*. He blushed when everyone around him applauded.

The new satin drapes fluttered as gentle breezes from the sound blew in through the open French doors. Following a group that was part of a tour, I headed for the dining room, which was now bright with peach-and-lavender chintz flowers. Even with its new, garish purple ceiling, it was cheerful and fit the mood of the evening. Off to the right was the newly restored billiard room, where several men in tuxedos were gathered around the massive, antique oak table, boisterously playing a game of pool. It proved to be the most popular room in the exhibit and was as close a re-creation of Woolworth's original as they could muster. Soft light glowed from a pair of antique silk, fringe-trimmed lamps that hung low over the billiard table. Fine old English-leather chairs stood about the room, and some of the strange mounted heads of jungle animals had mysteriously found their way back up on the paneled walls. I thought it curious that they had somehow escaped the auction block.

At that point I realized I was being rude and quickly returned to the main hall to join my date, who was busy posing for photographers covering the event for the local papers. It appeared he hadn't noticed I was gone, so I dashed up the stairs to check out the upper-floor rooms. They too had undergone drastic changes, and the general tone seemed to be our future in space. There were silver-lamé time capsules, space modules, pop-art extravaganzas, and other startling transformations. Such was the nature of designer showcases; still, it was a far better fate than having a building fall into ruin or to the bulldozer. I was heading for the room that had been under lock and key all those years when a loud gong sounded from downstairs.

I leaned over the second-floor railing to see what was happening. The gong sounded again, and people began moving towards the main door. Someone announced that dinner was being served, and touring guests were directed out to the massive white tent that was set up on the east lawn. The tent was lavishly decorated with garden trellises, fountains, miles of orange blossoms, and twelve-arm candelabras that rose five feet from the center of each lace-covered table. Crystal chandeliers hung from the thirty-foot ceiling. At one end an orchestra played vintage tunes from a stage above a spacious dance floor. Throughout the dinner Mr. Von Brunner continued with his duties as official host of the gala, navigating his way around gold chairs and six-foot urns filled with enough exotic flowers to fill a swimming pool. There was little time for conversation, though we shared a dance or two.

Just after midnight there began a great exodus as people milled about in a struggle to find their way back to their cars. When the last of them were pulling out of the drive, we walked the short distance back to the house. I gathered up the yards of trailing fabric of my gown to keep it from dragging along the damp grass. As we passed the belvedere and fountain, my escort paused to look up at his house for the last time that evening. The lights were blazing in each of the rooms, and the ballroom chandelier shimmered, its crystals gleaming as it reflected in the shallow pool outside the entrance.

"I've never seen anything so beautiful," I whispered.

"For now," he agreed, suddenly sounding very subdued. We returned silently to the now-empty house. An elderly security guard sat in a metal folding chair, reading the evening paper intently. Mr. Von Brunner walked up to him and said, "You might make yourself scarce, old chum; I'll be staying the night with my attack sheep."

The guard looked up at him uncomprehending. "I can't leave, sir," he said politely.

"So be it. I guess you have to guard all the fripperies," he said with a wide sweep of his hand. He then turned to me with one of his wide smiles and asked, "Which room shall we have a nightcap in?"

I was distracted by the question, looked about, then noticed the glassed-in room straight ahead. "The palm conservatory would be nice."

"Then the palm conservatory it is," he said in an indulgent tone, and he made his usual bow. I followed as we passed through the dining hall to the all-glass greenhouse that extended out onto the exterior terrace. The conservatory had been transformed into a veritable tropical jungle heady with the fragrance of hibiscus and jasmine flowers. An antique gilded cage housed a pair of colorful parrots who swung on their perches to the music of water splashing into a marble fountain. Amid this little Eden of greenery were Moroccan couches piled high with silken and tapestry pillows, lush Persian rugs, and dozens of scented candles that glowed softly in bronze bowls. It was as inviting as a room could get, but it took on a surreal quality as the light of the moon glazed down from the all-glass ceiling above.

"What an exhausting night!" my host said, opening the brass door to the birdcage as he reached inside to pet one of the birds. One of the macaws began to shriek as it inched its way along the branch towards him, then nipped his finger hard.

"Nasty little beast. If that guard wasn't out there, I'd feed him to—"

"Stop that! Those poor birds have been tormented by your guests all night," I said. He smiled back at me to let me know he was putting on a show, then held up his hand and pretended one of his fingers was missing.

"Very funny," I said under my breath.

"Do you think you could call me André?" he asked. Then he turned and headed into the kitchen. He soon returned with a bottle of white wine and a pair of crystal glasses. "Compliments of the staff," he said, pouring wine into one of the glasses. "They put in a wine closet and stocked it."

"Is that wine real, or are they stage props?"

"We'll soon find out," he said, reaching over and handing me the glass. "Here, try this."

"No, you go first. Then, if you keel over, we'll know it's probably cleaning fluid or God knows what. I've been on too many movie sets and events like this know all their tricks."

"Ah, in that case let's give some to the little birdies," and before I could stop him, he reached into the cage and poured some wine into their water trough. One of the birds shrieked and flapped its wings.

"Is that healthy?" I asked, jumping up to stop him.

"Not if they're driving you home," he responded, amused with himself.

"Are you always like this?"

"Like what?"

"Strange," I said as he sank into the soft pillows of the couch and looked up at the starlit sky above. He filled his glass and drank it down, then poured himself another.

"You know, you've done an incredible thing here," I said, turning to face him.

"It wasn't really my doing. Hell, I thought I was dreaming when those people approached me. I'd have been nuts to turn such an offer down," he said, taking another sip from his glass.

"I've seen hundreds of places like this go down, and this is the first time one has been brought back to life. You proved it was possible. Maybe it will start a trend."

"It would be a great trend if they left all their goodies here, but at the end of the month, it all goes back to wherever it came from, and I'll be left with . . ." He trailed off.

"The purple ceiling," I interjected.

"You haven't touched your drink," he said, looking at me intently.

"I was waiting to see what effect it had on you and your feathered friends."

"Well, they're still bright eyed and bushy tailed, and the wine's not bad," he said good-naturedly.

"Don't you have a wife to help you decorate this place?" I asked, wondering if I wasn't being too forward. He sat back and took another sip of wine.

"I'm between wives at the moment. This house is what ended the last one. She said it was bigger than both of us," he said, lowering his voice, for no reason that I could think of except perhaps not to further arouse the temperamental birds, who were both glaring at him warily.

"How many times have you been between wives?" I asked. He averted my glance, looked off to his right, and began to ponder a Boston fern. It was a while before he answered.

"Well . . . if you count the in betweens, four times, but five wives. I'm hoping wife number six will be normal," he said with a tinge of bedevilment in his voice.

"What made you marry so often?" I asked, suddenly needing that drink.

"Part of the problem is I travel a lot. I'm in shipping lines, with offices in five countries. It's a lot to oversee. But aside from that, I have a talent for picking the wrong women."

"What were they like?" I asked, intrigued.

"My first wife was a countess whom I met in Germany. She had great style and dressed impeccably, but she liked to gamble with my money — went through a fortune before I put a stop to it. Wife number two was a Paris model, beautiful, thin as a rail, but as soon as I married her, she began to eat and eat, and within a year she turned into a blimp." Taking a deep breath, he covered his face with one of the pillows, then let it tumble to the floor. "My third wife turned out to be a hit woman, and I was her hit. She tried to stab me in my sleep one night. Fortunately, I'm a light sleeper."

"You're not serious."

"I *am* being serious," he insisted in a miserable tone. I looked at him as he held my gaze. "I am being serious," he repeated, pouring himself another glass of wine.

"Perhaps you find something exciting in knowing your relationships are doomed," I said, trying to sound supportive, but it came out sounding arrogant.

"Are you a shrink too?" he said without affect.

"No. It's just that some people take comfort, perhaps unconsciously, in knowing there's an escape hatch built into the marriage, so they pick weird partners."

"That's drivel," he snapped. "Do you want to hear about wife number four?"

"Go on," I said softly, with a tinge of voyeur's curiosity.

"She was a stripper. They called her Candle Lily." I rolled my eyes, but he didn't notice. "I met her in a nightclub in Sweden. I've seen a lot of nightclub acts, but nothing like this. She had the biggest pair of . . . you know." He fumbled, gesturing with his hands in front of his chest. "She'd come on stage, red lights flashing all around her, and she'd dance to wild flamenco music while dripping hot wax all over her . . . you-know-whats. Then she'd snuff out the candles with her . . ." He stopped abruptly when he saw me leaving the room. He jumped up from the couch.

"I guess you don't want to hear about wife number five." I turned and glared at him.

"Let me guess: she was an extraterrestrial, and she glowed in the dark. Mr. Von Brunner, this is all very colorful, but it's getting late, and I find your choice of conversation a little tasteless."

"You asked me, remember."

"Yes, I did, but I never expected it would be so . . . sordid." I responded awkwardly.

"Well, I'm sorry Miss Prim and Proper," he said, sounding sanctimonious. He started to move towards me, but I turned and headed towards the front door. "Where are you going?"

"I'm leaving," I said coldly.

"How are you planning to get home, madam?"

"I can walk to the train station and call a cab."

"Dressed like that! This is Glen Cove. There are rapists lurking behind every tree, just waiting for someone like you to saunter by in an Edwardian ball gown." I continued towards the door, then caught my reflection in a tall Baluster mirror ahead. The man had a point. But I was out the door when he caught up with me.

"Please don't go. . . . I was trying to shock you," he said miserably. "I'm sorry, I just get nervous around American women. . . . You're all so independent. Ever since I moved here, those decorating broads, I mean ladies, from Great Neck have been throwing themselves at me. I mean literally attacking me in the closets, on the stairs, in the elevator." I suppressed a giggle and continued to hold his gaze while he bumbled on.

"Perhaps you should carry a cattle prod around with you to hold them at bay," I said as a faint smile flickered in his eyes.

"I like to think women find me irresistible."

"I can resist you," I responded icily.

He turned away and faced the heavy bronze-grilled door. Finally he looked back and said softly, his tone changing completely, "I'm sorry if my choice of words offended you before, but that has been my life, and I don't regret any of it." I just stood there, confused by his many shifts of mood. He was not someone you could easily size up or figure out. He had an oddball spontaneity I found refreshing. Though often aberrant and surreal, his mind seemed to draw from a jumble of Salvador Dali images. He sometimes reverted to speaking in other languages, mixing sentences and countries on a whim. He carried the aura of a land baron well, but there was an overlay of something unspoken, hollow, and melancholy just beneath the surface. I was determined to ferret it out.

"Just stay with me a little while longer," he said in a tone of despair. The massive door creaked open on its ancient hinges. The guard had not moved from his assigned post, nor did he look up from his paper as we passed. The house was so still, I could hear the fabric of my gown dragging along the marble floor. When we reached the conservatory, my host flung himself back on the couch and remained perfectly still. I took note of the birds, who appeared to be asleep or drunk on their perches. "Where is your furry companion?"

"Wooley? He's upstairs. They left me one room to stay in while all this is going on, but I'll be in the city on business most of the time. Can I get you something to eat? 'Cause I'm famished." No, I shook my head as he sprinted towards the kitchen door, returning a moment later with a silver tray piled high with strawberry and peach tarts left over from the evening's dinner.

"Voulez-vous des pâtisseries?" he asked, passing the tray in front of me. I waved my hand in dismissal. "I could send out for a pizza, or a twelve-foot hero," he said, munching down one of the glazed tarts.

"Have you heard any more strange sounds in the house at night?" I asked to get off the subject of food.

"Hard to tell. Up till now the men have been working and making a racket around the clock to get things finished on time. So this will be the first night when . . ."

"I think you're afraid to be alone," I said. He looked up and continued eating.

"Some of the painters took photos of the rooms they were working on, before they were decorated, and they claim to have gotten things on film that weren't there," he said in a reserved tone.

"Like what?"

"Like people who've been dead for seventy years."

"Did you actually see this?" I asked.

"No, but I know one of the guys. He's not the type to just make something like that up. There are other things about this place that are strange. Upstairs—any idea what all those eagles and bees are about, and the letter N carved into everything?" he asked with a grimace while downing another pastry.

"Those are Napoleon's symbols," I responded, relieved that the conversation had shifted to the subject of history. I sat down on the couch but kept my distance. "Years ago, when this was a girls' school, I found an old book lying around in one of the rooms. It was all about Woolworth's rise to fame and fortune. Apparently he was born into a poor farm family up in Jefferson County, New York. He hated the drudgery of that life and the bitter cold winters up north. He didn't own a pair of shoes, and his mother would wrap his feet in rags. His hands would burn from the cold when he shoveled snow to make a path to the barn at five in the morning, and there were suggestions of abuse. The only thing that kept him going were the stories he used to hear from the locals about how in the early part of the nineteenth century, Napoleon's brother Joseph Bonaparte had built a huge estate in Great Bend, not far from where Woolworth was growing up. He would ride over to the property in one of his father's farm wagons every chance he got and just stare at the castlelike fortress with the Bonaparte coat of arms emblazoned over the stone entrance. Young Woolworth listened eagerly to the stories told to him about the place, and about a great gilded Venetian gondola that floated on the property's lake, and about the lavish parties once given there. One of the legends about the place was that Joseph Bonaparte had masterminded a heroic plot to rescue Napoleon who was imprisoned at St. Helena and bring him to Great Bend to live in the castle and create a new empire in the United States. But Napoleon died before his brother could carry out the plan. Frank Woolworth was so impressed by what he saw and heard he vowed he would one day be surrounded by Napoleonic grandeur, with an empire of his own creation." When I looked down, André had his head leaning back on the couch, his eyes closed. "I seem to have put you to sleep," I said, leaning forward and raising my voice just a bit.

"No, you're wrong," he said with a start. "I was just thinking ... wasn't it Fitzgerald who said: 'The grand life is the best revenge,'" he said drowsily.

"Yes, something like that," I mumbled, then said the first thing that popped into my mind. "Was it revenge that attracted you to this house?"

"You ask a lot of questions," he responded in a brittle tone.

"Sorry. I didn't mean to pry. It's just that it has always fascinated me—

what drives some people to accomplish so much, to attain the unattainable, and others to be content with what they're given in life. There's always an intriguing story behind those who are driven. They're the ones we read about in books," I said, trying to turn my remark into a compliment, but he was not taken in and sat there aloof, staring upward as though a part of him had left the room.

The moon had drifted overhead, reflecting in multiples, like a kaleidoscope, across the glass prisms of the domed ceiling. André stared at it, transfixed, for a long while, its cold blue light seeming to draw something out of him. When he gathered his thoughts together, he surprised me by his candor.

"I knew the moment I saw this place that I had to own it. It was a symbol of everything one could possibly attain in this world, and if it were mine, it would make up for an unbearable past. . . . I had a father who taunted me—took every opportunity to let me know he didn't believe I would amount to anything. Just before the opening I sent him a plane ticket and flew him over here to see all this, thinking he'd change. . . ." His body stiffened as his eyes swept the room.

"Go on," I urged.

"I picked him up at the airport, and when he got here, he just sat in the car like a stone—didn't say anything. Not one word. He didn't even want to come inside. Finally I pulled him out by the arm and practically dragged him around. Nothing—no reaction at all. Then he up and left—just walked off across the lawn and vanished," he said in a voice resigned and bitter. "He didn't have a car—didn't even know what town he was in—but just like that, puff, he was gone. I had the cops out looking for him all night. Then the next day I found out that he somehow got himself back to the airport and took off without a word to me—then or since." André reached over for the bottle and went to pour himself another glass of wine, but it was empty. "The grand life is not what it's cracked up to be. It takes too much out of you, and, frankly, I find it exhausting," he said in a mordant tone. An awkward silence filled the room as I tried to think of something comforting to say. I understood only too well what he was feeling, but I had failed all my life to reckon with that kind of emotional abandonment, choosing instead to bury myself in work.

After a long pause, I came out with the inane response. "Perhaps your father was just overwhelmed by your achievement."

André sat there clinching his fist in a knot while searching the room with his eyes. "He could have said something . . . anything. I waited my whole life for that day . . . to show him he was wrong about me, but he was like a stone. Being around my father was like being surrounded by a great wall of stone," he said, his voice sounding corrosive as sandpaper.

"Now you've got this great wall of stone to protect you," I blurted out too hastily, then regretted it. He flinched slightly. He eyed me warily, pretending to dismiss my words, but there was something vacant in his eyes, as though he were no longer connected to the world around him. He gazed up at the glass ceiling, but now he only seemed to see the blackness beyond. I wanted to leave, suddenly feeling trapped in the fragrant, heady airlessness of the room. For a second, I was afraid. He had the dark, disquieting nature of a half-tamed wild animal; an unpredictable overlay of fury seemed to always be there, and you could never fully trust him or let down your guard. Feeling uneasy, I walked over to the birdcage, reached in, removed the glass dish, and refilled it with fresh water from the marble fountain. Some of the guests had thrown pennies and coins into the shell basin during the night, and I wondered what wishes they had made.

"Sometimes I think it's better not to have parents at all than to have the kind who abuse your spirit as a child," he said dully while a bright spot of color burned in his cheeks. I sensed the luminous intensity of his gaze, and I turned. His eyes bore into mine, and he seemed to regard me with the utmost suspicion. "What's your fascination with this place?" he asked, seeming far removed from where he'd been before.

"I had a dream about it once, long before I even knew it existed. That sounds crazy, I know, but it happened," I answered in a low tone, but I was not sure if he was listening. There was a long awkward silence.

"You are at this moment the only thing in this entire house that seems to belong here," he said in a slow, even tone of profound despair, and while I believed he meant it as a compliment, the intensity of his gaze was almost chilling. I didn't say anything but turned and looked at him. Something came and went, some enervating exchange of mutual attraction. I was surprised to find that I was both repelled by him and drawn to him at the same time. At that moment he rose abruptly from the couch.

"I'm taking you home," he announced suddenly, and he began pacing the floor like a panther. "I'm so grateful that you came," he intoned, as though addressing something invisible in the room.

We drove back to my house in silence. When we arrived, he got out of the car and walked me to my door. It was almost dawn, and the birds were beginning to stir in the trees.

"Madam, it has been a most pleasant evening," he said, taking my hand. I could not see his eyes as he was silhouetted by the iron entrance lamp behind him. I felt his hands on both my cheeks, then a warm gentle kiss like that of an innocent young boy.

Then he was gone.

Five months later André reappeared under very bizarre circumstances. I was working on a TV commercial shooting at the nearby Prybal estate in Lattingtown. The property was situated on several hundred acres overlooking the sound. It had been abandoned and had fallen to ruin after the original owners died in the sixties. The house had been on the market for ten years, but the rumor was that the property had just been sold. The spacious, brick Georgian mansion had a wide, sweeping circular staircase that the director needed for his shot, so I took a chance and drove over with the producer to check it out.

When we arrived, we were surprised to find an elderly man in a dress suit raking leaves in the large, circular drive. He motioned for us to enter the gate, then told us he had just purchased the property but hadn't gotten his staff together just yet. He worked in a hurried manner, as though his life depended on the removal of every offending brown, shriveled leaf. He never looked us in the eye, but as he continued working, he began to speak on the Zen of raking leaves, claiming it helped him stay connected to God, trees, and nature.

The producer pretended to be fascinated by such a concept, but he was getting antsy, as creative people often do when on a mission. He then explained that he needed to create a Hollywood-style fantasy using the sweeping staircase as a backdrop. The only catch was that the walls and stairs had to be painted bubblegum pink.

The owner looked up finally and stated that pink was one of his favorite colors, and that the house was in such a state of disrepair that this would give him a head start. Considering the eccentric ways of some of the landed gentry, we didn't think it at all odd when the man offered to give us a tour of the house, leading us in through a broken window out in back, claiming to have lost his key in the tall grass.

Several days later we paid the owner several thousand dollars in cash and watched him sign the standard property release. It took us two days to paint the vast entrance hall and get it ready for the scene that was being shot to sell a new line of evening gowns. On the day of the shoot, a young dance team was rehearsing a takeoff on a Ginger Rogers and Fred Astaire number. Someone turned on the bubble machine, and the couple began to tap-dance their way down the wide spiral staircase. The director had just begun to film their first take when the front door burst open, and within seconds the house was swarming with police.

"Don't anyone move—you're all under arrest," one of the officers boomed. Everyone froze and stared at the director; the director looked at me in horror.

"There's some mistake," I blurted out, feeling myself turn white. I quickly fumbled through my purse and handed over the property release and the receipt for the money paid. The officer glared down at the worthless piece of paper and announced:

"This person does not own this house; it belongs to the city of Glen Cove." In all my years of scouting for the movies, I have never thought to ask anyone claiming to be the owner to show me the deed to the property with his or her name on it. Being a trusting soul, I would never have thought of doing so. I stood speechless as the lights, camera equipment, and bubble machine were carried out of the building and loaded into police vans. Everyone on the crew, including the dancers, was herded out of the front door. We were informed that we were being charged with trespassing, vandalism, and painting city property pink. Just as I was being escorted to a waiting police car, André appeared in the driveway. He looked at me with an amused expression and said, "Madam, you seem to have gotten yourself into a bit of a pickle." To this day, I'm not sure what happened after that. He was involved in a conversation with the police in the drive, the mayor of the town was called, and within ten minutes we were told we could return to the house and resume filming. News of the incident spread like wildfire, and the local papers had a field day with the story. The phantom who had claimed to be the owner was said to have hopped a plane for parts unknown; according to the press he was unavailable for comment.

André had been tipped off about the impending police raid by one of the locals who had a CB band radio, and he figured I might somehow be involved in the TV shoot. We began to see each other almost every night after that. We would walk the grounds of Winfield at dusk, gather wood for the fireplace, and talk for hours before a roaring fire. He announced that he was finally ready to settle into the house and make it a home. But even with no furniture in sight, he had a way of filling the empty rooms with his boundless energy and vitality and never-ending strange stories. His complexity continued to surprise me, and while I came to know parts of him, I began to see there were many different sides to his personality. He seemed to enjoy and take pride in his ability to shape-shift and ride the wave of his own unpredictability.

In the ballroom there was an oversized dark green velvet couch with faded fringe and tassels running along the bottom. It had gone unclaimed after the auction, and it would have ended up in a dumpster had André not recognized it from one of the photos as one of the original pieces from that room. After the showcase ended that spring, he had it hauled up from the basement and placed before the massive fireplace. Then he installed a state-of-the-art sound system, with speakers hidden behind all the open filigreed walls. The music seemed enhanced by the alchemy and grandeur of that room, which was created to glorify it. Though I'd heard all the classics played elsewhere so many times, in that room of shining angles and blinding splendor, it was as if I were hearing them all for the first time. He spent days choreographing and arranging onto reel-to-reel tapes all the great Baroque classics he'd collected over a lifetime, and he worked like a sorcerer to weave a spell out of those celestial sounds. His knowledge of music and its history impressed me as he strung together haunting and lyrical pieces like Wagner's *Lohengrin* and Fauré's *Requiem Mass*. The walls would resonate with string concertos and languorous symphonies and operas. We listened for hours to works by Rachmaninoff, Mahler, and Brahms, but when the last act of Wagner's *Parsifal* began to play, the air in the room seemed ignited by electricity as sight and sound coalesced.

We sat studying the flamboyant shapes in the ceiling. André remained somewhat shy and reserved during that time. Sometimes he held my hand, but nothing more. Those evenings alone in that room were the purest moments of complete rapture I'd ever known, and though nothing was said, I knew I was falling in love with him.

One night I arrived late at the house and found André sitting on the couch. A row of lit candles stood flickering along the high rim of the mantelpiece as Vierne's *Tocatta* played softly in the background. He smiled when he saw me enter the room, but he did not speak. He reached out his hand, and I joined him. There was an imperceptible look of serenity on his face. When a passage of the music slowed to an inaudible pitch, his gaze moved up to the crystal chandelier directly over us. Then there were several loud bursts of sound as the notes held in a long crescendo, causing the chandelier to suddenly vibrate. André stood up, his eyes gleaming. Then he turned down the sound.

"My caretaker showed me something very interesting today," he said as he reached down and pulled a flashlight out from under one of the velvet pillows on the couch. He walked towards the alcove, pausing in front of one of the ornately carved panels. With a bedeviled smile, he began to tap gently around the wall. Then he turned the arm of a carved mythological creature. Like magic, a heavy panel opened with a slight creak, revealing a narrow wooden staircase. I watched him disappear up into the darkness. Then he called for me to follow.

There was a landing between the first and second floors, crisscrossed with narrow passageways. We found ourselves on a wooden catwalk with iron railings that shook precariously if you moved too quickly. André scanned the room with the beam of the flashlight as cobwebs hung like hammocks from ledges and stretched from one silver organ pipe to the other. Hundreds of long, vaulted chambers rose up from floor to ceiling, some with concealed little wooden doors with brass handles. From one of the stacks, an unexpected stairway rose into the darkness. There was a kind of *Alice in Wonderland* madness about the place, that seemed to fascinate André.

"I'd like to get all this working again, but, so far, I haven't found anyone who's up to the job, at least not in this country. I may have to bring someone over from Vienna, where they understand that music is life," he said. Reaching over with the metal flashlight, he began to tap a bank of hanging chimes. It produced a heavenly sound that lingered with a faint echo.

"Here, you have to see the best part," he said, grabbing my hand. I followed him along a narrow ledge above the room below. A faint light flickered through the open plasterwork panels, where the walls curved and joined the ceiling of the ballroom below. We found ourselves on the other side of the carvings of winged beasts and goddesses that glistened and were silhouetted all around us. We looked down and could see the entire room below, as though it were a stage set seen from a balcony in an old Broadway theater.

"It's amazing—it's like a lookout post," I said in a hushed tone as the music from below continued to play softly and float up to where we stood, with surprising clarity. We began to make our way back when suddenly there was a scuttling noise from inside one of the lengths of wooden pipe. Then something brushed past us and ran unseen down the narrow ledge. Terrified, I leaped into André's arms with such force that the flashlight flew out of his hand, hit the catwalk, and rolled off the ledge. A second later we heard it crash as it hit the basement floor some fifty feet below. "Oh, no!" I shrieked.

"It's all right—it was probably just a rat," he whispered, unfazed.

"I'm not afraid of rats. . . . It's the dark, and this high-wire balancing act, and if we fall, no one will ever find us," I said. Then I realized I was digging my fingers into his shoulders.

"Voilà," he said, producing a flash of light from a cigarette lighter. "Just don't move yet. I brought you up here for a reason."

"To scare me to death," I said, unraveling.

"No, to ask you to marry me," he said as we stood there amid the cobwebs and gloom. I stared at him in the faint light, having lost all power of speech. That queer, mischievous look played in his eyes.

"I thought you wanted someone normal this time," I stammered.

"I changed my mind," he whispered. There was a sharp snap as he switched off the lighter, then slipped both hands around my waist. He squeezed so hard I could barely breathe. Tiny flashes of light danced before my eyes.

"I'll marry you . . . but let's go back," I mumbled, too unnerved to be coherent.

"Say it—say you love me," he pleaded. I could feel his warm breath on my face. Before I could answer, his mouth crushed down on mine, and I was filled with such exquisite sensations that my legs almost gave way. The danger of the moment only added to his passion. I gripped the iron railing with one hand, thinking we were going to fall, and it was a long way down. As my eyes adjusted to the darkness, a faint flute of light began to appear around the open carved ceiling. Finally, I gave into the moment, reached up, put my arms around him, and returned his fervent kisses. All my defenses crumbled, and I willingly surrendered to him.

It would have been out of character for André to have chosen a normal place to propose marriage. A gazebo would have suited me just fine, but that was not his way. Once we were plighted, he decided to host a black-tie engagement party at the house the following weekend. He became like a child at Christmas, and he took charge of all the arrangements. On the night of the party, he seemed nervous and obsessed with last-minute details. For a dining table, he took three doors he found in the basement and set them up on sawhorses in the ballroom. He used old sheets from the linen closet for a tablecloth, then placed a large vase in the center and filled it with masses of vibrant, rose-colored hydrangeas. I offered to drive back to my house and pack up all my china and glassware for the occasion, but he assured me he had everything under control.

Moments before the guests arrived, he pulled out a silk handkerchief from his pocket and handed it to me.

"I think you should wear this tonight," he said, beaming. Then he stepped back nimbly as I opened it.

Inside was was an unusual, Victorian-style platinum ring with clusters of rubies set into several sharply pronged flower petals.

"It's beautiful," I said, with tears welling up in my eyes.

"It belonged to a Russian baroness who lived in the last century. When her lover was trampled to death by his horse, she threw herself from a castle tower and drowned in the moat. She was wearing that ring when they found her body."

I stood there in mute astonishment, waiting for him to tell me that he had made the story up. But he watched my reaction with an erasable smile on his face.

"What a charming story," I said while he slipped the ring on my finger. André could be very entertaining, but I was beginning to believe that his exotic narratives and curious reveries were a unique art form. He was the only man I'd ever known who sought the advice of fortune-tellers and took what they had to say seriously. One night he announced that a psychic he had seen used a crystal ball to describe his sixth wife, and that I fit her description to a T.

"We Europeans believe in dying for love," he said in an ebullient tone just as the guests were starting to arrive. He quickly turned and ran into the billiard room to call the caterer, which I found out moments later was the local Chinese takeout in Glen Cove. As his guests began to arrive, I thought them odd. My friends were late, and when he finally met them, he thought them dull. You learn a lot about a person when you see them with their friends for the first time. André was electric around people and would do almost anything to keep his guests amused.

One of his more colorful friends was a rather hefty-looking opera singer named Helvinka. She had wild orange hair and wore long black eyelashes that were so heavy, her eyes were never fully open. Sometime during the evening she and André began to sing an aria from a German opera, and once they began, there was no stopping them. They held each other's gazes as they flawlessly went through their lines. They sang their way up the stairs and out to the balcony, and then despite the cold they continued to sing outside on the open terrace. When a chilling wind began to blow Helvinka's royal blue sequined gown up around her, they finally returned to join the rest of us.

After dinner, there was ballroom dancing, though few of the guests knew how to waltz or could maneuver their way around the huge table. Those who were drinking seemed to have the best time of it. André loved to waltz, and he made it seem effortless as he covered the dance floor with a buoyancy that no one there could match. The party was a success. My friends loved it. They applauded with childlike glee when, around midnight, we ran out of firewood and André picked up one of the rented wooden folding chairs and hurled it into the fireplace. When it came time to clean up the mess from dinner, André opened the front door and let Wooley in. At a snap of his fingers, the animal proceeded to devour all the leftovers, then the paper plates, the centerpiece, and part of the tablecloth.

Everyone left around 2:00 A.M. André, now tipsy, continued to sing as he danced through the halls and made his way up the stairs.

"Who was that woman you were singing with half the night?" I asked, giggling as he draped himself over the balustrade.

"Sheeee's Wooley's moooother," he bellowed in an exaggerated operatic voice. I moved towards him and looked him straight in the eye.

"You are the weirdest man I have ever known."

"But you still love me," he insisted as he grabbed my hand and squeezed it. His eyes were still shining in the afterglow of his first party hosted with no help from anyone. I hadn't answered his question, so he squeezed my hand again.

"I do, but I'm wondering if perhaps you prefer the Brunhilda type. Maybe if I put on an extra hundred pounds . . ." I said, feeling giddy and light-headed from too much champagne. He dropped my hand, and before I could catch my breath, he picked me up and flung me over his shoulder like a sack of potatoes. I shrieked and giggled. Then, when I reached down and tickled him under his arm, he lost his footing, and we both tumbled down the stairs, still laughing. Marble stairs are not the best things for tumbling. We lay on the hard floor, still laughing, but too stunned and bruised to move.

"You okay?" he asked, sounding winded and out of breath.

"I don't know. Are you?" I mumbled.

"Remind me to have these stairs carpeted," he said, feeling his limbs to see if anything was broken. Nothing was, but he lay there looking somewhat contorted on the cold marble floor for a long while without saying anything. The amber glow from the tinted lantern above us put his face in shadow, making his eyes seem larger than they were. He scanned the empty hall.

"I've got to do something about furnishing this place," he said, struggling to sit up. Then he pulled me up to join him on the bottom step of the staircase.

"How many rooms are there?" I asked, feeling myself come alive with a plan.

"Too many," he responded ruefully.

"I think I can help you," I said, staring up at the ceiling but not wanting to move just yet.

"How?" he asked flatly.

"Can you get me some trucks and strong men?"

"What for?" He winced as he tried to stand. I started to giggle again despite the soreness I was beginning to feel, and as I leaned towards him, a whiff of his European cologne filled my nostrils. I kissed him gently on the cheek.

"Let me surprise you," I said, feeling a surge of secret power. That was to be the first of many times he would not take me seriously. Though I was partly to blame for it this time, for I had never gotten up the nerve to tell him about my former life as a pirate. Somehow I didn't feel that my girlhood antics of running rescue raids on the doomed mansions would fit his conception of women, and I was still too much in love with him to have begun to question just what his views might be. His being a foreigner made him even more of a mystery to me. Perhaps through the influence of movies, I held the belief that European men placed their women on a pedestal and expected them to look and act in a feminine manner. The idea of my scaling walls, crawling through broken windows, and driving a getaway car in a poodle costume I feared might just cause him to suspect there was something seriously askew in my nature. No, I decided, he wasn't ready for any of it, but Winfield was a gloomy house in need of furniture, and the time had come to take those abandoned treasures out of storage. I would figure out what I was going to tell him later.

It had been years since I thought about those heroic days. I missed them so much I could taste them, but all the grand empty houses were gone. Only J. P. Morgan's sprawling brick mansion, a short walking distance away, was still there. It too would come down in a few years, but for now a handful of Catholic nuns lived there. All of its original furnishings had been sold off after Morgan died in 1943, and now the building was filled with cheap, gaudy objects that looked as though they had been bought at the Salvation Army. Local preservationist groups would attempt desperately to save the landmark building, but in the end the developers were the ones with the most money, and they always won out, while we lost yet another piece of our history. I recorded the mansion's last days on film, walking over to the private island and crossing the medieval stone bridge that connected the property to the mainland.

Today the surging tide still sweeps through the narrow channel from Long Island Sound to the little bay on the south side, where dozens of swans surround the island banks like ethereal white sentinels. When Morgan was alive, he kept a herd of cows who were free to roam the vast lawns, claiming it gave his rolling acres a restful, bucolic look. His four-hundred-foot stone dock, where he kept his yacht, the *Corsair,* is long gone. The local library kept volumes of old scrapbooks filled with newsclips about the comings and goings of Morgan in his day.

In 1915, a young German instructor, convinced Morgan was about to get America into the First World War to protect his foreign interests, managed to slip past the security guards, staff, and cows and enter the house to fire two close-range shots at the financier. His faithful butler jumped the would-be assassin and saved Morgan's life. The intruder committed suicide in his Mineola jail cell while awaiting trial. Morgan, though nearly fatally wounded, was back in his office in less than two months. By the following season, Morgan was again hosting lavish parties for hundreds of noted guests on his quiet island.

Again, it seemed as though all the exciting and glorious things had already happened and all we had left were faded newspaper clippings found on dusty library shelves. No one knew what would happen to Morgan's fabled mansion, but there would be no daring rescue raids. The house was off-limits, and there was nothing inside to save.

In my mind I began to take stock of all the things that Chloe and I had saved from extinction. There were hundreds of pieces, many of them still hidden and covered with blue plastic tarps in an old carriage house in Brookville. In the meantime the objects I kept and used in my Oyster Bay home were much cherished, and I took pleasure in sleeping under Napoleon's gilded canopy, putting on my makeup at Empress Josephine's former dressing table, and serving tea to my friends on a wicker boudoir tray rescued from Farnsworth only days before it was toppled to the ground.

But there was a void in my life that even being in love couldn't fill. At the heart of it, I was insecure by nature, and I doubted I could hold André's attention for long, considering his history with women. But I felt a new purpose rising within me, and thought I could dispel those feelings of inadequacy by using my obsessive abilities and talents to transform and make homey his prized possession.

With some effort André and I managed to make it up the stairs that night, and we spent a sleepless evening in what was called the Ming dynasty room. It was an exotic room, smaller than the rest, with an Oriental carved black onyx fireplace that, when lit, reflected flickering flames onto the cinnabar red chinoiserie fabric covering the walls.

André had decorated the room for himself with a newly acquired brass bed, too new to really fit the room, and a black-lacquered dresser set—on sale, he said again, at Bloomingdale's. Though still sore from our fall, we curled up in each other's arms, and our night together passed as though in a dreamy haze. The next morning I was awakened by what sounded like heavy breathing coming from just outside the bedroom door. Shaking André, who was sleeping soundly, I asked him to listen.

"It's nothing," he grumbled.

"Nothing doesn't breathe," I whispered.

"Ignore it," he said, pulling the covers over his head.

But I couldn't ignore the slow rhythmic sound that was resonating ghostlike down the cavernous hall. I pulled on his brown-velvet robe and shivered my way to the door, opening it. There, lying on the floor, was what looked like a pile of that stuff you pull out of vacuum cleaner bags, only it was snoring.

"It's Wooley," I said, feeling stupid.

"Oh, geez, I forgot to let him out last night. . . . I hope he didn't. . . ." He trailed off in a muffled voice.

I looked back down at the animal, then closed the door gently so as to not wake him.

"I think he needs a bath."

"Come back to bed," André mumbled, extending his hand.

In the weeks that followed we were inseparable. He soon discovered and became fascinated by American shopping malls, and though he didn't cook, he took delight in buying sets of dishes, cookware, and colorfully handled flatware for the kitchen. He never seemed to get tired; his fervent vitality kept me on edge, and at times I found it difficult to keep up with him. His mind teemed with extravagant plans, which on one occasion included his building a secret gambling casino in the basement to amuse his friends. The next day, he was on to something else, having forgotten all about yesterday's ideas. Without warning he would entertain on the spur of the moment, and his hospitality often included anyone who came to the house for any reason—no matter what the hour, they were given the grand tour. There were several more parties of the Chinese take-out variety, at which he remained effortlessly poised, but not quite in sync with some of his guests, who often included the local merchant who had come to change the locks, or the glass cutter, or a UPS delivery man who had a pleasant smile and expressed an avid interest in the history of the house.

Several times a week I would drive back to my own house, partly to spend some time alone and recharge. I would check my answering machine and see that the lawn got cut and that cobwebs didn't accumulate along the high ceilings. The two boarding horses that lived in the old wooden stables on my property were tended to by their owners, but I would always check in on them to see that they were okay. When the weather was good, they were often out in the fields until sunset. From time to time, I would take Daphne, a gentle gray-and-white Appaloosa, out for a run through the open meadows along Woodbury Road, then on up the hill to catch a glimpse of the Otto Kahn Castle. The 126-room fortress rose up on Long Island's highest point. It had long since fallen to ruin, but from a distance it made your heart soar just to look at it.

The ride back was always slow and languorous, and though I'd made the trip dozens of times, the surrounding woods seemed newly created. Leaves turned color overnight, and forests resonated with the sounds of starlings and hawks. That idyll in Woodbury hadn't changed much since the Indians occupied it hundreds of years before, and as I moved across that rich land, the dull rhythmic clippity-clop of the horse's hooves hitting the soft wet earth acted as a tonic, and I would feel content and at peace.

Gradually something began to subdue André, and he became more and more preoccupied with his work. At times his eyes seemed dark and troubled, and there was tension in his voice. He seemed slightly detached from everything around him, and focused on matters that were going on thousands of miles away. Strangers would appear at the door, leave messages, then turn around and head back down the drive. He became moody and preoccupied, and there began to be highs and lows in our relationship.

One day a letter arrived for him. He tore it open and read it where he stood, showing no sign of emotion. Then he turned to me and calmly stated that he had to leave for France that evening. Even more disturbing, he was packed in less than five minutes. I drove him to the airport, but I didn't press him for answers. I assumed that because of his foreign roots he felt it somehow made him less manly to share his personal or business problems with a woman. On the drive back I realized I would miss his strange roller-coaster life, but I needed a rest and was almost relieved to return to my own house, where I began several painting projects.

Wooley was moved to a nearby estate that had a farm with other animals for him to play with. Within a few days André's letters began to arrive. On the envelope there was a curious seal or coat of arms of a large boat with what looked like a goat or wolf perched at the helm. His letters were illegible, written in Kelly green ink and punctuated with little drawings. I tied up all of his letters with a blue ribbon and kept them in a drawer of my dressing table.

When André returned two weeks later, he brought a bodyguard with him. At first I thought he was joking when he introduced Jovon, who did not look or act the part. He was tall, slim, stately, and impeccably dressed, and he looked more like an English professor from an Ivy League college than a bodyguard. He was serious and reserved, with dark good looks, and he wore a thin mustache that he fussed over constantly. There was nothing protective or sinister about him, and if he really was a bodyguard, I never saw him carry a weapon of any kind, though I was told he was armed and that his unassuming persona was part of his cover. He and André were about the same age and claimed to have gone to school together, though just what kind of school was never made clear. Jovon read a lot—mostly cookbooks. He spoke with an accent and was a fitness fanatic, often running around the property several times before and after eating, but for the most part he was never far away from André.

I was intrigued and puzzled by this curious new situation, which allowed for very little privacy, but something told me not to ask too many questions about it. There were no more quiet dinners in André's favorite local restaurants, but Jovon turned out to be an accomplished gourmet chef and quickly took over the sprawling kitchen, taking delight in the ancient ten-foot stove. He cooked elaborate and exotic meals, and we drank foreign wines he and André had brought back with them. Each night we ate and laughed together and listened to music, and if any of the staff were about, they were invited to join us. André would often sing, and Jovon would propose toasts in French, Hungarian, or German—I was never sure which—and once he threw a new crystal glass into the fireplace. These were very versatile evenings that left me confused, for I had never given any real thought as to what living with André would be like on a day-to-day basis. André, realizing this, pulled me aside one night and begged me to be patient with him, claiming he was working on something important that would secure the future of his shipping lines and our future together.

The following week I saw them both off at Kennedy Airport, and the next day a telex was delivered to my door in Oyster Bay by one of André's new gardeners, hired to help with spring cleanup.

April 22, 1978
Dear Monica:
All went well:
Transfer self and all worthy possessions to Winfield:
Will return shortly:
Warm loving regards:
André

I stared at the message, and as I did, Sunny's words echoed in my mind: "Be careful what you wish for; it might come true." She had said it in an ominous tone, as if it were a warning, but in that moment I was elated.

The house never looked more beautiful as I pulled up the drive on that foggy day in May. A silver haze was beginning to lift from the lawns and the surrounding trees as the house began to take form. Winfield stood in the distance.

Chapter Seven

The Gold Rose

The movers were late. When they finally pulled up to the entrance, they were agitated and claimed to have passed the house by several times, thinking it was an institution of some kind. It wasn't the first time that had happened, and though I had mentioned to look for the stone arch beforehand, they were probably thinking of McDonald's twin arches rather than a thirty-foot replica of the Arc de Triomphe. It stood out, aberrant, on an avenue of mostly split levels and a Victorian cottage or two. Moments later I stood on the second-floor landing and watched as the two men carried the heavy rosewood furnishings up the stairs. As I directed each piece into its assigned room, I wondered if the ancient furnishings were happy to be home again in the rooms where they belonged. It was a silly thought, but I had always had a tendency to personify inanimate objects. "Welcome home," I said under my breath, and smiled gratefully as the men trudged by with their burdensome loads.

The Empress Josephine room at the top of the stairs was an exact replica of the original that Napoleon had designed for his beloved empress at their country estate, Malmaison, just outside of Paris. Despite its formality, it was cheerful and sunny, with French doors that opened out to a large terrace extending out over part of the driveway entrance. The room needed very little in the way of decorating, as it had been painted a warm beige color with upholstered inset panels of pale blue and peach flowers for the recent showcase exhibition. When I arrived that morning, there was a thick, powder blue rug rolled up on the floor in the downstairs hall with a card attached. "Hope this goes with your new room. Love, André." It was perfect.

When the movers finally left, I opened the glass doors of the terrace to let in some air. Everything outside was still engulfed in a gray vaporous mist, and you could no longer see the entrance gate, which was off to the left, or the Neptune fountain to the south. I stood there for a long time breathing in the salt air and fog, wanting to hold on to that moment for as long as I could. A seagull who had been perched unseen on the balustrade suddenly winged his way across the lawn and headed towards the beach.

I began to think about all the stories and rumors I'd heard during the girls'-school years and before that. It all seemed so long ago, and in that moment none of it mattered. Nothing was going to cloud my being there—not that day or any other. I continued to watch as the seagull flew and then vanished into the milky surreal whiteness that engulfed everything as if to cleanse and make everything new again. Sunny may have believed this was a sad and tragic place, but I was determined to make it a happy one. "Mind over matter," I said out loud, as if the bird now invisible could hear me. "Mind over matter," I repeated as the new phone in my room began to ring.

"How are you surviving moving day?" the voice at the other end asked breathlessly.

"Katia, you're my first call." I said, happy to hear an old friend's voice. "So how's it going?" she asked again.

"Well, I've got one room down and fifty-six to go," I said cheerfully.

"You're crazy, you know. I give you until dark before you freak out. You have to be a little nuts to stay in that place alone," she said, popping what sounded like bubblegum in her mouth.

"Katia, it's so beautiful here. I feel like I'm living in art, in esthetic overload. You must come for the weekend and see for yourself. I'll have another room pulled together for you by then."

"Do you hear anything odd?" she asked in her mischievous tone.

"Just an occasional frog croaking out by the pond," I answered.

"Well, you know I'm here if anything strange happens," she said.

"Nothing strange is going to happen. Thank you for calling." I said, eager to get back to work on the room.

"By the way, that's not the best phone number for you numerologically. It would be better to get a number with three fives in it. You should call and try to get it changed," she said insistently.

"Anything else?"

"Well, come to think of it, you should have waited until tomorrow before moving in," she said with her usual dramatic zeal.

"Too late now," I said.

"Not really. You could always spend the night in the car. But park outside the gate, at least until midnight," she shot back in an amused tone, not expecting me to take the suggestion seriously.

"Think about the weekend," I said, hanging up.

Katia and I had been friends for years. She was a numerologist, and one of the best astrologers in New York City. I had seen her on a television talk show and was impressed by what she had to say, so I called her for a reading, and we'd been friends ever since. Katia was also psychic and full of information on the subject of the paranormal, but the term *numerology* was new to me when I met her. Katia explained that it had to do with helping people pick the best dates and times to make important decisions in their lives. She said that all numbers vibrate on a certain frequency and that those vibrations could influence the success or failure of any given thing. Our addresses, license plates, and phone numbers, she claimed, all work together to play an important part in our lives. Katia was great fun to be with, but when she spoke of these things, she became very serious. Her earnestness was part of her charm.

The room felt damp and musty from nearly a year of not being used, but within a few hours everything was scrubbed clean, including the closets and a wall of glass shelves in the adjoining dressing room. I carefully unpacked a box of antique perfume bottles and arranged them on the now-gleaming shelves. I fussed over the placement of table lamps, silk scarves, and knickknacks, and put a pair of brass candelabras and a porcelain bust of a Victorian woman on top of the mantel. I found some daffodils growing wild in the surrounding woods and put them in a cut crystal vase to keep on the night table. When everything was finished, I took out the old photographs and was amazed at how quickly the room began to look the way it did in 1917.

After making up the bed, and covering it with an off-white, tufted satin bedspread, I sat back on it and studied the room, then noticed for the first time that the main door off the hall was missing. Back at the turn of the century, it was the custom for all the country houses facing the sound to have two sets of doors. One was used only during the summer months and was made of heavy oak, with open louvered slates to allow the ocean breezes to flow through. It was sturdy enough, but it hardly provided that sense of security one got from a real solid door, though I noted it did have a brass handle that could be locked from the inside only. The main doors had most likely all been removed during the showcase tours and were probably being stored somewhere in the building. I made a note to go on a search for the door in the morning. In the meantime I had no intention of sleeping that first night, so it hardly mattered if the doors were locked or not. I had waited so long for the opportunity to photograph Winfield at night, and I had brought along half a dozen rolls of infrared film to experiment with long time exposures.

Years before, at the Strand Bookstore in Greenwich Village, I had come across a curious book on how to photograph so-called haunted houses. The author of the book suggested using infrared film because it responds to heat rather than to light. It's a tricky thing at best as there is no ASA reading to work with and no way to control the results. Camera stores rarely stocked the film, so I had to special-order it. With high hopes I set the camera on a tripod at the top of the stairs and held the release button for ten- and twenty-second intervals.

I didn't really believe you could photograph ghosts, and the many pages in that questionable book that alleged that those were real ghosts caught on film in various castles and dungeons in far-off lands looked phony to me. But I was always drawn to the odd and unusual and was going to photograph the house anyway; if anything spooky turned up, all the better. I shifted the camera a few times, but the only light in the hall was from the ancient chandelier, which looked like an Oriental temple with bronze sentries standing guard all around the sides.

I worked my way down the hall in the east wing, climbing over unpacked boxes and furniture I'd yet to sort out, and I began taking shots of each of the rooms. I paused in front of the Marie Antoinette room, which had always been locked before. There was a deathly stillness about it that made me want to move on, and it felt twenty degrees colder than any of the other rooms. Delicate wisps of cobwebs obscured the tiny crystal pendants that hung from the chandelier, but I didn't turn it on. Instead, I waited for gray, haunted things to appear in the shadows, but there was nothing there. A cold, blue lunar light played on the brooding faces of the marble angels that supported the mantel. I took a shot of it in the dark, holding the exposure for a full two minutes. Then I found myself counting out four minutes. Secretly I felt I was playing with them, whatever they were. I was inviting them to dance with me, daring them to make themselves known through a camera lens. I was open to anything; it was only film. I thought about what they might look like, and childhood taunts played back in my head: *Come out, come out, wherever you are*. The silence made me leave that room and move back into the hall. From the staircase landing there was a spectacular view of the formal gardens below. The moon was shining like an auroral sun, illuminating the stone pavilion with its labyrinth of interlacing boughs of hanging foliage.

As I was carrying the camera and stand down the stairs, I thought I heard a tapping sound coming from the basement, but when I moved towards it, it faded. *Old pipes,* I thought, and continued down the open hallway to the ballroom. I slid back the huge oak pocket doors and turned on the chandelier. The room was musty with the smell of stale ashes and burnt wood, having not been used in several weeks. The light from the raw bulbs amplified by hundreds of glass pendants seemed to overpower everything, and I considered turning the chandelier off and shooting by moonlight or even candlelight. Then I looked around and began positioning the camera near the alcove when suddenly I heard the faint crash of falling plaster. Something nearly hit me in the head. Looking down, I noticed a small, gold-leafed plaster rose lying at my feet. Above me in the ceiling there was a carved angel with voluminous wings, her arms outstretched to where the rose had broken free from her nerveless fingers. I bent down and picked up the rose and held it in my hand. Normally it would have appeared to be just a piece of plaster that had fallen from the otherwise-crumbling ceiling; such things happen in old buildings. But in that moment, the rose took on the most profound significance, and I was seized with all kinds of curious thoughts. The first was that some ghost unable to contact his local F.T.D. florist to send a welcome bouquet had decided to drop a plaster rose on my head instead. I also pondered the possibility that someone living there in spirit was trying to let me know that he or she liked roses, and that I as the gracious guest should run out and plant some in the garden. The last thought was that I might be telekinetic and that I had caused the plaster posy to fall myself. I opted for the first theory and left the room believing that some ghost liked me. I took the rose upstairs and placed it on the nightstand next to the vase of daffodils, forgetting all about photographing the rest of the house. There was plenty of time for that, but it hardly mattered, for I was never to see the results of the film I'd shot that night.

The next day I dropped off the three rolls of film at the local camera store. And just to cover myself with the spirit world, I also stopped at Martin Viette's, the nearby nursery, and picked up some pink climbing roses. Later that afternoon I planted them around the gazebo.

At ten o'clock the next morning, I went back to pick up the film and was informed that the night before the small private plane that was used to fly the film for processing in Rochester, New York, had crashed, killing the young pilot. Everything on board had gone up in flames. The clerk behind the counter imparted this information in a matter-of-fact tone, as though it were just another tragic news story. Then he quickly offered to replace the lost film, looking closely at my claim ticket to see what kind it was. A chill went through me. "That's horrible," I said lamely, and turned to leave, ignoring his offer to replace what I knew they didn't stock. I tried to put it out of my mind, and there was no mention of the crash on the evening news, but I decided not to say anything about it to Katia, fearing she might see it as an omen. I summoned the strength to block it from my mind, convincing myself it was just an unfortunate coincidence, as any sane person would. It would be illogical to think otherwise.

André was due back any day, and in my eagerness to surprise him, I raced about unpacking boxes and moving things into place. Taking stock of what was still in storage, I had only enough furniture to authentically fill perhaps three or four rooms with original pieces from the house, including a fine set of white-wicker settees and plant stands originally from the conservatory. During the building frenzy on the Gold Coast, most of the large houses in the area had been furnished in basically the same style and period, and many of the owners used the same design firms. When looking through old copies of *Town & Country* from that time, many of the estates' rooms looked alike. They were all exquisite and in perfect taste, but Woolworth went for something more exotic, and he commissioned the design firm of Hoffstater & Co. to re-create his one-of-a-kind rooms. All I could hope for was to pull some of the remaining rooms together in a pleasing manner true to the look and overall style of the times.

By the end of May, things began to come alive in the garden as all kinds of colorful flora began to sprout, and I found myself drawn outdoors rather than puttering around in those stagnant, dreary rooms. The heady scent of lilac, jasmine, and roses began to attract birds and butterflies. The cottage roses I'd planted the week before had taken and were beginning to inch their way up the stone pillars and wrought-iron arches along the rear garden wall. I spent long afternoons wandering about the grounds, picking bouquets of foxgloves whose lavender bells were splattered with bright touches of red, and mixed them with lush fronds of ferns that arched over the round reflecting pool at the bottom of the west staircase. Etched on a slab of a marble garden bench that stood nearby was a piece of poetry:

Bind me, ye woodbines, in your 'twines,
Curl me about, ye gadding vines,
And Oh so close your circles lace
That I may never leave this place.
  — *The Last Essays of Elia* by Charles Lamb

Those words had a strangely prophetic ring. In the surrounding woods, I could hear the sounds of pheasants and peahens as they ran about and roosted in the ancient oaks and black pine trees. I spent long hours in the gazebo writing letters to André and wondering if he ever got them.

As the garden continued to flourish and peak, it was as green and lush as it would ever be all summer. I began to feel restless, and decided it was time to share it all with some friends.

For years I had belonged to a group of artists and writers from the area. We met on Sunday afternoons in abandoned gazebos to share our love for the art, beauty, and style of the last century. We hadn't gotten together since the summer before, and, since everything was in bloom, there would never be a better time to plan something in the garden. I spent the night calling everyone, including one or two former members of the Gold Coast Rescue team and anyone else I thought would enjoy an old-fashioned garden party. I left a note on the back door for the gardener about the intended event, and the back lawn was freshly cut by the time I got up. It was to be a jubilee celebration of bending time, at least visually. We now had the perfect setting, the vintage costumes, and the willing spirit of a unique group of artists.

On a bright sunny afternoon, a dozen guests pulled up to the house dressed in authentic turn-of-the-century costumes. The ladies wore silk-flowered and veiled straw picture hats and white-linen gowns trimmed with embroidery, and they carried lace-edged parasols to shield their faces from the sun. The men sauntered up the steps in light cotton jackets and straw boater hats, greeting everyone with make-believe English accents. One carried a mahogany walking stick topped with the brass head of a griffin. Caught up in the spirit of play, he pretended to use it to knight everyone who stood near him. The women had each brought some Victorian-style dish to eat. Katia, a dedicated career woman who prided herself on never setting foot in a kitchen, surprised everyone with a colorfully decorated potato salad molded in the shape of a pineapple. She had painstakingly trimmed it with olives and a spray of scallions that sprouted out from the top. Then she had packed it in a large ice bucket and carried it all the way from the city on the train. Though she was seeing the house for the first time, she showed no reaction to it. I led her to my room and helped her find something to wear for the occasion, then left her alone to change. She emerged moments later on the veranda in a long, white organdy-embroidered gown, her waist-length dark hair and pretty oval face framed in a wreath of white-silk flowers.

Alicia, a noted concert pianist and my best friend of many years, brought a salmon mousse set in a bed of ferns and fresh dill on an antique silver platter. That morning I had filled a large crystal bowl with fruit ambrosia laced with peach brandy and set a white wicker tray filled with strawberry tarts on the table. The men brought champagne and long loaves of French bread from a local bakery that swore they were flown in from Paris that morning. In the center of the garden, I set up a large table covered with a white damask cloth and edged it with garlands of orange blossoms, having gotten the idea from an old vintage photo. Some of the women helped as I carefully unpacked a box of gold-edged crystal wine goblets that I had rescued years before from a house that was later bulldozed. We carried the English china and silver down from the house in a big wicker hamper. In the old days that would have been the job for the butler, but we could only carry our fantasy so far. At the last minute I hung some Japanese lanterns from the teahouse arches and placed a huge basket of fresh-cut flowers in the center of the table.

Whenever we got together, we always picked a theme, and everyone would do a little research, write something original, or speak about someone they admired who lived before us. Alicia, a regal dark-haired beauty, was the first to get up. She spoke about George Gershwin, and how she had recently discovered that his greatest work had been altered and mutilated: what the world had come to know as the *Rhapsody in Blue* was merely a shadow of the original. She spoke passionately about this man she admired, and she vowed she was about to set the world straight by going on a world tour and performing his masterpiece from his original manuscript. We all applauded, knowing she would do what she set out to do. Then she was followed by Kim, a visual artist from Huntington who gave a talk on *Madame Bovary*. Katia followed with an enlightening history of the Fox sisters, who were known as great psychics during the mid–nineteenth century. The two sisters, Margaretta and Katherine, grew up in a house where a ghost began to give them messages when they were very young. No one believed them until the ghost told them he had been killed years before and buried behind a brick wall in the basement. When it was discovered that the story was true and the body was found exactly where they said it was, the Fox sisters became world-famous.

As the afternoon wore on and the sun became too hot, we moved the table and wicker chairs into the teahouse pavilion, where bowers of fragrant wisteria vines overhead protected us. It was a relaxed and languorous afternoon, visually breathtaking in its authenticity. We looked as though we had stepped out of a canvas by Monet, and even if the garden had lost some of its luster, we brought something new to it. At one time rare and exotic roses of every kind flourished in a blaze of flaming color that was framed by clipped, parterre boxwood borders. Woolworth, who fashioned the parklike setting after the famed Borghese gardens in Rome, was said to have employed a staff of seventy men to maintain everything in perfect order, right down to the last blade of grass. But on that day butterflies danced over our heads, birds chirped contentedly in the trees, and you could hear the buzzing of bees as they gathered honey in the shadowy arbors, and that was perfection enough for us.

We had some more champagne, and then John, an architect and

graphic artist who lived up the road in a French château called Malmaison, spoke about the nineteenth-century architect Ogden Codman, who designed it as a replica of the château Napoleon built for Empress Josephine. He had picked the subject after I told him about the room I was staying in. Next up was Howard, the oldest member of our party and the only one to wear a tux and top hat. He spoke about his friendship with Ernest Hemingway, whom he met while a reporter for *Life* magazine during the Second World War. We all encouraged him to publish the stories he shared with us that day, but Howard was a modest man and said there was little he could add to what had already been written about the brooding author.

There were several more readings and presentations. One male guest read a poem he had written about Harry Houdini, then went on to perform one of his magic tricks. We were astonished, but he refused to tell us how he did it, claiming it was a trade secret. Ella, an art collector, spoke about several of her favorite painters and their work.

When it was my turn, I did a reading on Isadora Duncan, one of the greatest visionaries and dance performers of her day. Then I took out a page that had been reprinted from her journal after her tragic death in 1927 and read her own words:

" 'I do not doubt that someday someone will discover an instrument which will do for sight what radio does for hearing, and we will discover that we are surrounded, not only by sounds, but also and invisibly to our eye, by the presence of all that is no longer. The music and the voices that we hear over the radio do not cease to exist, but travel in space indefinitely and, in time, attain other stars, therefore gestures also travel endlessly in space. So each word we speak, each gesture we make continues in the ether on an immortal voyage.' "

My hands were shaking when I finished reading. How true her words would prove to be, and though I didn't know it yet, they would play out within the very walls of the fortress that stood before us.

When all of us had shared whatever work we had brought, I turned on the portable sound system and played a tape I had choreographed for the occasion, splicing the soundtracks from the films *Somewhere in Time, East of Eden,* and *Elvira Madigan,* then adding some Palm Court music transferred from old seventy-eight records. One couple got up and slow-danced on the grass. John, the architect, had brought an old croquet set. He set it up on the lawn next to the fountain, but despite our efforts, none of us knew how to play a serious game. With the bubbly flowing freely, the game quickly deteriorated into a free-for-all in which the colorful wooden balls, hit with too much bravado, zigzagged in all directions and got lost in the boxwood hedges. One of the girls, giggling uncontrollably, tumbled accidentally into the fishpond to retrieve a red ball, emerging moments later with algae covering her antique gown.

"It's washable," she said good-naturedly. Then she grabbed a mallet and continued to play, soaking wet.

Our behavior hardly followed the strict codes of decorum of the turn of the century. By late afternoon many of us had kicked off our shoes, and the men pulled off their bow ties. We toasted to a new beginning for Winfield. I ran about taking photographs of everyone, and looking into the camera lens, realized that together we had re-created one of the faded images that I'd seen in the old magazines. We were all enjoying the nostalgia of the scene when suddenly out of nowhere the sound of a shotgun blast shattered the mood. It came from somewhere up on the roof, and with it dozens of birds panicked, making an explosive noise as they scattered in all directions. We could hear several shrieks, which sounded like they came from teenaged boys off in the woods to the west, but from where we stood we couldn't see what was going on. We all froze in our places.

"What was that?" Katia shouted, covering her face with her hands as the others ran to safety behind the stone walls of the teahouse.

"I don't know. There is a guard. . . . He might be trying to scare some kids off the property. Sunday is a big day for trespassers," I said. Then ran into the house and up three flights of stairs to the roof, but I could find no one.

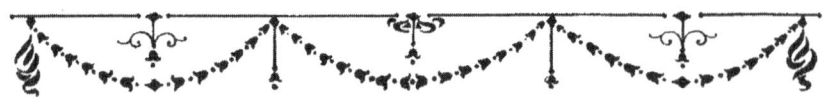

Chapter Eight

Voices in the Night

Aside from the sound of the shotgun on the afternoon of our picnic, life at Winfield in those first few weeks was idyllic and peaceful. Most mornings I'd awaken to the erratic rumblings of a power mower off in the distance. With the exception of the gardener, Pete, I had seen very little of the other inhabitants of the house. Willard, the caretaker, lived on the third floor with his reclusive wife, who spent most of her time cooking large quantities of food. The whole house often smelled of cabbage that she left simmering in huge pots for days on end. Sometimes I'd catch sight of her hanging clothes on a makeshift line near the back kitchen door. She'd wave politely but rarely smiled. Willard was never seen during the day. At night I thought I heard him scuttling about in the dark, labyrinthine chambers of the pipe organ; I assumed he was replacing burnt-out lightbulbs. I was never really sure what role he played at Winfield. André had once told me that Willard was not his real name, that he had changed it at some point and came to Winfield to hide from creditors to whom he owed a great deal of money. André was a compassionate soul and seemed to have an unlimited tolerance for people with strange problems.

Willard struck me as a sleazy sort, with dark weaselly eyes set into a round blowfishlike face. The faint smell of garlic and cabbage always hung about him, and he looked as though he had just gorged himself on half a dozen pizzas. He was always polite to me in a controlled sort of way, but I felt from the beginning he could not be trusted. From what

I could see, he had very little to do with the maintenance and running of the house or grounds. Most of the work was done by Pete, a friendly, cheerful fellow with an unruly mop of salt-and-pepper hair that covered most of his face. He was small in stature but seemed to have the strength of ten men. The eighteen acres of lawns were a constant challenge. The grass seemed to grow faster than the ancient cutting machine could mow it down. But Pete tackled it as though it were a game — a little bit at a time, so that it was never even. When you looked down at it from the upper-floor windows, it took on the odd appearance of a green checkerboard. Pete lived in a small, sparsely furnished room on the third floor. It was filled with old hunting and rifle magazines. He was overly protective of the property and watched over it like a hawk. It didn't take long to solve the mystery of the gun blast on the day of our garden party. I soon discovered that, when not cutting the grass, Pete spent part of his time marching along the edge of the roof, shotgun in hand.

"Trespassers," he said when I confronted him. "You got to get tough with trespassers, or else they take over. Nothing like a little buckshot in the butt to get the message across. Of course . . . I never shot no one — I just fire into the air and watch them varmints scatter over the wall." He sounded exhilarated as he lifted his rifle up over his shoulder like a sentry. I stared at him baffled, not quite knowing what to make of the situation.

"Pete, that's not legal. There are houses all around us, and those bullets are eventually going to land on someone's head even if you shoot into the air," I said in a mollifying tone. He looked up with very gentle eyes and brushed a lock of hair away from his face, but he didn't speak.

"You scared us half to death the other day," I said softly.

"Sorry about that, ma'am," he responded, looking down at the floor. There was something endearing, but misguided, about him. Even though the gun thing made me a little nervous, I found his presence there comforting. Even on the hottest days he worked harder than anyone should. When the pressure of his chores, or Willard's eccentric ways, got to him, he would let off steam by taking potshots with a BB gun at the broken statues that lay in a heap at the bottom of a gully on the far side of the woods.

One morning I was preparing breakfast in the kitchen when I heard someone muttering out in the hall. When I went to see who it was, all that was visible was a huge carved French door being carried up the stairs by what looked like a pair of phantom legs.

"Pete, is that you?" I called out.

"Yep, it's me," he answered, sounding out of breath but continuing to move with slow pantherlike steps.

"What are you doing?"

"Thought you might feel better at night with a real door on your room."

"Where did you find it?" I asked, running over to give him a hand.

"Those dumb decorators took all the doors off for their fancy show last year and left them in the basement sloshing around in two feet of water," he said, resting the door on the top step to catch his breath.

"I really appreciate your going to all this trouble," I said, watching him as he coaxed and shifted the door into place. Then he fumbled with a rag he had rolled up in his pocket, pulling out a dozen large brass screws and some tools. I held the door in place as he worked to bolt everything down. Minutes later he had the door back on its hinges.

"There, that should do it," he said, swinging it back and forth several times. "There ain't nobody going to break in that door—that's three inches of solid rosewood. Yes, sir, they sure knew how to build 'em in those days," he said, giving the door an admiring pat. He then began searching his threadbare jeans pockets for something else, then finding it, with a triumphant expression he handed me a thick brass key.

"Thank you, Pete," I said, taking the key from him and turning it in the lock plate several times. Then I noticed that he had taken the time to polish the brass door handle. I was at a loss for words. He reached over and slid the thin, louvered summer door back into the wall as though to banish it.

"You'd be wise to keep that door locked when you're alone here at night . . .'cause you never know what's creepin' about this place," he said, slipping his tools back in his pocket.

"Have you ever known any trespassers to get into the house?" I asked, never having given any thought to it before.

"I'm not talking about trespassers, ma'am," he said, hesitating. I looked at him, puzzled, and I got the feeling he wanted to retract his words, but he went on as best he could. "Well, I don't want to give you the heebie-geebies, but sometimes when I'm working down in the basement, there's this banging sound, like something's trying to break through the wall, and every now and then I see these fuzzy lights. . . ." he said, shifting his weight from one foot to the other nervously.

"Fuzzy lights," I repeated.

"Yeah." He stopped communicating in words for a while, and with his hands raised and his fingers wiggling teasingly in the air, he began to hum a few bars from the soundtrack of *The Twilight Zone*. I laughed out loud, but something told me he was serious.

"Pete, how long have you been here?" I asked to change the subject.

"Well, I'm only here part-time in the summer, you know, to take care of the lawns and stuff. I was here for the first time last year, and I saw them then too. There was another guy before me, but he left 'cause he was scared to death of the place. But me, I ain't scared of nothing. You don't have to worry when I'm here 'cause I got my gun . . . but those fuzzy things . . . bullets don't stop 'em," he said with gloomy relish.

"I'll keep that in mind." I said, taking a long deep breath. "Well, at the least, I owe you a home-cooked meal. How about breakfast? I was about to fix a ham-and-cheese omelette when I heard you out in the hall." He smiled broadly as his eyes registered delight. He then followed me into the kitchen, where I'd left the skillet on the stove; the omelette was now burnt to a crisp.

I was in the house for almost three weeks when I began to hear the sound of voices late one night. At first I just assumed it was the caretaker and his wife, who lived off in a wing on the floor above me. But as I tried to focus on these sounds, I sensed they were not the voices of living people. Though strangely muffled, one sound resembled the sobbing of a young woman, and it was broken now and then by indecipherable murmurings and whispers. The sounds continued on and off through the night, intermingling with the echolalia of the cold, dispassionate walls. The sounds would fade, then return, rising and falling in disturbing cycles. I lay there on the bed as though paralyzed, feeling as though a slab of marble were pressing down on me, holding me there. Again came the chorus of unearthly voices, and then it stopped. It wasn't really fear that I felt, but something else, for the more I listened, the more the sounds seemed to be repeating themselves, as though they were on some kind of tape loop having nothing to do with the here and now.

I was determined to prove to myself that I wasn't imagining the whole thing, so the next day I bought a small portable tape recorder and placed it on the floor near the door to my room. I turned it on and waited, but nothing happened. Nothing happened the next night or the night after that. By the end of the week, I began to think I'd dreamt the whole thing.

It was about ten days before I heard the sounds again; the voices seemed to be coming from outside in the hall, along with the faint, measured footsteps of someone walking up the stairs. I reacted the only way I could, and that was to face whatever was on the other side of the door head-on. I was curious as hell to know what, if anything, was out there. After all, stories about ghosts have been around since the beginning of time, yet no one is known to have ever been killed by one. A few may have died of fright, but that hardly seemed likely to happen to me as I really wanted to finally meet one. A full-blooded, ectoplasmic, engloomed, demented-eyed, phantasmagorical, possibly fanged, cobweb-enshrouded transcended ghost! I flung open the door and heard myself gasp, but there was nothing there.

But there was no mistaking the faint creak of a rusty hinge rubbing against raw metal. I moved to the edge of the staircase balcony, looked down, and saw the hall chandelier swinging ever so slightly on its ancient hinge. Even as I stared at it . . . it stopped.

Katia agreed to come out that weekend, but it took a little coaxing. She had made a lifelong study of these matters, and like myself she believed there were logical explanations for everything. We both knew that strange things happened in certain houses, but we believed these occurrences followed some logical order that often eluded scientific understanding. My own fascination with the paranormal began after meeting Sunny during the charm school years, and after that I signed up for every class I could find on the subject. There was even a workshop given at New York Tech by a well-known author, Dr. Hans Holtzer, on how to capture ghosts on film. The following year I flew to London and spent most of the summer at the College of Psychic Studies, learning things that changed my views forever. I witnessed phenomena while there that simply boggled my mind. A haunting was looked upon as simply an imprint of something that had taken place in the past, which appeared to have a way of playing back the original event no matter how long ago it occurred.

One of the most fascinating experiments conducted at the college had to do with the curious nature of marble and granite, which are similar on the molecular levels. Two professors—one an electrical engineer, the other a specialist in computer-chip technology—were called in to investigate sounds and voices that were overheard in a seven-hundred-year-old building on the outskirts of England. The science team went to the site and connected several electrodes to the marble wall where the voices were heard, then fed twenty thousand volts of electricity through the electrodes and recorded the sounds of conversations they believed had taken place hundreds of years before. That conclusion was based on the fact that the dialect hadn't been used in centuries. The scientists theorized that, because of its high content of quartz crystals, silica, and ferric salts, all substances used in the making of modern recording equipment, marble had the ability to trap vibrational sounds for an indefinite period of time.

Apparently, Russian scientists have known about this phenomenon for a long time and made clever use of it during the Second World War. They discovered that buildings act as natural sound resonators and that the sound of the human voice causes subtle vibrations that linger and are trapped in the walls, windowpanes, and other parts of buildings. They discovered that conversations could be played back by reflecting infrared waves at precise points. Soviet spies were then able to eavesdrop on top-secret conversations taking place in our government buildings, including our American Embassies. Understandably our government was horrified when it finally discovered the Soviets' ingenious use of this little-known natural phenomenon. (*Smithsonian* magazine, July 2001, page 55.)

Winfield was built almost entirely of marble, so, as I was aware of these experiments, hearing random sounds coming out of the walls seemed no more scary to me than turning on a record player. But I would soon find out that knowledge can be a shallow illusion at best.

I waited for Katia at the Glen Cove railroad station. It was one of those charming Gothic stone buildings built during the last century. There were only a handful of them left on Long Island, as the cruel hand of progress had not yet reached the old Oyster Bay–Glen Cove line that ran along the North Shore. For the elite commuters it provided a grand tour of the old estates as it moved along, at a snail's pace, on its way to Penn Station.

That Saturday afternoon, Katia was the only passenger to get off the train. She struggled down the steel-grated steps with two huge bundles of luggage and a large portable tape recorder. As the train pulled out of the station, spewing puffs of steam from its sides, her long black hair blew about wildly. Her dark, exotic eyes lit up when she saw me wave to her. She was all in black and wore a long, full skirt with a wide band embroidered with pink flowers at the hem. When I reached over to help her with her bags, her wrists jangled with silver-and-gold bracelets. She was smiling triumphantly as though getting there was half the battle and we were about to embark on a grand adventure. I was glad she was excited about the weekend and about the firsthand opportunity to work with a house rich with hidden and challenging possibilities.

On our way back to Crescent Beach Road, I handed her the tape I'd recorded of the strange sounds outside my door. Impatient to hear it, she popped it into her cassette player and held it up to her ear but then said she'd have to play it again later with no distractions. Once we were back at the house, I helped her carry her bags up the stairs and showed her to the Chinese room, which was only a short distance from mine. She asked a lot of questions about André — what he was like, how we met — and I found myself not wanting to talk about him. He'd been due back weeks before, and though he continued to write from places I'd never heard of, I was beginning to worry. I assured her he wouldn't mind at all if she stayed in his room. She put her things down on the king-size brass bed, walked over to the window, and gazed out at the long drive and the belvedere at the far end of the garden.

"I feel like I'm in a foreign country, in a different century," she said softly, stretching her arms up over her head and taking a long deep breath. Then she turned, smiling happily. "I'd like to orient myself to the house again. I never really had a chance to see much of it the last time — we were so busy with the party and all. Do you mind if I just wander around a bit?" she asked as she moved across the Oriental rug and peered out into the hall.

"Make yourself at home; you have all the time in the world," I said. "I'll go make us some tea and meet you in the ballroom when you're ready." I watched her disappear down the darkened hall. By the time tea was ready, she had already settled herself on the couch in the center of the ballroom. I entered carrying the tray and found her gazing up at the huge round crystal that hung from the center of the chandelier. She continued to stare at it, her eyes clear and comprehending, her face inscrutable as it formed tiny lines of concentration. Katia brought her distant gaze from the chandelier and reached over to where tea was set on a small table.

"He was into magic . . . your man Woolworth, but there is a coldness here, something untouchable. I get the feeling we're not welcome," she said in an ominous tone.

"You can read that in the crystal ball?"

"No . . . not really, but I can feel it. There are signs everywhere you look. The walls are studded with cryptography disguised as art. It's a kind of mystery language made up of random shapes, ancient symbols, hieroglyphs, ciphers, and cartouches."

"What does it all mean?" I asked, never having heard half those words.

"I don't know, but whoever built this was into some pretty heavy stuff," she said, pouring herself a cup of tea. "Those rooms upstairs — most of them are empty. What happened to all the furniture?"

"There was an auction three years ago, and everything went. Years before the sale I managed to save some of it from the greenhouse,

"What was Woolworth's connection to Napoleon?" she asked, twirling a lock of her hair around her finger.

"How did you know about that?"

"He's all over the place," she responded. I told her about Woolworth's childhood, how he grew up poor but lived a short distance from Napoleon's devoted brother and the great stone castle he'd built in Great Bend, New York.

"That's interesting," she said, reaching over the table to pour herself another cup of tea. "Napoleon was into the occult sciences in a big way, but they seem to gloss over that aspect of his life in most of the history books I've read."

"I was told that Woolworth was convinced he was the reincarnation of the great emperor, and that before he built this place, he would make regular pilgrimages to France to visit every palace that Napoleon had ever lived in. Then he ravaged all the antique shops and galleries to buy anything he could that had once been owned by him," I said, giving her a cynical glance. "Do you believe there could be any truth to that?"

"It's possible—anything is possible," she said dispassionately.

"Katia, in every mental institution in the country there are at least a dozen inmates who believe they are Napoleon, or Joan of Arc, or the Virgin Mary."

"True, but look around you—this is no delusion. This is real. I want to try something. Do you know when both of them were born?"

"It's not exactly something I carry around in my head, but I brought a lot of books with me, and one of them is on Woolworth. I'll run up and get it, and you can look up the little general in the *Encyclopedia Britannica*. There's a set in the library," I said, pointing to the next room off the hall. When I got back downstairs, she was thumbing through an old red-leather volume.

"Got it," she said, tapping the page with her long, red-painted nails. "Napoleon was born August 15, 1769 and he died at St. Helena May 5, 1821."

It took me a while to find it, but I finally gave her the dates she needed from John Kennedy Winkler's book *Five and Ten*. "Woolworth was born April 13, 1852, and he died here in this house on April 8, 1919."

Katia seemed lost in her own thoughts, but her mind appeared to be going a mile a minute. Then she reached down into her overstuffed canvas bag, pulled out a yellow notepad, and began scribbling numbers, slowly at first, then faster as she mumbled numbers under her breath. "Double nines," she said, her hand moving frantically now as her gold bracelets flashed and jangled and caught the light from the chandelier above. She wrote in broad, thready strokes across the paper, then turned it and continued running her pen along the margin edge until there was no space left. She stopped suddenly, took a deep breath, then looked up from her notepad.

"You don't happen to know the exact time of Woolworth's birth?"

"No. I don't think they kept detailed records back then," I responded.

"I guess not," she said glumly, staring down at what she had written. "Then none of this is really conclusive, but I can tell you this much: they were like two peas in a pod—brilliant, grandiose, and lived lavishly. There's something else that's interesting. Bonaparte was believed to have died while in Egypt—one of those near-death experiences: his heart stopped; no pulse. His men thought he was dead. Then suddenly he came out of it. That was 1799—double nines again. After that, he believed he was invincible, as if he knew everything before it happened, but then his life took a turn and everything went wrong," she said, stuffing the notepad back in her bag.

"I was here when that Empire room was still intact and filled with Napoleon's things: a throne from the Palace of Fontainbleau; a life-size bust of the emperor posing as Julius Caesar. There were lots of Egyptian things: a stone obelisk, a brass sphinx on the mantel, and rare Egyptian figures carved from malachite. I remember seeing something else that was unusual: a door in the Edwardian room had a panel that looked like black onyx. It was Woolworth's private dressing room. It's not in there now," I told her, noticing her eyes flicker with interest.

"A black mirror—that fits right in with a gut feeling I had before."

"What do you mean?" I asked, but she didn't say anything more about it. Instead, she leaned back in the soft velvet cushions of the couch, staring up at the huge carved mantel, scanning it with her eyes, going over every detail.

"He's still here, and very strong—not one to let go of his possessions. Before we go out, later tonight, I'd like to leave the tape recorder on in this room . . . over there by the alcove," she said, pointing with her long graceful fingers towards the south wall. "I can feel a lot of energy in this room, but if nothing picks up on the tape, we can try recording upstairs in the hall where you heard the sounds the last time."

We chatted for a while longer. Then, around eight, Katia moved the recorder to the alcove and turned it on, and we headed into the village to have dinner at one of the local restaurants. As we approached the gate at the end of the drive, I spotted Willard's blue van parked on the opposite side of the gate. He was about to lock it when he saw us. He stopped what he was doing, shrugged his shoulders as if our being there created a minor inconvenience, then pushed back the steel gate to let us through. A wide ring of keys hung down from his belt, which revealed a ballooning stomach. He was chewing on something as he walked over to my car.

"My wife and I will be gone till Monday, and Pete's gone upstate to visit his folks, so be sure to keep the gate locked at all times," he said, staring up at the trees as though addressing the squirrels. Then he shifted his gaze and peeked into the car, and looked at Katia, who was trying to suppress some private amusement.

"Willard, this is my friend Katia. She'll be staying over." He nodded, eyeing me cagily, and without saying anything further, he waddled back to his van, his keys jangling in rhythm with each step. Katia finally let out a giggle as she watched him drive off.

"Who was that?"

"He's the caretaker, or something like that."

"His name is Willard? You've got to be kidding," she said, laughing.

"André told me it's not his real name; he's incognito," I said. She was still snickering as I pulled out onto the main road. Then she got serious when it hit her.

"So, was he trying to tell us we're going to be all alone in the house tonight?" she asked.

"Hello?" she said in a raised voice when I didn't answer. I pretended to fumble with the rearview mirror while thinking of something stupid to say.

"It's you, me, and a few furry bats," I finally said as she let out a groan.

It was dark when we got back to the house several hours later. We headed into the ballroom, where the lights had been left blazing. Katia walked over to the recorder, where the tape had long since run out. She pressed the rewind button.

"I hate waiting for these things to rewind," she said, fumbling with the drapes in the alcove just to keep herself busy. After what seemed like a long time, she bent down and pressed the play button, then carried the machine over to where I was sitting and placed it on the small table. We sat and listened in silence. There was no sound at all. After ten minutes Katia got up, seeming mildly frustrated and running her fingers through her mane of hair.

"It's probably too early in the evening. You said you heard voices after midnight. So we'll try again later," she said, sinking back down on the couch. She started talking about some movie we'd seen recently, and we forgot that the tape was still running. Katia stopped mid-sentence and leaned forward, staring down at the recorder, which had suddenly come to life. We heard what sounded like a faint breathing sound, low and steady. Then, after a few minutes, the breathing became labored and heavy—almost a gasp for breath. Towards the end of the tape, it died out and was followed by what sounded like the rhythmic sound of a human heartbeat: *thump thump . . . thump thump*. Katia looked up at me wide-eyed, not saying anything at first.

"Tell me you heard that too?" she asked finally. I nodded and held her gaze.

"It's a different sound from what I heard before," I said, slightly shaken but more fascinated than anything else.

"When's the next train to New York?" Katia asked, her voice husky.

"There are no trains back at this hour. It's the weekend—they stop running at eleven forty-five, and you're not going to chicken out on me now. You're so unpredictable, Katia! A few hours ago you were expounding on the revelations of astrology, black mirrors, secret languages, and whatever as if this was all old hat to you. Now that we're on to the very thing we came here to investigate, you're starting to show signs of unraveling!" I had run out of breath. Katia sat straight up on the couch and rolled her eyes nervously.

"You forget I'm a city girl. You don't find very many haunted houses on the streets of Manhattan. And, yes, I've studied this stuff for as long as I can remember, but it's one thing to read about ghosts in books, and another thing . . ." She didn't finish the sentence.

"Are you telling me this is your first haunted house?"

"Yes," she squeaked, sinking further into the folds of the couch. I looked at her, suddenly feeling like the bravest woman on earth.

"You know what those sounds are; we've talked about it. They're nothing—a mere echo from the past. Do you think I'd stay here if I thought for one moment that it was something alive, with a will of its own? Katia, where's that adventurous spirit of yours? You're supposed to be the expert on these things," I said, raising my voice.

"Yes, and as an expert I'm telling you there's something in the room with us!" she said, sounding irritated. I tried to make light of it.

"That's why we're going upstairs and locking our doors," I said, turning to leave the room. I noticed she was right behind me.

"Are you bringing that thing with you?" I asked, referring to the recorder.

"No. I've heard enough for one night."

Sometime later that night something woke me—a faint moan at first; then I heard someone cry out. It took me several seconds to realize that it was coming from Katia's room. As I rushed down the darkened hall, I had the vague feeling something had just turned out of sight and was scampering down the servants' stairs on the left. When I got to Katia's room, she was sitting upright in bed, shaking and clutching the bedcovers. Her eyes were wide and black with terror.

"What happened?"

"I saw a cat with hideous eyes." Katia was shuddering almost convulsively.

"Katia, there is no cat. Nobody has a cat in this house!"

"I saw it, and I felt it crawling up my leg on top of the bedcovers," she said, raising her voice.

"Katia, maybe you had a bad dream, being in a strange place and all. Besides, your door was locked."

"No, it wasn't, 'cause I don't have a door!" she said, pointing towards the hall. "I mean, it's not a real door like you have," she moaned.

"Oh, I forgot about that," I said a little sheepishly. "But the summer door was locked; nothing could have gotten in."

"Well, it got in, and it got out. I saw it run out into the hall only seconds before you came in," she said, still shaken. I sat there on the bed, regarding her a moment, suddenly believing she had seen something that frightened her; she wasn't prone to hysterics.

"Try to pull yourself together. It was probably just a mouse." She looked up at me in stunned astonishment as if I'd suggested it was the Easter Bunny coming to deliver chocolate eggs.

"A mouse!" she repeated, baffled. "What do you feed your mice around here? Elephant chow? I felt the weight of that thing on my leg—all twenty-five pounds of it!" she insisted.

"Okay, Katia, you win. It was probably a mountain lion; the town of Glen Cove is overrun with them," I said, trying to get her to laugh. But she was not amused, and she began to rock back and forth, pulling the bedspread around her even tighter.

"Well, whatever it was, try to put it out of your mind. There's a comfortable couch in the dressing area in my room. You can sleep safe there for the night—at least we can lock the door." She sat there for a while longer, still rocking herself, the terror still apparent in her eyes.

"I'd rather spend the night on a cold wooden bench down at the railroad station and catch the five forty-five train back to New York."

"Not a good idea. There are rapists lurking behind every tree. A pretty young thing like you—no, I wouldn't suggest it," I said, stealing a line from André.

"Okay, we'll try your room," she said as she rose slowly from the bed, pulling all the bedcovers with her. I grabbed her pillow and put it under my arm, then waited as she hesitated at the door, looking out into the unlit hall before entering.

"That thing knew what it was doing, I tell you... and its eyes glowed," she mumbled as we walked.

"All animals' eyes glow in the dark," I said, picking up the bedspread that was trailing on the floor behind her.

"Yeah," she said glumly. "I don't know how you stay here alone."

"I feel right at home."

"You're very strange."

"I know," I said as we headed back to my room. All was quiet: you could hear a pin drop—there were no pipes banging in the cellar; there was no chandelier swaying in the stairwell. But I could see Katia's mind was still on whatever it was she saw—rat, squirrel, mouse, or weasel. It was the country, after all. She stood close by, watching me intently as I slid the hidden louvered door out of the wall and latched it, then closed and locked the main door, turning the old brass key in the lock plate as the tumblers clicked into place. We padded barefoot across the thick blue rug and headed towards the dressing room. She stopped at the nightstand and picked up the framed photograph of André, studying it intently for a while before putting it back down.

"Is that him?" she asked, sounding tired and depleted of all energy.

"Yes," I nodded, but she didn't say anything more, which was unusual for her.

I helped her pull a bed together out of the rose-colored couch, which was set into a wide marble alcove. We sat there in silence for a while.

"What time is it?" she asked in a quivering voice while she fidgeted nervously with the satin binding on her blanket, pulling at the threads until it became undone.

"About three," I answered absently, seeing she was still restless. "How did you get into the psychic field?" I asked to get her mind on something else.

"I was born with the gift. Even when I was very young, I had these dreams . . . and they would come true. I thought it was normal, and then as I got older, I realized I was different. I was an only child, and my mother . . . well, she could be very distant at times, and there was little to distract me from the things that were going on in my head. I guess lonely children have to find ways to entertain themselves, so I started to read a lot about esoteric subjects—metaphysics and spiritual things. The more I read, the more fascinated I became, and somehow I just fell into becoming professional at it. It's an ability that seems to get better the more I use it," she said with a nonchalant air.

"You're so lucky to be able to see things before they happen."

"Not always. Sometimes it's a double-edged sword. Not everything that I see is good. It may be a gift, but it carries a heavy burden of responsibility. I can sometimes see where people's lives are going, how they're going to end up, and I know that those people are not going to fulfill their dreams. It affects me to know they're going to mess up their lives."

"What about your own future?" I asked.

"It never works for me; I can only use my gift to help others. I have to fight the urge to advise too much, or control people. Sometimes I want to say, go in another direction, try another field, do the thing you love, or find another husband, but I can't do that. People always do what they're used to doing, like they're stuck in dysfunctional glue that binds them to patterns that make them unhappy. What always amazes me is the resistance I get when I'm working with clients, the women who will stay in a crazy, abusive relationship for years on end, yet who keep coming back to me to see if things will get better. I can't figure it, can you?" she asked with a certain brusqueness.

"No, but maybe they're just glad to have you to turn to," I responded, realizing her mind was finally off whatever it was that scared her. "What do you see about my being here?" I asked. Then wished I hadn't.

"Do you really want me to answer that?" she asked, leaning back on her pillow.

"That depends on what you're going to say," I said, wondering if she could read my mind too. "I don't want to hear anything negative. I'm really enjoying the fantasy and the mysterious man in my life. Remember, I grew up around a lot of fairy tales. I always wanted to be like Grace Kelly sailing off into the sunset with her handsome prince." Katia gave me a look that made me feel like a misguided twit.

"There is something called reality, and I think you're missing the mark just a bit. I don't mean to put a damper on things, but I do feel something negative in this house. I felt it the first day I came here, and whatever it is, it's very strong. If it's a spirit of some kind, it could just be toying with you, allowing you to be deluded by the beauty of the place and the fantasies you've built up in your own mind. These things have a funny way of taking hold of your thoughts until you have no will of your own. It's very subtle. You don't feel it happening. Believe me, I've seen it all before," she said gravely.

"To what purpose?" I asked, leaning toward her.

"Who knows? To suit their purpose, whatever that may be. They need your energy, your soul essence, like vampires need blood. Without you, the living, they have nothing to play off. They exist in a kind of limbo . . . waiting. . . . So there: Your wise adviser has spoken. Now are you going to pack your bags and leave?" she asked, sounding all too cynical for me.

"You know, Katia, I don't know if what you're saying is true, but sometimes you have a way of putting things that's scarier than all the creepy, crawly things that might come a-slithering into my room at night!" I stood up to leave.

"See what I mean—no one ever listens to me," she said, moving her hands into a prayerful position.

"I thought we were going to approach this situation logically, as if it were a science project."

"There are some things that defy understanding, and I think this house may be one of them. There are lots of theories to explain all kinds of phenomena, but none of them are proven, so no one really knows," she said, shifting her body to face the wall.

"When you stand back and think about everything, nothing really horrible has happened. A few voices caught on tape, and some poor little animal that wandered into your room."

"You can say that calmly 'cause it didn't wander into your room and crawl up your leg and scare you out of your wits," she said. Then added, "And by the way, I locked my door."

"It could have fallen down the chimney," I responded.

"You can rule out the chimney unless it was dropped in by helicopter."

"Okay, but that vampire bit, the analogy to needing blood—that's really pushing it."

"It was just a metaphor," she said into her pillow, her voice muffled. Then she turned to face me. "Look, if you're really planning to live here, there is something I think we should do, just to check the place out further. I know a husband and wife—they're professionals at this and very gifted. If there's something here that needs to be dealt with, it's not going to get past them. Entities or spirit forces can be very tricky. They're just as devious and clever as those of us who are earthbound. If it's alright with you, I'd like to call them and arrange a séance as soon as possible," she said in a confident tone.

"A séance, like in the movies? You're not serious?" I asked, trying not to laugh.

"It's not like anything you could imagine—trust me. I'll call tomorrow," she said, leaning her head back again and closing her eyes.

"Sleep tight," I said, and went back to bed as the birds began to chirp outside. Sometime later I heard the whistle blow as the first commuter train sped through the quiet village on its way to the city. Katia wasn't on it.

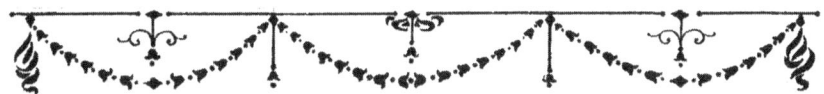

Chapter Nine

The Séance

June 17, 1978: I thought of nothing else for over a week and was plagued by misgivings and doubts. It all seemed too silly. My only familiarity with séances came from what I'd seen in cheap Hollywood movies that often made a mockery of anything having to do with the subject. I couldn't help but assume that the people involved in conducting this event were attracted to this odd practice out of a neurotic need to express some theatrical side of themselves. Part of me couldn't take it seriously, for, whatever the outcome, they could say and do just about anything and fabricate any story, and no one could prove or disprove any of it. On Katia's advice I was to have no contact with the members of the group beforehand, and she agreed not to give out any information about the house or its history. She would meet everyone at a church about half a mile away and escort them to Winfield, so that even the address and location would be kept from them until they arrived.

That night I was restless and paced back and forth on the front terrace, alert for any signs of headlights pulling in the front gate. I jumped every time I saw a car head north on Crescent Beach Road, as the hours seemed to drag on. It was very hot and muggy. The air was full of summer smells, and in the distance I could hear the gentle rumble of motorboat engines purring on the nearby sound. For a moment, I envied normal people doing sensible things like going for a late-night swim in their pools, jumping off the decks of their boats, or gossiping about the day's events over a cold beer. Standing in front of an open freezer naked seemed like a sensible thing to do that night.

One thing I knew for sure: no one else in Glen Cove was getting ready to host a séance. The Long Island Sound seemed to be calling me, and I suddenly had the urge to run down to the beach and join the normal and sane people, but I just continued to pace.

The group was late, very late. Finally around ten thirty, they pulled into the gate in one long caravan. The sound of half a dozen cars crunching and spitting up gravel along the drive was deafening after the hours of silent waiting. Then there was the clicking of car doors opening and closing in quick succession. I held my breath. All night I had envisioned being visited by a group of weirdos, like a cast of extras from *Rosemary's Baby*. I expected to see orange afros, garish makeup, and lots of dime-store jewelry.

I couldn't have been more wrong. As they emerged from their cars, one by one, I was met by the most ordinary and pleasant-looking people—family types of the kind you see all across the country mowing their lawns and attending church and PTA meetings. Katia introduced them as they gathered on the front porch and moved inside the main hall. I searched each of their faces with the eagerness one has for strangers entering one's home for the first time. I can only remember some of their names. Andrea had a warm, round face and smile. She said she taught school somewhere out in Port Jefferson. Arlene was a travel agent from Smithtown. Jerry, who was all in black, was a civil service worker somewhere out on the island. Leonard, the tallest of the group, said he was a buyer for a department store in Commack. Richard and Janice Diana, the husband-and-wife team who were to lead the group that evening, remained silent during the introductions as if to conserve their energy for what was to follow.

As a group, they did not react to the opulent surroundings the way most people did but instead came across as unimpressed by material things. I felt an openness about them that put me at ease. They had a wide range of ideas that seemed to go beyond conventional thinking, and as a group they projected a strength and maturity that impressed me. Katia and I began to show them around, and they soon became very intent on exploring what I took to be the soul of the house. There were no theatrics, no words were spoken, nor did they exchange glances. Instead, they proceeded to move about, fading in and out of the faint light as they passed from room to room. After awhile, Katia left them alone to do whatever it was they needed to do, and she came over to join me.

"What are they doing?" I asked, trying to keep my voice down.

"They're tuning into the electromagnetic energies. . . ." she said.

Then Richard came over to us and said, "We're ready to begin." The others nodded silently. Richard then opened his arms wide and motioned for us to follow him into the music room. Once inside, we gathered in the south end in a round alcove flanked by two white-marble pillars. Each of the members of the group (six women and three men) carried a collection of candles and small bronze or metal containers that they were now arranging to form a circle. It was beginning to look like *Rosemary's Baby* after all, but there was no turning back.

I felt a strange energy already gathering in the air as Richard took his place off to my right. As the candles were lit, my eyes settled on the gilt cherubs carved into the dome ceiling, which appeared to dance and move in the warm, flickering light. On either side of us were two ornately carved doors with missing handles. One of the men asked where they led. I was about to warn him about the pipe organ and its dangerous drops when he somehow managed to get the door open and slipped into the darkness. There was the faint sound of padded feet climbing up the narrow wooden stairs, but the others seemed oblivious to his disappearance and continued setting up in silence.

Then, out of nowhere, with sharp metallic strokes, the pipe organ chimes rang out like an unexpected storm. They pierced the silence as loudly as a rifle shot. The guests all froze where they stood as the room filled with majestic sounds of music. As suddenly as it began, it stopped. Andrea and the others looked up, startled. "He's going to wake up the dead for sure," she said. We heard his feet thudding back down the wooden ladder, and he reappeared in the doorway with a sheepish grin. "I found this on the landing, saw all those chimes, and couldn't resist. I could have played a Bach fugue if there'd been more light up there." He placed what looked like a small thin rod on the floor, then sat down and joined the others.

Janice then placed an antique, bronze oil pot in the center of the circle and filled it with strange-smelling incense that looked like amber crystals. It reminded me of the glass pebbles you see at the bottom of tropical fish tanks. When she lit it, it glowed strangely. The smell was intoxicating and unlike anything I had ever smelled before. Richard's face caught the light, and his eyes fixed on one of the candles before him.

The incense crackled and burned. Its smoke rose up and formed a misty haze about the room. Richard wore black from head to toe, and in the darkened room he appeared to have no body at all. Only his face could be seen, as it was lit by a hazy flute of light. He had dark features, with deep penetrating eyes that were at once alert and intensely electric, and when he closed them, he no longer seemed to be of this world. His wife, Janice, sat opposite him to my left. Her long, flowing waves of chestnut hair framed a pretty oval face with deep doe eyes and a cherubic nose. She looked at her husband and then around the room and said, "I think we can join hands now." We all did as she asked. "We must not break the circle for any reason once we begin. What will happen if we are successful tonight is that one or more of us may act as a channel for a disembodied spirit or entity. We will have no control over which of us he or she may choose. Any one of us could become the complete embodiment of a lost soul, and our voice, and even our physical features, can be altered while in that state. It's called a transfiguration. By our being here performing this sacred ritual, we are opening a door for the spirits to enter and hopefully heal whatever they need to resolve."

I had the feeling she was saying all of these things for my benefit, as it appeared that everyone else present was already aware of what was going on.

"Is there anything I should do or not do?" I asked, feeling somehow off center and uneasy about my inclusion in this secret gathering.

"Just go with your feelings," Richard said softly.

"This reminds me of the encounter groups I attended in college," I said, trying to relax.

"In a way it is. Unresolved conflicts affect the living as well as the dead. We're all here to learn from them and move on," Richard said, placing his hands together in his lap.

"But how can we change what happened maybe fifty or a hundred years ago?" I asked.

"Sometimes when there is a sudden death and no time to prepare, spirits get stuck and cannot move on without help. They can remain attached to a building or place even long after the building is gone. The etheric energy, which we're all made of, can linger for centuries; it's all around us. It's all recorded—the good and the bad. Entities, or what some people call ghosts, only appear in houses where they have suffered a traumatic death or some tragedy. When someone dies, they carry their personalities with them. They can choose good or evil, just as we do. If they valued material things above all else, they can remain prisoners of this plane and stay with their possessions, guarding them to prevent anyone else from enjoying what they left behind. In cases where someone has taken his own life, the spirit can remain in a living hell, reliving the horror of what he didn't want to face in life, over and over again. Our being here is an offer of help, but help must be accepted.... They have to make that choice. Let us begin," he said, taking a deep breath.

The candles flickered and played on the somber faces in the room. Richard began a soft chant in a far-off voice that was barely audible as the smoke from the burning incense rose up around him like formless phantoms. I did not know how well the others knew this man, but they seemed to follow his every move reverently. I was the last to close my eyes. With all hands joined together, I became aware of a wonderful sensation, like floating off into an unhurried dimension where there were no limits and everything was possible. The others joined in his chanting, and there was a faint humming sound. It began to build like a wave of energy with the rise and fall of their somnolent voices. Slowly it increased in volume, then leveled off into a steady hypnotic and powerful force. There was something strangely familiar about it, as if I had experienced this all before, though I hadn't. Perhaps it reminded me of being in church when I was a child.

Richard's voice stood out above the others. He repeated words of a language I did not recognize, but which I assumed was Latin. An hour may have gone by—there was no way to know, no sense of time, just peace and a linking current of nameless energy that seemed to flow between our hands and all around the circle as though we were on a raft drifting peacefully on a calm sea. With every nerve in my body sensitized, the chanting continued and seemed to engulf the room. I let their hypnotic voices take me as I sank deeper and deeper into some unfamiliar place. Just when I thought it would go on forever, there was an unearthly pause.... Somewhere off in the room I thought I heard something—the swish of an invisible gown—and the room seemed to fill with the faint fragrance of roses.

"We are here in peace; we are here in love. Let us know who you are?" Richard asked in a gentle, but commanding, tone. "Tell us how we can help you. Let us know who you are." he repeated. After a long silence, suddenly there was a pitiful choking cry from someone to the left of me. Then a muffled sob rose from her throat as if from a tomb, and opening my eyes, I realized it was Janice. She was now struggling for breath.

"Do not be afraid. You are in God's light. No harm can come to you here," Richard said.

The incense crystals were glowing red-hot and cast an eerie beam of light upon the woman who was trying to speak. It was not the Janice I had met an hour before. Her face seemed strangely altered by an expression of sickening fear as her eyes grew wide as though lit with anguish.

"Do not be afraid. We are here in peace and love," Richard said, again reassuringly. Her mouth grew wide as if some terrible struggle were going on inside her.

"Will you let us know who you are?" Richard repeated, leaning slightly forward. She looked bewildered, as though she had been wrenched from some dreadful hiding place.

"Go away from here," she said in a miserable rasping whisper. Her head began rocking from side to side in an invertebrate fashion.

"Please, go away from here!" she cried again.

"Tell us who you are," Richard demanded firmly.

Her eyes widened; speaking at all seemed an unbearable effort. Then in a hoarse voice she said, "Edna Woolworth!"

My heart leaped. This was no game. I stopped breathing for a moment and could feel my hands trembling, though they were held in a firm grip by my two partners, who sat unwavering beside me.

"Edna." Richard repeated her name softly and with such visible compassion that she looked straight at him as her whole body seemed to tremble. "All of us came here to be with you, to help you in any way we can. We need you to tell us what we can do; we need you to guide us."

She stared back at Richard for a long time, her face ashen, her eyes black with fear.

"You can't help me," she said finally, in a hoarse whisper. "You must go from here . . . now," she pleaded. "This is father's room. You must not be in one of his rooms."

"No one can harm you; we are here, and no one can harm you. Tell us why you are afraid," Richard asked the strange young girl who had entered our circle. She just sat there, her shoulders rigid, continuing to question us with her eyes. She had the haunted, spirit-broken look of a lost child and seemed to jump whenever Richard tried so gently to question her. She trembled at the sound of her own voice, echoing in that cold hollow room. She looked down at the floor and began to stare into the flame of one of the candles. For a brief moment she betrayed an eagerness to speak, but she held herself back as though at any moment she might splinter and vanish into the airstream of heady incense smoke.

Richard closed his eyes as if praying for a way to reach her. Several minutes went by. "Can you tell us anything you remember about this house?" he asked with careful solicitude. She continued to stare into the flame of the candle.

"A special place—perhaps there was a special place you liked to visit here," he said gently, in a tone that revealed his own indifference to such pretentious surroundings.

Edna looked up at him as her demeanor seemed to change. "I hated this house and everything in it," she snapped. "I only came here to be with . . ." She hesitated. "I only came here to be with Mother. Mother was kept a prisoner in this house. I would not stay here; I came only when Father was away. . . . Then I came and took mother out of her room for walks in the garden. There were the most beautiful rose gardens," she said as her eyes seemed to soften reminiscently. "There was an old wooden playhouse out back that we used when we were young. My mother and I would sit inside that tiny house with the white-lace curtains. We felt so safe there," she said, speaking in a low, childlike voice and with her eyes downcast.

"Mother no longer talked by then; she only listened and nodded her head. No one else in the house talked to her; they didn't think she understood what was said to her, but she understood everything that was going on." She leaned forward slightly and gazed into the flame for awhile before speaking.

"There was a lamb, a small white lamb. Amber . . . his name was Amber. It belonged to one of the gardeners, and it used to follow us around in the garden. Mother used to like to touch its soft fur. She was so much like a child herself by then. Then one day, it was all gone."

"What was gone?" Richard asked.

"Everything . . . it all went up in flames. Only the charred pillars were left. The playhouse was gone, too. . . . I cried and cried for Mother, too, because I could no longer take her for walks in the garden after the fire. Only the gardens survived . . . and the roses—they were all covered with black soot . . . nothing but black soot everywhere. It was the end of everything. . . ." Her voice trailed off, and her face became an expressionless mask.

"What happened? Why was everything destroyed?" Richard asked.

"There was a fire, a terrible fire. You could smell the smoke all the way in town."

"What caused the fire?" There was no answer.

"Do you know what caused the fire, Edna?"

"I was not here when it happened," she said quickly, as though to dismiss the memory.

"You don't have to talk about it if you don't want to," Richard said.

Edna's eyes sought his but seemed to go out of focus for a moment, as though his presence encroached on something she was thinking.

"Mother was angry . . . so angry, she couldn't breathe. This house choked the life out of her, but it got worse after the fire. She no longer got to see the roses . . . though they continued to bloom for her. Through all the soot, they continued to bloom . . . but she never got to see them, 'cause now there was a guard posted outside her prison room." She began to cry softly as she sank down into the folds of her thick, dark sweater, as if trying to wrap herself into a cocoon with it.

Richard seemed confused; and he waited a moment before asking, "Did your mother's room survive the fire?"

Edna raised her head from out of the folds of fabric that all but covered her face.

"The house was gone; only the foundation was left. Father built this house over the old one. It went up very fast—faster than any house like it was ever built. He was crazy, frightening, obsessed with getting it built. He never slept. He worked everyone to death to get it all done. He would cry for hours when work was delayed, when something had to be shipped from somewhere or never arrived. He was obsessed with those rooms—always those rooms, more and more rooms. They had to be perfect replicas—of what, I never knew. He ran all over the world collecting things, all kinds of things to put in those perfect rooms. The building went on around the clock; there was no resting for any of the workers. Father never slept; he studied his books all through the night, always researching, perfecting, always striving for more and more, always wanting the impossible. Then he brought something back from Egypt . . . only then did he rest."

"What do you think he wanted?" Richard asked solemnly.

Edna was silent for a long while, her gaze turned back to the burning embers of the incense as the smoke rose up like powdery wings. Then her voice broke in unexpectedly. "To be immortal . . . I think he wanted to be immortal. Before the house was even finished, he became obsessed with the emperor's room. Everything in it had at one time belonged to Napoleon. No one was allowed to go in there, not even the servants. He would lock himself in there for days and lie there in Napoleon's gold bed, staring off into space. One day I came to see Mother; I thought he was away. I was upstairs in the hall when he came out of that room. He saw me, but . . . he was different. It was not his voice or his walk. It frightened me more than anything."

As she spoke, these images seemed to come out of her in fragments and cautiously, as if she were walking on pieces of broken glass in her bare feet. She took a deep breath before going on.

"It became more and more difficult to see Mother. I knew a way to get past the nurse who sat in a chair outside my mother's room. The nurse would leave several times a day to get what they called my mother's medicine, but it was laudanum that they gave her. It left her too weak and confused to go out. It broke my heart to see her. She would just rock back and forth staring out the window, day after day. I wanted so desperately to help her break free from the hold he had on all of us, but I felt paralyzed with fear . . . fear that he would find out and lock me up, just like Mother."

"Find out what?" Richard asked.

She pressed her head up against her knees as she sat on the cold marble floor, looking like a crumpled rag doll, her head lost in the folds of her long dark skirt.

"There was someone else . . . someone else I came to see. He worked here for my father . . . and he . . ." She was barely audible; then she fell silent again.

"Edna, no one is going to harm you; there is nothing to fear," Richard kept repeating softly. But her eyes closed as if she had gone into a stupor, and we watched as her face seemed to change and she began to slip away.

There was a long pause, and I knew we were losing contact with her. Richard kept repeating her name, but there was no response. Suddenly he turned to me.

"Talk to her; bring her back," he said urgently.

I was caught completely off guard. So far she had spoken only to Richard, as though unaware of anyone else in the room. I felt safe there only as a spectator, but now I was being asked to talk to a ghost. I felt flushed and at a loss for words. How could I comfort this tortured woman haunted by a childhood of neglect, with a mother too drugged on laudanum to speak and a father who thought he was Napoleon?

I looked up at the ceiling awkwardly and wondered what had brought me to this bizarre circumstance.

Then I heard Richard's voice. "Take a deep breath and follow your instincts."

"Edna," I said, clearing my throat self-consciously. "Were you in this room with me several weeks ago? Did you drop the rose?"

She sat there unmoving. Then her eyes opened slowly; they seemed dull and unfocused, almost catatonic. I went on feebly. "When I first came here to live, I walked into this room, and a gold rose fell from up there in the ceiling. Did you want me to have it?"

She stirred and pulled herself up from the fabric of her long skirt and looked at me as though she did not understand what I meant.

"Did you make it fall?" I asked again. Then, without thinking, I pulled free from my partner's hand, breaking the chain, and I pointed up to the place on the ceiling. Her body jerked slightly as though she'd been given an electric shock, and I quickly rejoined my hand to the person on my left. She gazed at me with such intensity, as though my being there nourished some nameless part of herself. Part of me sensed the presence of her in the wordless safety of silent knowing, and though it came as an eerie thought, I felt we shared the same demons.

Then her head dropped slightly, and in a hushed tone she said, "It pleases me that you are here. I'm not afraid when you are here." There was a long silence as she continued to stare. Then she asked fervently, "Promise me you will stay here with me forever?"

I looked at Richard, feeling uneasy, but all his concentration was on her. I did not know quite how to react at this point, or how seriously I should be taking any of this. It felt pretty serious at that moment, but then we were not in this world anymore. I shifted uneasily, feeling the cold hard marble of the floor.

"Edna, I'm only a guest here," I said, beginning to feel weird.

"No. Forever—you must stay with me forever," she pleaded with heartbreaking sadness. It was her eyes that continued to hold my attention; they seemed so filled with earnest life. It was a look I shall never forget.

"I promise," I whispered, unable to resist her childlike plea but not sure what I was getting myself into.

"You have your mother," Richard quickly added as if trying to distract her. He spoke as though her world were part of the present.

"Mother can't help me!" she said, almost spitting out the words. She drew in a breath, then lifted her head. "Mother loves me, I know, but it's as though she is dead." Her voice cracked as tears began to stream down her face. "Father made her that way. . . . She is locked up because she knows about the secret things."

"What secret things?" Richard asked.

"Leave me alone. . . . You must go now. . . . It's too late. There is no hope. I can never be free." Her eyes squeezed shut, and she broke out in loud hoarse sobs. I wanted the whole thing to end right then, but I didn't know what to do.

The whole night had been so surreal, I didn't want to believe at that point that it was really happening. They could have all been part of some cleverly staged hoax, the whole thing could have been rehearsed and planned out. I had gotten so caught up and fascinated by the drama of what was happening. But it had gone much further than anything I was prepared for.

I had never expected to intrude so intimately on the life of another. Whether that person was dead or not, it felt wrong. I knew we had gone too far, and it began to scare me. It scared me that we had the power to do that. But at no time did I believe that any of us might be in any danger that night.

I glanced over at Katia to try to get her attention, but she seemed lost in a trance. As I continued to stare at her, I suddenly became aware that the room had filled with the smell of the sea. Then Edna's hands rose up and flailed at the air as if she were warding off some invisible oppressor.

Suddenly some of the topaz-colored crystals from the incense sputtered, and some sparks from it shot across the circle, revealing the face of a man I had not seen before. But that was not really the case at all. It was one of the men in our group; he had been there all along, only now his face seemed hideously altered somehow. Not so much in the physical sense, but it appeared as though every muscle and facial nerve was now frozen in a fugue of rage.

Edna's mouth opened wide as she heaved a deep gasp, but terror silenced her. The room went dead cold. My eyes were fixed on Edna when the stranger broke the circle of hands and lunged savagely for my throat. He was grabbed instantly by the other men and held down before he could reach me. A cry of anger rose from him.

"This is my house!" he roared, his eyes wild and feverish. One of the candles burst with a sharp crackle, and the flame wavered wildly. "I worked and slaved all my life to build this. . . . This belongs to me alone. Get out!" The veins at his temples were pulsating beneath his swelling anger.

"Mr. Woolworth, I presume?" Katia called out in a sardonic tone, unscathed and unafraid of his words.

Richard cut in and tried to calm him. "We are here in peace."

"Get out . . . get out . . . this is my house—mine for eternity," he roared, as his steel gray eyes seemed to burn into me. "This is mine, all mine, you meddling bitch!"

I don't know what came over me in that instant, but it suddenly struck me that his childish shrieking was his only weapon. He was beginning to get on my nerves.

"You pompous megalomaniac!" I screamed back at him. "You built this mausoleum and filled it with your ego. There was no love here, no human kindness. It brought nothing but unhappiness to your family, and you never even noticed."

Without warning he jerked forward with such violence that he almost broke free from the hold two of the men still had on him. Several others, including Richard, quickly joined them until they formed a mass of dark shadows, intent on stopping him from strangling me. A look of vengeance welled up in his face unlike anything I'd ever seen. I had to look away. The marble carvings of grotesque beasts and serpents on the fireplace wall seemed to stir for a moment in the flickering candlelight as he continued to boom in a brutal shower of rage.

He'd been watching us all along, I thought, inhabiting his dark sanctuary above the alcove. Now there was the murderous coming apart of all restraint. I froze where I sat, unable to move. The rest of the night seemed to pass in slow motion. I felt displaced and faraway, and no longer part of it.

Richard, while continuing to hold down his prey, took over and immediately began the rhythmic chanting again. The others quickly followed. Richard's words stood out over the hypnotic chorus of voices. "We wish you no harm. . . . Go back in peace," he said forcefully. "It's not our place to judge you. This will always be yours and yours alone. . . . It has your mark on all its beauty and will stand in your memory always. This house breathes your soul and no other," Richard said in a hypnotic tone that seemed to have the power to subdue him.

My eyes were still on the desperate man opposite me, who was slowly being taken over. Whoever or whatever he was, the rage that had all but disfigured his features only moments ago seemed to vanish as he backed off.

He sat shaking uncontrollably, staring mutely at Richard as if absorbing his words in recognition. Richard continued to hold his gaze as the droning voices reverted to the strange-sounding phrases I'd heard earlier.

The walls around the room were a bevy of shadows as the candles flickered and played upon the members of the circle who had quietly returned to their places. Richard nodded his head in farewell, then reached out his arms and rejoined the circle of hands.

The solemn chanting went on for what seemed like an hour or so. Again there was that dreamlike floating feeling, but I never closed my eyes again that night. I kept watching the man opposite me, though he seemed to have turned back into the gentle stranger who had walked through the door an eternity ago. I couldn't help but wonder if he would remember that sometime during the night he had acted as if capable of murder.

One of the candles sputtered as the last of the wick smothered in a pool of wax. The chanting came to a stop, and Richard closed with a prayer, then broke the circle. No one spoke or moved for a long time, and it seemed to take some effort to shift back into the here and now. The pale blue light of dawn was beginning to filter softly through the tall glass windows. Someone finally got up and turned off the reel-to-reel tape recorder that had been running silently since midnight. I rose unsteadily and left the room to get coffee for everyone. Katia, calm as usual, came into the kitchen to help as though nothing had happened.

When we returned with the coffee moments later, everyone was kneeling on the floor listening to the tape recording being played back. There was the chanting at the beginning, which lasted a few minutes, then seemed to fade away. The only sound after that was a dull throbbing rhythm of what sounded like a human heartbeat.

Still no one spoke. Then Richard saw me standing in the doorway with the tray filled with steaming cups. As he reached over to take one, he said, "It's not uncommon; these events are rarely recordable." I never understood what he meant, and when I tried to ask, I found that I'd completely lost my voice. He mentioned something about emotional hysteria and traumatic stress and advised me not to worry. Katia and I saw everyone to the door. They waved good-bye, and we watched them drift away.

"Well," Katia said in a resigned low tone. "I don't know about you, but I'm exhausted. These little gatherings can be so draining."

I looked at her incredulously, wanting to ask a lot of questions, but I could not speak.

"Oh, don't worry about the old man," she said, glancing back towards the room where we'd spent the evening. "Without us, he's powerless. He only got to us because you broke the circle when you pointed up to the ceiling. That's how he got in. The energy field we created by linking our hands was for protection. . . . It's no big deal. It was your first time," she said, as she turned and headed up the stairs.

The house was quiet again. Outside the birds were beginning to sing while a silvery mist rose up from the warm damp grass.

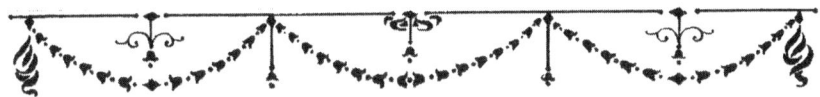

Chapter Ten

The Czar Comes to Winfield

Katia returned to New York that afternoon, and I was left to pick up the pieces of an evening that seemed as far removed from reality as anything could get. I'd seen the whole thing as a fascinating experiment. We were, after all, searching for clues through fragmented descriptions of earlier events, hoping to fit them together. I had believed that in the faded atmosphere of that room, we could somehow purge the house of its toxins—a few prayers, some chants, the right affirmations. It all seemed so simple, but I was totally unprepared for the effect that night had on me.

It was several days before I regained the use of my voice, and I avoided the room where the séance took place as much as possible. The events of that night remained disturbingly alive in my mind, and the look on Edna's face or Janice's face transformed was as real to me as anything had ever been. I decided that no matter what she was—a living spirit, an entity, or a lost soul—since I knew of her presence, I would regard her with the same respect as I would any living human being; and since on that night I made a promise, I would try to keep it.

Once having made that decision, the house seemed different somehow, and I found myself more and more subdued by the beauty and witchery of the place. Inside the house the atmosphere seemed altered somehow, but, more than that, I became vaguely aware of a melancholy presence—who like a nameless shadow seemed to follow me about whenever I was there alone. With it came what I perceived to be the faint scent of roses.

The garden was flourishing from my feeble efforts, and Pete was happy to have an extra hand. I built extra trellises to hold the new marauding vines that were starting to burst forth with colorful blooms. Because of these improvements the commercial studios were starting to call trying to book the house and grounds for photo shoots. I began to feel for the first time that the house was beginning to attract people rather than repel them.

In June a photographer friend called to say that he had just landed a big job doing ads for a well-known vodka company. His client was looking for an estate to represent the czar of Russia's winter palace around the turn of the century. After the company saw pictures of Winfield, a deal was made to do the entire year's campaign there. These ads were to be some of the most elaborate ever staged, with a cast of about fifty extras, including actors playing the roles of the czar and his czarina, two white Russian wolfhounds, and a horse. In one scene the horse was to charge into the ballroom, then stand at attention under the chandelier. The director claimed this was historically correct, and he went on to say that in olden times the czar, following victory in battle, would often gallop into his palace, making a flamboyant entrance.

I was excited about working on the project, but one problem remained. The contract had to be signed by the owner of the house, and that meant having to convince André that a horse galloping through his living room wasn't going to damage the rare parquet floors. No matter how well trained and pampered the beast might turn out to be, it did not sound like a good idea.

Tracking André down proved even more difficult, but about a week before the photo shoot was to begin, I received a six-page, completely illegible letter from him, and decided to take a chance and try leaving a message with his secretary in his German office. I was shocked when, on the first ring, André himself picked up the phone.

"André, I can't believe it's you."

"Hi, love," he said, chewing on something brittle.

"I just got your letter, but I can't read a word of it," I said, knowing I sounded a little bit nervous.

"I wrote it on the plane; it was a bumpy flight—I'll type next time." He sounded detached.

"What does it say?" I asked eagerly.

"They're love poems. I'll read them to you when I get back."

"You've been gone so long, when—" He cut me off.

"Soon—I'm having some trouble over here—should end any day now."

"Is Jovon still with you?"

"Like a shadow."

"Give him my regards," I said, beginning to lose my nerve about the real purpose of my call.

"How are things at the house?" he asked as some static intruded on the line.

"It's wonderful. I can't wait for you to see the new rooms, and the garden. . . . André, I booked the house for a magazine campaign, and we need to bring a very well-mannered, pedigreed, slightly oversized pet into the ballroom," I said sheepishly.

"Do what you will" was his response. "What kind of pet?" he then asked, as I feared he would.

"A horse," I said, hearing him crunch down on something that sounded like a carrot.

"Why?"

"It's historically correct," I said. Then I went on at great length about the Russians and their curious habits during the last century as they had been related to me only days before.

"What if the horse takes a crap on my floor?" he snapped, raising his voice.

"It's against royal protocol," I demurred.

"Humbug," he snorted. "A horse is a horse!"

"Well, can we do it?!" I asked. Then I told him about the twenty-thousand-dollar location fee. He continued chomping, or maybe it was the static on the line.

"What the hell—get the house booked as much as possible. It'll help pay the taxes."

"You won't be sorry—the ads are going to be great."

"Okay, babe. Will you take care of something for me?" he asked.

"Anything."

"Have the pool pumped out and cleaned. It'll be nice to go for a swim when I get there."

"I'll take care of it. Just hurry back. I miss you."

"Miss you too." There was a click as André hung up the phone.

The studio crew arrived the following week in several buses filled with actors, hairdressers, wardrobe people, and photographers. Next came trucks and vans filled with props and lighting equipment and all that makes up the business of making pictures for advertising. About seventy-five people soon filled every room in the house. The palm court was taken over by the makeup artists, the library became a dressing room for the male models, and the women used my bedroom upstairs. Outside, on the lawn, men were unloading ten-foot palm trees, their faces hidden behind the lush branches as they filed into the house. About a dozen or so gilt ballroom chairs followed. Off to the side of the drive was a white van on which was printed in bold black letters: CAPT. HOGAN'S TALENTED ANIMALS. EVERYTHING FROM DANCING BEARS TO WALTZING ZEBRAS.

Two men stepped out and opened a side door. One of them bore a striking resemblance to the actor who played Goldfinger in the James Bond movie. At the snap of the trainer's finger, out leaped two magnificent white Russian wolfhounds, their plumelike tails swaying in rhythm with their graceful feet. At the trainer's signal they would stop in place, rear up, and pirouette as though performing for the czar himself. It was clear that they were the real stars of this whole production. The younger of the two men waved to me, then introduced himself and the two hounds, Jeraldine and Frostbite. Happy to be free of the confines of the van, they soon took to racing across the lawn at terrifically high speeds, then leaping over the statues along the drive. When they had exhausted themselves, they returned, panting, to their trainer, who pulled an antique silver brush out of his back pocket and began brushing their long silken manes. One of the female models was walking by and gushed, "Nice doggies," extending a hand laden with jangling jeweled bracelets.

"Don't upset the dogs. They are high-strung," one of the assistant trainers said sternly.

"But they're such nice doggies," she squealed again, reaching down to let one of them lick her face.

"Lady, please, they got a case of nerves today. When they get upset, their hair starts to fall out," he said dryly.

"Really," said the girl playfully, pulling one of their ears. "Bye, bye, doggies," she said in a sing-song voice. Then she turned and headed back up towards the house. Just then, another huge van pulled up in the driveway, and a handsome white horse soon made his appearance on the front lawn. Within seconds it took to sucking up huge clumps of grass, then eating them, dirty roots and all. I was glad André was out of the country. When he did return, it might be days before he'd notice the lawn missing. Surely Pete would help me out and swear he saw a herd of boll weevils having their way with the lawn.

Two crew members carried a pair of ten-foot, ornately scrolled gilt torchères up to the house as other regal furnishings followed. At this point I noticed something rather curious. As everyone was milling about at their assigned chores, I spotted Willard making one of his rare daylight appearances. He stood at first in the open doorway, surveying what was going on. Then he slowly descended the stairs, carrying himself with a bearing that was out of character. Not only did he walk differently, he was wearing a suit, his hair was combed back neatly, he'd stopped drooling, and altogether he looked almost human. I watched from a distance as he proceeded to introduce himself and shake hands with crew members as though he were an ambassador of goodwill. He carried on like this for a while, then disappeared, and he was not seen again for the remainder of the shooting. I thought it strange but dismissed it from my mind.

Inside the house people were everywhere. To the right of the main hall stood a ten-foot rack filled with lavish turn-of-the-century ball gowns. Three wardrobe girls were busy stitching long strands of pearls to silk-and-lace bodices. Next to them was a long worktable covered with gaudy diamond crowns and glittering costume jewelry. On the floor below were dozens of satin dancing slippers laid out with tags attached that bore the names of the models who were to wear them. Upstairs, hairdressers arranged elaborate wigs on the female models, who were being made over into Russian nobility.

The tall and handsome man who was to play the czar sat in another room and made faces while being fitted with a full beard and waxed mustache that were being attached painfully with barber's glue. He was then dressed by two attendants who helped him with an elaborate red military jacket, gaudy with gold braid, and a glittering profusion of medals. He stood up and was handed a gleaming sword that was to be bound to his waist with a braided sash. Once it was tied, he walked over to one of the mirrored doors and beamed at his transformation.

Finally, when everything was set up in the ballroom downstairs, the photographer climbed a twelve-foot ladder, gazed about the room solemnly, and yelled, "Let's get the show on the road. Everyone take your places."

The women filed into the room first, their long trains trailing silently behind them, diamond crowns balanced on their heads. Then the male extras, decked out as noblemen, ambassadors, counts, barons, and the like, emerged from the outer hall. Some were asked to stand on small wooden boxes in order to appear taller than the ladies. Only after everyone was in his or her place did one of the animal trainers enter; the wolfhounds followed. There was a hushed sigh from the onlookers. The trainer talked softly to the hounds the whole time as they took their place alongside the beautiful czarina, who stood just under the chandelier.

As dozens of candles were being lit in the torchères, the room took on the glamour and romance of another age. The photographer seemed happy.

"Where is the horse?" someone yelled.

"He's coming, he's coming," came the answer.

The horse appeared in the doorway, his harness crowned with a lavish spray of red plumes. The czar, not used to the stiff black-leather boots, walked awkwardly across the polished floor, squeaking leather accentuating each step. He was then assisted into the saddle, accidentally stabbing one of the crew members with his sword as he mounted.

"Is everyone ready?" the director yelled. Everyone stood at attention. "Let's have some fog."

There was a sudden swooshing sound just outside the open doors on the terrace, and within seconds the entire room was engulfed in heavy white smoke.

"Cut!" the director yelled, as the fog continued to pour into the room. "Cut the fog—too much fog!" he yelled again.

Something had apparently gone wrong with the fog machine, and it was now out of control.

"Keep your places!" an unseen voice shouted.

"Don't anybody move."

"Kill the fog," an angry voice boomed as everyone became lost in the thick blinding vapors. It was eerie.

The dogs began wailing, and there was a sudden loud thump. Some of the female models began shrieking off in the corner. You could hear the horse as he began galloping around the room knocking over whatever was in its path.

"Pull the plug, damn it!" came a cry. Several minutes later, when the fog cleared, the horse was the first to come into focus. He stood motionless under the chandelier. The czar lay on the floor under him. Crew members clung to the outer walls, their hands outstretched against the paneling. The two wolfhounds stood frozen in fear next to the horse, their eyes bulging half out of their heads. One of the dogs was completely covered with horse shit. Everyone watched in horror while long strands of its white hair began falling from its fragile body; his trainer stood by, turning noticeably pale. "Oh, my God!" he whispered under his breath as he picked up the shaken creature and carried it off into the servants' wing to be cleaned up. Several production assistants ran into the room with pails of soapy water and a mop and swooped down on the offending pile of manure still steaming on the floor. By the time everyone was ready to shoot the picture, one of the wolfhounds was nearly bald. The crew worked well into the night, with arc lights blazing to simulate daylight.

The next morning I walked down to the pool, which had not been used in three years. It had become so loathsome that no one ever went within fifty yards of it. The water was stagnant and foul smelling with algae scum and decomposing leaves. From the looks of it every crawly thing for miles around had for some reason found its way to the pool and managed to fall in and drown. Floating on the surface were six dead rats, two birds, and an assortment of moths and spiders. The only living thing was a large box turtle who was sunning himself contentedly on a moldy log floating at the shallow end. I went back to my room, checked the local yellow pages, and called the Happy Porpoise Pool Service, who arrived that afternoon to pump out the water and scrub the walls down with acid. Surprisingly, within a few hours it looked like new. A green garden hose was draped over the side of the diving board, and fresh water began to gather at the deep end. To make the pool area more inviting, I repainted a pair of wrought-iron chaise lounges that I had kept in storage over the years that came originally from the Woodward estate in Oyster Bay.

It also occurred to me that the Victorian gazebo we had rescued from the bulldozer years ago would look very attractive at the far end of the pool and could double as a cabana. I made a note to ask Pete to help me truck it over and reassemble it as a surprise for André.

Throughout that summer we did dozens of film shoots, including a Gatsby-era party scene with vintage costumes and antique cars and an Estée Lauder perfume commercial. With the pool restored and sparkling, filming at Winfield was even more appealing, since crew and production people could take a dip to cool off from the summer heat during their breaks.

Willard began making random appearances whenever a shoot was taking place, and on occasion he proved himself quite useful. He would turn up unexpectedly whenever the studio crew blew a fuse or needed a twenty-foot ladder or extension cord. He would emerge from the bowels of the house with whatever was needed. Doors and windows that had not opened in years were suddenly back in use, and he would produce keys to basement rooms I didn't know existed. Most astonishing, he somehow got the Neptune fountain to spring back to life, and once again water began to gush out of the mouths of the marble dolphins. The fountain hadn't worked since the sixties, and it was assumed by everyone that the pipes had long since rusted out. But now, with one deft turn of a corroded wheel buried in the earth, the pool basin began to fill, and the gold-and-blue tiles began to shimmer as the water played around them.

I assumed from Willard's newfound diligence that he enjoyed the attention of the production people, who on occasion paid him for his efforts. It came as a bit of a shock, however, when, while shooting a scene on the lawn, the director came over to me and said that the grass was too high. Pete was away at the time, so I was at a loss as to what to do. Then one of the production assistants, who had been conversing with Willard earlier, suggested we ask Mr. Woolworth if he wouldn't mind getting one of his men to give the lawn a quick trim.

"Mr. Woolworth," I responded incredulously, "has been dead for over sixty years." The man looked at me oddly.

"But I just spoke to him an hour ago," he said.

"That would be quite impossible. He's buried at Woodlawn Cemetery in the Bronx."

"But he was here," the man insisted. "The heavyset fellow. He said he owns the place."

I stood there thinking I'd heard wrong.

"You must mean Willard. He's the caretaker."

"He said he was Mr. Woolworth. I just assumed he was a descendant or something."

I didn't know whether to be amused or alarmed, but again I put the incident out of my mind and assumed he heard wrong.

At dusk the studio people loaded up their trucks and headed back towards the city. Feeling exhausted, I decided to go for a swim. The pool was almost filled, and by now the water level had reached the skimmers, and you could hear the hum of the filter system working. It was dark, and I had to fumble around in the pump house for the underwater light switch. The water sparkled like turquoise glass and shed an eerie glow onto the trees that surrounded the terrace around the pool. I was too exhausted to go upstairs to get a bathing suit, and so I stripped down to my slip and dove in. The water was freezing, and after a few laps I climbed out and stretched out on top of the diving board, thinking how there's nothing quite like the first swim of the summer. After a few moments, the pool grew still, and I listened to the wind as it moved softly through the trees, blowing leaves across the water's surface. As I lay there, content in the warm night air, my mind wandered back to the recent séance. That night still haunted me with its images of seemingly disembodied faces floating in a haze of strange, musky, perfumed air. It seemed like a dream, and I wondered if I'd distorted the memory of it in the few shorts weeks that had passed. I never spoke of that night to anyone. No one would have believed me if I had. Even Katia never brought the subject up.

I thought about the tortured woman who claimed to be Edna. She was either the best actress I'd seen in a while, or a gifted channeler. (I wasn't quite ready to believe in possession.) and was grateful for all the distractions and work going on around the house, which had left me little time to think about it—until now. The memory of that night had left me profoundly shaken and humbled and forced me to think about things in a whole new way.

I knew very little about Edna and her two sisters, really. There seemed to be almost nothing recorded about them. Years before, when I was living in the Woodward Playhouse, Edna's suicide came up while I was visiting my Woolworth neighbors in Oyster Bay. They said she had a beautiful singing voice and longed for a career in music, but that the daughters of rich and powerful men were often denied such dreams.

From birth, a girl from such a family was conditioned to live for one thing only—a successful marriage, that being determined by the wealth and status of the man. Any woman rebelling, following her heart, and marrying for love was often immediately disinherited. It seemed unlikely that anyone as remote and frightened as Edna would have had the strength or emotional stamina to put up a fight.

From what I remember of that ineffable night, she conveyed a debilitating passiveness and incompleteness of spirit. Her only daughter, Barbara Hutton, was the one who garnered all the attention in the press, with several books and a movie about her tragic life. The beautiful Hutton was married seven times: there was an assortment of questionable princes, a baron, a count, a famous gigolo, and Hollywood heartthrob Cary Grant. Grant was the only one who didn't take her for millions. Woolworth's granddaughter died alone and penniless in her hotel room at the age of sixty-six. Cause of death: malnutrition. A story in the *New York Post* said that she had lived on nothing but Coke and chocolate chip cookies for years. She was quoted as saying: "All the unhappiness in my life has been caused by men." For all her glamour, in every photograph published of her, there was a sadness in her eyes so profound, it seemed like the very life had been drawn out of her. Despite her perfect features, her face had an aura of sorrow about it, as if every wound and act of betrayal were etched on her frail papery skin.

I had almost dozed off on the diving board with these thoughts floating through my mind when I was jolted awake by a splash coming from the far end of the pool. I looked up and saw some tiny animal splashing around in the frigid water, trying to find its way out. I didn't really want to move, but as I watched it struggle, I could see it was a little field mouse. With no choice but to rescue it, I jumped down from the board and ran for the net and fished it out. It was still kicking for dear life when it jumped out of the net and scampered off into the darkness.

As I was heading back towards the house, I spotted Willard leering at me from behind the pump house. Startled, I froze where I stood.

"You like rodents, I see," he said in a sniffling tone while exhaling smoke from one of his cigarettes. There was no end to his creepiness, I thought. Then I realized I was standing there in my undies.

"What are you doing here?" I snapped.

"Just making sure you don't forget to turn the pool lights off," he said in an unconvincing, lethargic voice. Willard's face seemed distorted as his features caught the cold blue reflection of the pool light. With one of his large pudgy hands, he reached over and switched off the light, throwing everything into darkness. I rushed past him to get back to the house, shaking and out of breath.

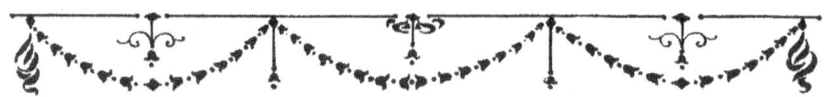

Chapter Eleven

The Homecoming

At dusk the following evening I left the house to go for a walk along the beach. When I returned several hours later, there was light coming from the ballroom. The front door stood open. Thinking I would find Pete or Willard, I walked into the room, but there was no one there. The fireplace was ablaze with burning logs despite the temperature having been in the eighties that day. Resting precariously on the wide arm of the couch was a half-empty bottle of scotch, the scent of it lingering unpleasantly in the air. Just as I was turning to leave, I felt a massive pair of hands closing tightly around my eyes, and I quickly slipped from its grasp. I turned and was shocked to see André. He was drunk, had grown a beard, and was barely recognizable.

"Madam . . . I've returned," he said in a cloying tone. Then he bowed, but he was unsteady on his feet.

He looked as though he'd aged; gray smudges ravaged his eyes. I froze where I stood, gazing at him in stunned silence.

"Why didn't you let me know you were coming?" I blurted out finally. He moved towards me, then stopped as some sap from a burning log burst and crackled loudly in the hearth. "Have you lost your mind? It's stifling in here," I said, raising my voice. He stood there, wavering a bit, but he still didn't respond. The intense heat didn't seem to bother him as he walked over to the couch and took another drink from the bottle. The amber glass glittered for a second in the firelight. Despite the sweltering temperature, I felt myself shiver with fear.

"What's wrong with you?" I asked in a mollifying tone.

"What's wrong with me?" he repeated, as though addressing the flames.

He continued to gaze into the fireplace through narrow, discordant eyes. Then he turned to me.

"This house has brought me nothing but bad luck. Do you believe in such things? Of course, you would believe in such things," he rambled contemptuously. "There's something about this place. Nothing ever goes right. It's like there's this little black cloud hovering over Winfield, and it sucks everything out of you," he said, glancing about the room with sudden loathing. Then he grabbed the bottle and took another gulp. There was something brutal and aberrant in his face that I hadn't seen before, and I thought back to the night of the séance and what I saw in that stranger's face. It was the same look. I suddenly felt queasy.

"But you," he went on, picking up the poker and waving it in the air as though it were a baton. "This place is like a lucky charm for you. You seem to bloom here . . . bloom like the flowers in the garden. They didn't bloom for anyone else. Last year everything we planted died, but for you they bloom. You little witch! That's what you are, you know—a witch," he said, flailing about with exaggerated bravado. Seeming exhausted, he sat down, hunched forward, and began jabbing violently at the glowing logs. I felt myself shut down in a way that seemed familiar, and the whole scene took on the light of a hallucination.

"You've had too much to drink," I said in a low, steady tone, but no longer recognizing my own voice. There was an aura of fear about him, and I suddenly knew he wasn't lashing out at me but at something else. He started to lift himself from the couch. His eyes appeared to be bloodshot, but he collapsed with a thud into the sofa, and it lurched backward, scratching some of the varnish. I moved towards the couch and took the bottle out of his reach. A potent glint of rage shuddered through him.

"You might feel better if you went for a swim," I suggested, out of my compulsion to fix things, regardless of whether it made any sense or not.

"I don't want to go for a swim; I want you to show me how glad you are to see me." His eyes were glaring, appraising me. I didn't answer. His odd behavior had shaken me to the numbing point. I ached with a sense of loss and confusion, and suddenly I felt like a trespasser. I was there because of him, but no longer knew who he was.

"You're not happy to see me," he said coldly.

"You've been gone a month; and then you appear out of the blue and creep up behind me looking like a fucking werewolf."

He started to laugh but caught himself.

"That's good," he said, pointing his finger mockingly. "I look like a werewolf to you . . . *that* coming from a witch."

"You're drunk," I said, sounding mean. Then I turned to leave the room. With that he lunged forward and caught me by the hair, pulling me down towards him on the couch. I rolled down onto the floor, nearly landing in the fire. Then I stood up and leaped behind the couch out of his reach.

"It's this room. . . . This room is making you act crazy. It was *his* room," I said, forgetting that it's foolish to try to reason with someone who's had too much to drink. But then what I'd just said didn't exactly sound reasonable either.

"What the hell are you talking about?" he sneered with irritation.

"Woolworth—he doesn't like anyone using this room," I said.

"Christ, are you going to start with that ghost bullshit again?"

"Like it or not, I think this house is haunted. That lunatic caretaker of yours walks around here thinking he's the five-and-dime king himself, and now you're acting just as nutty."

"I don't want to hear any more of this garbage," he snarled.

"You can call it garbage if you want. I don't think ghosts care if we believe in them or not. They just seem to exist no matter what we think. You don't have to believe in trains either, but if you stand on a railroad track long enough, sooner or later you're going to get squashed," I said, turning to leave.

André rose from the couch. A look of pomposity washed the haggardness from his face.

"Ghosts, squashed trains, squashed spooks," he slurred, "you know, I've met some pretty strange women in my day, and I admit I've picked some pretty flaky wives, but you may turn out to be the wacko of them all."

"Don't bet on it," I hissed. Then I ran up the stairs, bolted my door, and started packing up my things.

Sometime during the night, I thought I heard a loud splash. I got up, walked out to the terrace, and saw the pool lights glowing through the trees. There was another splash, and rays of flickering light spread and shimmered across the shadowed lawn. I put on a robe, walked down the stairs and out the open door, and headed towards the pool. André was swimming from one end of the pool to the other, rising at each side to take desperate, deep breaths, then swimming the whole length underwater. He continued swimming at a feverish pace a while longer. Then, finally exhausted, he pulled himself out of the pool and lay facedown on the tile floor, gasping for breath. I walked towards him, but when he saw me, he covered his face with both hands.

"Something happened that you're not telling me," I said.

"Jovon is dead," he said in a choked voice. "He was shot in the head two nights ago by someone who mistook him for me."

His words cut through me as if ice water had replaced the blood in my veins.

"But why?" I asked, kneeling down beside him.

He began to shake, then broke down in great heaving sobs while shivering from shock and cold.

"Why, André?" I asked again.

"I have enemies," he said, looking up finally, his eyes red and swollen with tears.

"Who?" I asked softly.

"I just have them—leave it at that. Nothing has gone right since I bought this place. I don't feel I can trust anyone. Jovon I trusted. He saved my life once, and now he's gone. You're the only one I have left who's not out to get me," he said in a voice that sounded inconsolable, frightened, and bitter. I watched him as he dried himself off with a towel left on one of the deck chairs. I struggled to think of something to say that would be of comfort to him, but I was too confused myself to speak. He stood up to leave, and I followed as he walked, marble limbed, back up to the house.

"Are you safe here?" I asked finally.

He stopped and blinked. "As safe as anywhere. This is my Fort Knox. I'm sorry about the way I acted before. I'm not myself. You can understand that," he said, reaching for my hand.

"Of course. I wish there was something I could do," I mumbled.

"You've done enough. The house looks great. Where did all that furniture come from?"

"Here and there," I said, knowing then that I would probably never tell him.

André was subdued and moody in the weeks that followed. He stayed close to home, running his business affairs from his room and sending out for everything. Occasionally he would take the train to New York, and he wouldn't return till late at night. There was tension between us. To make matters worse, I had booked the house for a week-long recording session for a rock group, the Top Hats. Originally, they had come to Winfield just to photograph the cover of their new album. Then they discovered that the acoustics in the ballroom were better than those of any recording studio in New York. At first we were excited about the idea and the handsome fee they agreed to pay, but they recorded all night long, making it impossible to stay there. The neighbors complained about the noise, and the studio people were forced to seal up the room with thick Styrofoam and cork paneling. It cut down on the sound, but the whole house vibrated with the ceaseless pounding of the drums.

Willard never emerged from his quarters the whole time André was at the house, and except for a light or two in the upper floor windows, he was out of sight, out of mind. Not wanting to burden André with any more problems than he already had, I never brought up the subject of Willard's strange behavior weeks before. Pete continued to mow the lawns in his unique fashion, but he no longer stalked the rooftops with his shotgun in hand.

Katia's prediction about the phone proved true. Whenever I tried calling her, there would be a steady clicking static at the other end. That seemed to be the case with any number with a nine in it. Katia had three nines in hers. I reported the problem, and the phone company would send someone out to fix it, but within a few days it would start again.

One day, while hanging a painting in one of the rooms upstairs, I discovered there was a secret door connecting it to the Marie Antoinette room, with a space of about two feet between them. There was no knob or anything to indicate that the door panel was moveable; I had simply leaned against it, and it popped open. I tried in vain to contact Katia to tell her about it, but I could only reach her through a phone operator who had to make the call from the control station.

By summer cobwebs began to form all over the house. It may have been the heat and humidity, or an unusual breed of overactive spiders, but even with Pete helping it was impossible to keep up with clearing them away. One night I was alone in the house, standing on a ten-foot ladder, sweeping away the faint wisps of cobwebs that clung to the chandelier in my room. The radio was playing softly in the background when the sky began to flash like a strobe light. There was no sound at first, just pulses of light to warn of a threatening storm. Then a soft summer rain began tapping on the dry hot tiles of the terrace outside. Thunder sounded from far away as dark gray clouds curled ominously and swept across the blackening sky. Then great rods of lightning pierced the clouds, and a loud clap of thunder exploded with such intensity, it seemed to quake the foundation of the building. I was halfway down the ladder when the lights went out. Lightning struck again and again, and with each flash of light I inched my way down the ladder and towards the dresser, where I kept a carton of candles left over from the czar shoot. I fished around for some matches and got two of the candles lit on the mantle.

Outside, the trees lashed back and forth against the sky. Rain began pouring down against the windows, flooding the terrace. Water shot out through the drain openings along the balcony balustrades, spilling jets of water out onto the drive below. From the staircase landing I could see water falling in wide sheets from the roof of the teahouse pavilion, causing the pillars and arches to appear as though they stood under a shimmering dome of glass. An exhilarating energy filled the house as the rain beat down on the copper roof above and swept across the glass ceiling of the palm conservatory.

My room took on an eerie quality as thin gray wisps of smoke from the candles flickered in the mirror above the fireplace. I searched around for more candlesticks and decided to remove the lightbulbs in the chandelier and put candles in the sockets. As I lit each one, it created a magical effect as the flames flickered on the porcelain roses entwined around each arm. I was staring at them when suddenly there was a creaking noise as torrents of rain slashed furiously at the terrace doors. The glass panes trembled in the aged wooden frames. Then the doors blew open with such force, I thought they were going to snap off their hinges. All the candles blew out at once, and the restless wind entered my room. It seemed to gather strength, and gaining power it raced into a gale wind through the room and out into the empty hall. Rain began pouring in, soaking the rug and satin bedspread. It took every ounce of my strength to push the doors closed and hold them in place while I turned the key in the lock. I was relighting the candles when I thought I heard a woman crying out in the hall, but it was soon drowned out by the thickening din of the rain. Taking one of the candles with me, I walked out into the hall and listened.

Whatever I had heard was gone, but the air around me felt charged with electricity, and I felt lighter somehow. I stood outside Edna's old room and noticed that the lightning outside had begun to die down. A faint mist or haze seemed to linger within the room — a strange vaporous glow that appeared to move on its own like a phantom promenade floating slowly across the panels of the pale blue and cream-colored walls. I squeezed my eyes shut, and for a moment the room seemed to shift away from me.

"Edna," I heard myself whisper as the phone began ringing down the hall. I turned and ran towards it. It was Katia.

"How are things at Hell House?" she asked brightly.

"I've been trying to reach you for days," I said, relieved to hear the sound of her voice.

"I'm in Atlantic City, trying out my numerological skills on the slot machines."

"Did they work?"

"No. I lost three hundred and sixty dollars and decided to pack it in and go sight-seeing instead. You won't believe what I found. I was walking along the beach and stopped to rest at one of the seaside pavilions, and I got to talking to one of the old-timers who knew everything about the area from way back. Anyway, I can't even remember how the subject came up, but this guy started to tell me about the Barbara Hutton mansion that's boarded up down here. It's called Bahia Mar, and it's been abandoned for years. He said Hutton never really lived in it, but everyone calls it by her name because she stayed here from time to time. It overlooks Lakes Bay and has a great view of all the new casinos on the boardwalk. It was built by Barbara Hutton's aunt Grace Middleton, the sister of Edna Woolworth's husband, Franklyn Hutton. I was told that everyone around here says this place is haunted too," she said capriciously.

"People say that about anything that's big and boarded up. Did you get to see the place?" I asked, intrigued.

"I only got to see the outside, 'cause it's all boarded up, but it's huge and looks like a Spanish castle, with sand dunes all around it. Over the entrance there's a crest like the one at Winfield, only this one has a carving of Bacchus. My new friend said he's been inside several times and there's a large stained-glass window with a coat of arms with the hex sign on it, and above it he said there's an inscription in Latin that translates: 'Regard the Demon.'"

"Did you actually see it?" I asked.

"No. Like I said, all the windows are boarded up, but there's one more thing. This guy said that there's a black mirror set into a wall upstairs and that it's hollow on the other side. Apparently that whole family of Woolworth's was into some kind of weirdness."

"The Huttons are not Woolworths—only through marriage," I added. "Did you get any photographs, even of the outside?"

"No. I didn't bring a camera, but it's all down here. You can come down and see for yourself. Oh, and I was told the place has a history of bad luck. A few years ago someone bought the place and turned it into a restaurant called the Sand Castle. Seems everything went wrong, and it had to close down," she said, finishing her report triumphantly. "What do you make of it?"

"Only you would walk into such a situation."

"There are no accidents," she said, half joking. But then she repeated the words in a reverent tone.

"You did good, Katia—it's an amazing find. I'll look into it if I get a chance to go down there."

"What's happening at the house?"

"I wish you were here. There's no electricity, candles won't stay lit, the wind is howling, and there are funny lights in the next room—it's your kind of night, Katia," I said tauntingly.

"No, thank you," she said just as some wax began to drip from the candleholder and gather in a pool on the new blue rug. I quickly reached for a magazine to catch it with, but it was too late.

"When are you coming back?" I asked.

"I'm just going to stay another night and try to catch a tan in the morning. I'll call you when I get back to the city."

"Oh, Katia, you were right about the phone."

"You sound surprised," she said, hanging up the phone. Just as I put the receiver down, the lights went back on and the stereo shattered the mood with the soundtrack from *Saturday Night Fever*.

Chapter Twelve

Pembroke

The following day temperatures rose into the mid-nineties, making it too hot to work or do anything other than find a shady spot down by the beach. Winfield had the advantage of being surrounded by water on two sides. To the north there were Welwyn and Crescent Beach, and to the west there was a huge tract of land that was still in private hands that ran along the water's edge. I decided to take a walk, slipping out the west gate, then crossing a brambled path that led out onto Red Spring Lane. On the edge of that road there stood a huge vine-entangled gate with the name "Pembroke" emblazoned across its wrought-iron arch. I had not visited the property since the main house had been razed in 1968. Now only the outbuildings remained intact, about a dozen or so structures half buried in vine overgrowth. To the left of the drive stood a stone gazebo, where a marble wood sprite sat on a toadstool playing a flute. Along the road, trees grew in perfect rows that led to a clearing where the earth appeared to drop off into a vast open void. At one time the main house stood on that spot. Now I could feel the emptiness of it as though it were a palpable thing. The sight of it brought on the memory of its destruction and the sound of the wrecker's ball as it exploded into the maze of pipes and the chimes of the interior pipe organ. The sound rang in the air, like a steel blade smashing into a wall of glass.

There were still traces of the house in the heaps of rubble—a few bricks, some carved capitals covered with weeds. But the Long Island

Sound that stretched out beyond had not changed at all. There was the steady hum of motors while boats of every kind were coming and going. Several huge yachts were bobbing with the waves as the tide came in. Through the haze, you could see Sands Point, or East Egg, as Fitzgerald fans sometimes referred to it. Standing on the opposite side of the bay was Jay Gould's 125-room Scottish castle, looking as it did when it was first built around the turn of the century. I watched as some kids moored their launch at the dock, then ran laughing along the beach, paying no mind to the NO TRESPASSING sign posted along the water's edge. I had taken my shoes off and was walking barefoot in the sand when the sound of a man's sharp voice startled me.

"Hey lady, didn't you see the sign?"

I turned and saw an old man who looked to be in his seventies.

"Yes," I answered glumly as he rolled his eyes in disgust. His face was tanned and wrinkled. It was a kindly face despite the harsh tone of his voice. He wore a navy blue T-shirt, worn overalls, and heavy work boots that were covered in mud.

"I know you," I said, walking towards him. "When the house was coming down, you let me photograph it."

He stood there and scrutinized me through narrowed eyes.

"Can't say I remember you, so many folks comin' around here trespassing — no stopping 'em on a hot day like this," he said, wiping some sweat off his brow with a plaid handkerchief.

"Joe — isn't your name Joe?"

"It is, so I guess maybe I did meet you," he said in a less-threatening tone.

"You're one of the gardeners, aren't you?"

"I do what I can. There's not much to garden around here anymore. Some of the old family still come to stay for weekends in the beach house, so I keep things in order as much as I can — don't want the place to look abandoned. How did you get in here, anyway?"

"The gate was open."

"My wife must have forgot to close it when she went out to the store this morning. It's always kept locked," he said in a way that let me know I'd broken the rules.

"It's not the same place here with the main house gone, is it?" I said, not knowing if I was opening up an old wound.

He didn't say anything as he stooped down to pick up a broken beer bottle from the beach. "Damn kids," he muttered under his breath.

I considered my running into him a stroke of good fortune and decided to take advantage of the opportunity to talk.

In all my years of active trespassing, I never met an estate worker who was not charming, friendly, and full of interesting stories. The key to winning their trust seemed to be a reverence for the past, and on that subject my willingness to listen knew no bounds.

"I never showed you the photographs I took when it was going down. Pembroke was beautiful even as a ruin," I said.

"Please don't remind me. That was the end of the world for us. All the help was let go after that. They were like family, you know. Gets that way when you work side by side for so long. Used to be over a hundred of us when I first came here as a boy," he said. He'd been turning the glass bottle in his hands for a long while. Then, with surprising strength for a man his age, he raised his arm and threw it towards what looked like an entrance to a cave that extended out amid some huge gray boulders. The green glass caught the light, then shattered into a hundred pieces against a rusting steel door half-hidden in a brambled embankment.

"Where does that lead?" I asked, pointing in its direction.

"Used to be a tunnel, but it got filled in after the war. The old captain . . . Captain Delamar, the man who built all this, put up a real fine bathhouse right here where we're standing. Kind of a mini palace, I called it — real fancy for a bathhouse. You could change and shower downstairs, and on the second level there was a teahouse where they used to dance and have moonlight parties. Well, at some point the captain decided to build a tunnel going from the bathhouse up to the main house. Mostly 'cause guests didn't like to get wet when it rained. A lot of the big places around here had tunnels going down to the beach or from one building to another. But the one over there was used to bring the coal from the barges that came up the sound. They would unload the coal into these small railroad cars that ran on tracks along the floor of the tunnel and carried the coal up into the basement of the main house. That's how they used to heat these monster buildings — with coal furnaces. Most of them are gone now, but back in the twenties, during prohibition, they started to get used for a lot of other shenanigans. I remember the gangster Waxy Gordon pulling up one night in a speedboat full of booze. He and his men with their Tommy guns tied the boat to our dock. I think they went to the wrong house 'cause they turned around and headed up to the cove. The bootleggers and rum-runners used to stash their booze in them—even hid stills down there, 'cause the police didn't know those tunnels existed. Every now and then there'd be some gangland killing, and they'd bury the bodies down there too. Most of them were never found, but you'd hear about it occasionally. With all the excavating, and new homes being built in recent years, you hear about skeletons turning up on a lot of these old estates. I heard of one case where this rich doctor bought one of the old mansions around here a few years back and found a body buried in an old coal chute in the basement."

"What did he do?" I asked with morbid curiosity.

"Didn't do anything so far as I heard. People like that don't want publicity, or police poking around, when it was most likely a sixty-year-old homicide involving a bunch of thugs," he said nonchalantly.

"Wouldn't you feel creepy having a corpse in your basement?"

"Well, he didn't leave it there. He had the gardener remove the bones and plant them out in the rose garden. Them old dried bones make good fertilizer."

"Charming solution, but isn't that illegal?"

He shrugged. "Who's gonna know," he said as his eyes followed a sleek black sailboat as it began to move into the cove. "Had a body in a coffin wash up on this beach once—I'll never forget that," he said with his hand poised midair. I stepped back, not sure I wanted him to go on.

"There was this hurricane back in the forties," he said as he began walking along the beach, not paying any mind to the water running up along the tops of his shoes. "You see, out there is Hart Island," he said, pointing west. "The city buries its unclaimed dead out there in shallow graves, but this storm caused the tide to rise six feet higher than normal, so when it receded it washed away the earth and all the graves along with it. There were bodies and coffins floating around all over the place. Most of them ended up on City Island or Kings Point. But one ended up here and got lodged in those rocks. The Coast Guard came and fished it out, but there was never anything in the papers about it. I guess you were lucky if you didn't know about it," he said with a hint of repugnance, then he snorted as if trying to blow the salt air out of his nostrils. I was relieved to hear the sudden dismissal of the subject in his voice. For a man his age, his energy level seemed high as we walked along the beach for a while longer. Then he stopped and kicked over a hollow shell of a dead horseshoe crab.

"You from around here?" he asked finally.

"I live next door," I said, pointing east.

"In Woolworth's old place," he responded, glancing in its direction.

"Yes."

"I thought that house was closed up for good—figured it would be going down soon, like they all do around here," he said with a touch of hopelessness.

"No, not Winfield. They'll never take that one down," I said with conviction.

"I used to say that about this place. Then bang—one day it's gone, like it never existed. Taxes and all is what kills them."

"It must be hard on you. I mean, to live here still, and it's all so different."

There was a long silence after that. When he finally spoke, it seemed as though he had no feeling about it one way or another, and yet he paused and swallowed. "I got me memories," he said. "My dad worked here before me when the sea captain owned the property. It was mostly woods and farms around here then—I'm talking around nineteen-fourteen or thereabouts. Woolworth wanted this land desperately. He would have gotten it too, if it weren't for Delamar. He was a sly one who always got what he wanted. Woolworth was furious. You see, they were cut from the same cloth, those two. Both started out poor and all, then became millionaires. There was a lot of competition between the rich in those days; one tried to outdo the other. Wasn't long after that that the captain's palace went up—biggest house ever built around here. Must have had over eighty rooms. Half the building was taken up with that palm conservatory. Do you remember it?" he asked.

"I remember it only as a ruin."

"When it was new, it looked like the Crystal Palace in England. I saw a picture postcard of it once, and that's what it reminded me of—Queen Victoria's Crystal Palace. I remember, when I was a boy, that building was filled with all kinds of exotic birds. Some of those birds spoke French, Italian, and Spanish. The captain had them brought in special to amuse the guests. There was one bird, Pecco—whenever he smelled perfume, he'd say 'Bella Señora' in this deep slow voice. He sounded so human, the girls went nuts over him. They'd walk around with him on their shoulders all night. There were palm trees some thirty feet high.

Then in forty-nine there was an ice storm, with hailstones the size of silver dollars. Well, they came beating down on that glass roof like rockets, smashing some of the windows. Those birds took off all over the place. The next day you saw tropical birds all over town, roosting on telephone poles, on the rooftops of houses. We got some of them back, but a lot were lost."

As I listened, it was almost impossible for me to grasp the full reality of the times he witnessed. Had I not once seen the glass palace with my own eyes, his tale would have sounded like a hallucination. I considered it a rare and sacred privilege to have run into him that day—he was the last of his kind. I listened in rapt attention, gratefully absorbing every detail, fragment, innuendo, and nuance of a time recorded only in the memories of those who lived it.

"There must have been a lot of parties then," I said.

"Oh, were there parties. They'd float orchids in the indoor pool, which was the size of a lake. There were hundreds of paper lanterns hung in all the palm trees, and there'd be movie stars staying up at the house for the weekend. Pauline Frederick was my favorite—a real looker she was. She walked into the greenhouse one night dressed in a long silver gown and asked if I'd give her a white orchid to wear in her hair for the party. So I showed her around and let her pick one out. She kissed me real proper, and I never forgot her," he said, looking in the direction of where the building once stood.

"Did you ever meet Mr. Woolworth at one of the parties?"

"No, he never came here—was never invited. He never got over losing the land to Delamar. Woolworth kept to himself mostly. Half the time he was off sailing around the world buying stuff for his stores. When he was here, he used to dock his monster ship up near the cove, by Morgan's Island. He had thirty or forty in crew, mostly lowlife foreign types from the West Indies. They lived on the boat, but every night they'd come into town and raise all kinds of hell, with drinking and brawling. By morning, most of them would be in jail. The whole town always knew when Woolworth was back at his house: you'd hear the pipe organ playing all night."

For a brief moment, a much-needed breeze blew across the stifling beach, rippling the wavelets and causing seagulls to screech with excitement. One of them swooped low to the ground as it flung a half-eaten mussel shell from its beak, nearly hitting Joe in the shoulder. He ducked, looking up at it.

"Damn gulls—they make a bigger mess of this beach than those drunken teenagers." he said, gesturing towards them.

"Were you here when the first Winfield burnt down?" I asked as we continued walking.

"We were the first to see it, 'cause there were no tall trees to block the view back then. The smoke drifted over this way, causing all the horses to go wild with terror. A lot of our men ran over to help. They were lucky to have so many people on hand. I wanted to go and pitch in, but I was just a boy and had to watch from behind the gate. Everybody formed a line and managed to save most of the stuff inside the house. Not that it mattered; nothing they saved was good enough for Woolworth after that. Once he got a gander at Delamar's new spread, he had to do one better. That's how it was back then. You can't imagine the rivalry that went on between those bigwigs. They couldn't stand to be outdone by anyone. Woolworth had to sail past this place to get to the cove. It must have eaten at him. Some of us thought maybe he burnt his old place down himself, but who knows—his old house was a firetrap, like a lot of those older mansions. It was strange though, 'cause almost immediately the new house went up, like it was all planned out ahead of time. The men worked around the clock in three shifts to get it done in a matter of months. I'd walk over there at night, and the place was lit up with these Hollywood-like arc lights, so bright they could blind you. The new building was built right over the old one, so the basement and layout remained the same. It was one of the grandest houses ever built—all that white marble. You know how you can see it from the main road? He wanted it to be out in the open like that, to show it off. He always did things in a flashy way, like those fur coats he wore. The maid up there was friends with some of the help here, and she said he had over twenty fur coats in his closet. Not to mention all those weird antique military costumes he collected."

"Military costumes?" I repeated. "He probably wore them to all the masquerade balls they had around here."

"He didn't go to masquerade balls—wasn't the frivolous type—took everything he did very seriously. After the house was built, he made a lot of trips to Europe, even Egypt, I heard. He'd come back, and that ship would be so loaded down with cargo, it's amazing it didn't sink. We'd hear stories from the crew—the few who spoke English, that is. Some of our live-in help liked to go down to the local pubs on their night off, and they'd come back with all the latest on what everyone else was doing. Servants loved to talk over a few beers. There was one story that Woolworth brought back a stone coffin with a mummy in it, and that he was going to put it in his house, just 'cause no one ever done that before. Some said there was a curse on it, but half the stuff you heard was just beer hall stories; no one ever paid them no mind."

"A sarcophagus . . ." I said, amazed. "He brought back a sarcophagus?"

Joe looked at me with a puzzled look. "Don't know what that is."

"A stone Egyptian coffin. That's an odd thing to put in your house."

"I don't know—odd was kind of normal in those days. One guy had a stuffed elephant in his trophy room. Then there was Vanderbilt, with his house of stuffed fish and sea monsters," he added in a tone that let me know he probably could have given a hundred other examples before running out.

"Did you ever meet any of Woolworth's daughters?" I asked, changing the subject.

"They were away a lot, but Jessie, his youngest, she stayed there the most and took care of the place after her father died."

"What about Edna?"

"She was grown up by the time her father built the new place you're in now. That Hutton fella she married was something of a philanderer. You'd read about all those showgirl types he was running around with. It's kind of sad, 'cause no matter how unhappy anyone was, divorce was impossible in those days. I only saw Edna once. She came down here for a walk along the beach. She was with a nice-looking fella—wasn't her husband, though. They just sat and talked down by the bathhouse. She seemed happy that day."

"Did you know who the man was?" I asked, vaguely remembering her saying something the night of the séance about a man who worked for her father.

"No, never saw him before, but he wasn't one of the rich folks, 'cause he was wearing a livery. A short time later we read in the papers that she was dead. Didn't say too much about it either—just that she died of something. But in time word got out that she took her own life. After that, her daughter, Barbara, moved in with her grandfather. She had a nanny and all, but she seemed sad and undisciplined. She was always running away—would come down here and took up playing with the McMannis kids, who lived next door. They were a wild bunch—were always getting into the barns here and letting the chickens loose. In all kinds of weather they would jump into the fountains with their fancy clothes on, then tear up all the flowerbeds, just to get attention. Of course, you couldn't say nothing about it, 'cause no one was going to stop them. They'd just come back and do it again. There was something so loveless and empty about their lives. No wonder they ended up the way most of them did. They had the best of everything, yet couldn't enjoy it—couldn't see what was before their own eyes. We were the ones who could appreciate the surroundings and marvel at the sights and all, but then we had real families to go home to at night. There are a lot of people around here who could tell you stories—people who lived here all their lives and worked on the estates, in one way or another. Before the Depression, we had over a hundred men just working the grounds here alone. Some of them are still around, just like those marble statues of Greek gods that disappeared over the years from Woolworth's driveway. If you drive around this town, you'll see them here and there in people's backyards."

Just then, a seaplane flew over us. It landed out beyond the stone pier. We watched it bob rhythmically in the waves. Then slowly it began to move again, gliding out towards the sound.

"What do you miss the most?" I asked, realizing it was time for me to get back.

"Everything . . ." he responded. "When we had it all, we took it for granted—didn't really believe those times would end. The rich had so much money—more than you would think could ever be spent in one lifetime, but it all went so fast. It was the war that did it—war and taxes. You woke up one morning, and it was all gone."

Chapter Thirteen

The Greenhouse

It was several days before the air finally cooled down enough for me to get back to working on the house. I decided to check out the long-abandoned greenhouse to see if there was anything in it worth salvaging. I had not visited the rotting building since the auction in seventy-five, and it was a hopeless ruin even then. An unsuspecting buyer, caught up in the moment at the sale, had bought the entire contents of the building, sight unseen, for five hundred dollars, but he never came back to claim any of it. The greenhouse, for all its clutter, had an emptiness about it so profound, it settled in the vast empty rooms like toxic dust. Nevertheless, I was determined, and thought there might be something in there I might have missed.

The wind sang gently in the hemlock trees as I headed out across the open lawn towards the south end of the property. Dandelions were sprouting up where the uneven grass was again in need of cutting. The belvedere loomed ahead at the far end of the long drive.

A stone balustrade running along the top of it was lost beneath a tangle of wisteria vines that cascaded down over the fountain of mythological statues that graced the center. Water splashed from the gaping mouths of a pair of winged marble horses that rose up from a small mosaic-tiled pool. A huge statue of King Neptune with his scepter stood on a pedestal supported by stone dolphins. At night it was lit like a stage tableau against a background of gold-and-blue tiles reflecting like jewels in the rippling water below. I set about to find the old path to the greenhouse that was just beyond the wall of statues, but the way was blocked by a huge pile of dead bushes and tree branches. Thorny rose twigs tore at the threads of my skirt as I got closer to the greenhouse. The door hung on one hinge and made a creaking sound when I opened it. Inside there was a rusted wheelbarrow turned on its side, with hundreds of broken flowerpots all around.

Most of the glass from the roof was gone. Someone had tried to cover the open roof with a huge tarpaulin that now flapped in the wind where the ropes had rotted and come undone. The smell of decay filled the air as cobwebs and mold enshrouded what was left of the furniture in that graveyard of forgotten things.

In one corner, a jumble of velvet draperies, valances, and gold-braided tassels was unceremoniously strewn about. A feeling of sadness came over me, but as I stood there scrutinizing every object in that desert of rubble, I was even more determined to find something that could be saved and put to better use up at the house. Just then a squirrel scampered out of a rotted piece of furniture and ran across a beam in the open roof. I followed him with my eyes, then spotted something half-hidden under a torn piece of canvas. Standing against the wall was a ten-foot armoire, its doors beautifully carved with a peacock. Years of exposure to the elements had bleached and warped the mahogany finish. Broken picture frames and shattered lamps with rotted silk shades lay cluttered all around it. Dresser and bedroom chests were stacked ceiling high, one upon the other, where layers of veneer had peeled away. Trees and vines were growing up out of the dirt floor around them, their blackened branches making their way up like claws through some of the open drawers of the ruined cabinets. Nearby there were half a dozen overstuffed chairs, piled high with faded cartons and boxes. At the top a handsome Regency-style chair caught my eye. Looking at it more closely, I knew I'd found what I was looking for. Chair legs had jammed one into the other, and as I struggled with the resisting load, everything began to tumble down at once. The chair finally broke free along with a tangle of other objects, I felt a sharp pain as it landed on my left foot.

All the boxes and broken glass from the ceiling continued to fall noisily to the floor. Crawly things scattered and ran for cover as their dank nesting places were exposed. A large box, spewing sawdust as it fell, landed with a thud next to me. I gasped at the sight of the half-rotted, stuffed head of an elk, its wild glass eyes staring out at the gloom. I recognized it as one of the mounted heads that had once hung on the wall in the billiard room. When the dust finally settled, I studied the chair and noticed a deep gash in the side where something sharp had pressed against it over the years. I gave a yank at the rotted upholstery, and as I did so, a piece of folded paper fell out from the lining and landed on the floor. I picked up the thick, cream-colored stationery and carefully opened it. At the top, engraved in fine black lettering, was "Mrs. Richard S. Reynolds." The handwriting was crusted with smudges of mould and faded almost beyond recognition, but I could read some of it where the dampness had not reached it.

In this bleak hour of gathering gloom
Can faith outsoar impending doom?
The mind, seized with nameless fright,
Spars at shadows in the night.

Storm-tossed waters seethe at sea
Down the road, demonic trees
Stretch out their arms toward me.

On the back in what seemed like a different handwriting, it continued:

searching the darkness for his tomb.

As I stared down at the writing, I realized that it was in that very spot that I first met Mrs. Reynolds almost two decades ago. How alive and verdant the greenhouse was then! I put the paper in my skirt pocket, dusted myself off, and headed back up to the house. The chair could wait; I was eager to tell Katia what I'd found.

When I reached the front door, I found it locked, though I knew I had left it open. There was a spare key in the glove compartment of my car, and, after retrieving it, I tried it, but the handle still wouldn't turn. I tried again and again, then began to panic, thinking Willard might have changed the lock while I was gone, but no one was there that day. Willard's van was gone, and if anyone had come through the gate, I'd have heard the car in the gravel drive. There seemed little choice but to wait. When it began to get dark, I decided to take my chances and break a window. To the right was the servants' wing, where a large, screened-in porch concealed the only small-size windows in the entire house. There was a shovel leaning against some cardboard boxes, and after hesitating a minute I picked it up and swung it as hard as I could. The window exploded, sending glass flying in all directions. With a rag I swept away the broken glass from the sill. Then, standing on a box, I crawled into the window.

In that moment, car lights flashed across the drive, illuminating the porch. I froze as I recognized the sound of Willard's van, with its faulty muffler sputtering loudly as it turned into the service drive. Despite the circumstances, I had invaded his end of the house, and felt a wave of panic as I heard him slam the van door then the jingle of his keys. His massive form was in shadow as he headed towards the porch with his familiar disjointed gait. I quickly jumped back out the window and called out before he had a chance to react as one might to a burglar caught in the act. I stood there in the shadows of the unlit porch as he turned on his flashlight.

"I was locked out and had to break a window," I said, nearly choking on my words. He didn't say anything but continued to move towards the house. Then he pulled the screen door open, and it scraped noisily along the cement floor. He shone the light on the broken window, and I thought I saw him raise his hand as if to strike out. But he only moved closer to pick up the shovel, placing it carefully back in the exact spot where I'd found it.

"Someone changed the lock. I went out to the greenhouse, and when I came back, it . . ." I started to say.

"Where's your key?" he demanded, his flashlight still aimed at the broken window. Though his face was still in shadow, for a second I thought I caught sight of a flickering light that danced, dark and wicked, in his eyes. I stepped back and turned to leave as I handed him the key. Without saying a word he passed through the screen door and down the steps and turned to the right towards the front of the house. I followed and watched as he shoved the key in the lock. It rattled into the keyhole, caught the tumblers, and revolved with the familiar click, and the door popped open. There was a sense of sick excitement about him, as though he was enjoying a private triumph. He handed the key back to me.

"I trust you'll fix the window by morning," he said smugly. Then, before I could answer, he turned and headed back to his side of the house.

I stood outside the door, staring at the lock and trying it again several times. It turned as it always had. It was a long time before I could bring myself to go inside.

Katia's phone rang at least twenty times before she picked up. She answered brightly, and hearing her voice helped calm my frazzled nerves. She seemed unmoved by Mrs. Reynolds's writing but suggested, "Why not get in touch with her and ask what she meant?"

"The house she moved to in the cove has been boarded up for years," I told her, doubting Mrs. Reynolds was still alive. She had once told me that she was born in 1882—almost a hundred years ago now.

"Maybe Mrs. Reynolds just liked to write about morbid things. Hell, if I lived in that gloomy place for over thirty years, I'd be going over the edge," Katia said in a flippant tone.

"Maybe, but something about what she wrote disturbs me. I can't put my finger on it, and it looks like two different handwritings."

"Why don't you take it to a graphologist to have it analyzed, and while you're at it, take along a sample of Woolworth's handwriting. That should prove even more interesting," she suggested.

"I never found anything of his in the house."

"Try the Woolworth Building down by Wall Street; they must have tons of letters and business transactions written by him on file."

"I'll look into it this week and let you know."

"There's my doorbell. I've got a reading to do—catch you later," she said, sounding out of breath as the phone went dead. Just as she hung up, another idea occurred to me—the possibility that Woolworth might have filed his will in the city of Glen Cove, that being his primary residence at the time. Back in his day wills were often written by hand, then signed by their attorneys.

The Woolworth Building, located at 233 Broadway, was listed in the phone directory, but by the time I got through, it was after hours, and a janitor answered. He was quick to mention that he had worked there for almost forty years, and in the next ten minutes I was given all the statistics on the building: the square footage of each floor, the source of the rocks used in the foundation, the elevator weight capacity, and how much the tower swayed during a hurricane.

Realizing he had a captive audience, he launched into a vivid account of how on a moonlit evening in April 1913, a grand banquet was held on the twenty-seventh floor for eight hundred of the most important people of the day, including Nikola Tesla, who developed the innovative alternate current that was used to light the building. The high point of the evening came when President Woodrow Wilson pressed a button and suddenly illuminated the building in a blaze of light. The guests dined on turtle soup, terrapin, and caviar, then raised a toast to Franklin Winfield Woolworth, the poor farm boy from upstate New York whose dream was to create the tallest building in the world. The informative janitor was about to tell me how many people had jumped to their deaths from the fifty-fourth floor when I cut in to ask if there might be a Woolworth history room that was open to the public. He informed me that most of the twenty-fourth floor was devoted to the Woolworth Museum, and that it opened each morning at ten o'clock. His final words were: "So come on down; we have the best view of the Brooklyn Bridge."

I was on the first commuter train out of Glen Cove the next morning, arriving at lower Broadway just before the building was open. Little had changed in the area since the turn of the century. Woolworth's skyscraper, known as the Cathedral of Commerce, stood on the edge of a small park at the foot of the Brooklyn Bridge. Looking up at the towering monument, I saw it had Woolworth's mark all over it. Grand and Gothic, it rose eight hundred feet into the sky, with crouching gargoyles perched along the ornate facade. Everywhere you looked were strange and curious carvings of bats, frogs, owls, weasels, and pelicans, commingled with several stone images of Woolworth hunched over, greedily counting his nickels and dimes. The entrance hall was so lavish, it was almost blinding, with walls of gold and veined marble imported from the coast of Greece. The vaulted ceiling was set with brilliantly colored patterns in glass mosaics that glowed like a million jewels.

The twenty-fourth floor turned out to be a treasure trove of memorabilia Woolworth had collected throughout his lifetime. It could just as easily have been called the Napoleon Museum, for as in the Empire room at Winfield, there were several gilt-and-red velvet thrones encrusted with the gold letter N encircled with laurel leaves. I recognized the priceless bronze statue of the emperor reared up on his horse from an old photograph taken when it stood on a table in Mr. Woolworth's bedroom. Dominating one wall was an eight-foot oil painting of Napoleon glaring down in his royal ermine robes and holding a scepter. I had the feeling that no one ever came into the massive room, and yet it smelled of furniture polish, and there was the ghostly scent of cigars. A shaft of sunlight filtered through the heavy red-velvet drapes that hung from the tall glass windows, setting off the rows of ancestral portraits that covered the walls.

I spotted a mahogany-and-glass bookcase off in the corner with a thick, green-leather album with the name Winfield stamped in gold on its cover. The cabinet was locked, but, overwhelmed with curiosity, I had to work up the courage to go back outside and ask if the case could be opened. A moment later a young gentleman with a red mustache and thick horn-rimmed glasses came in, unlocked the glass case, took the album out, and placed it on top of Woolworth's old mahogany desk. When I opened the front cover, several loose eight-by-ten photographs fell to the floor and scattered at my feet. One was an exterior view of the rebuilt Winfield taken at the time of its completion in 1917. Its marble facade gleamed in the sun, along with perfect rows of life-sized classical statues that lined the length of the drive. There were several photos of an elegant party in the rose garden, with tightly corseted women posing stiffly in their enormous picture hats. Two of the gowns I recognized from the collection that Mrs. Reynolds had almost discarded from the greenhouse so many years ago. There were dozens of shots from every angle of the garden, with every blade of grass, tree, and shrub clipped in perfect order.

Then I came across a photo of a charming children's playhouse that apparently once stood in a glade of trees by the west lawn. It was a small, clabbered-wood structure painted white, with tiny shutters and window boxes filled with pansies. Standing outside the front door were two young girls in white dresses and ruffled hats, with a lamb. A chill went through me as I thought back on the night of the séance and remembered the story of the little lamb named Amber. No one in the photographs was identified, nor were there any dates to indicate when they were taken.

As I continued to turn the pages, there was a picture of the glass palm conservatory, with a clear view of Long Island Sound and several luxury yachts floating past. It had apparently been taken before the trees had blocked out the view. Towards the back of the book was a large rectangular print taken of Winfield under construction, with thirty or forty men working together on the skeletal steel girders. Some hung suspended like aerial artists from rafters, fearlessly defying the laws of gravity. Several men laid tiles along the many terraces, while others cemented balustrades along the roofline.

When I came to the end of the photographs, tucked away in a folder and tied with a string were some floor plans and architects' renderings of the house and grounds. I unfolded the faded papers, laid them out on the massive desk, and studied them. The carefully drawn blue lines and code symbols made the house seem even larger and more complex than it appeared in reality. On the paper, extending out beyond the walls of the main building was a series of dotted lines. There was one to the carriage house and another to the garden pavilion, and a third appeared in the area of the west staircase. Remembering what the caretaker at Pembroke had said about underground tunnels, I began to make note of them, then noticed another series of dots just under the west staircase, indicating a possible room below it. The measurements of thirty-three feet by sixteen were clearly marked in blue ink. I knew of no such room. It was not uncommon for architects' drawings to be altered as work progressed, and fanatical owners changed their minds at every turn. On the chance that it might mean something, I pulled several sheets of thin paper out of my briefcase and attempted to make tracings of the location of those lines.

I had lost track of the time, and I was only halfway through the tedious task when the young man came back into the room and said he had to go to lunch, indicating he had to lock everything up before he left. He helped me gather up all the photographs and floor plans, carefully placing them back into the leather album. As he was locking the book in the glass case, I asked if there were any old letters or records of any business transactions written by Woolworth and was told there were none available for public viewing. I thanked him for his help, and he turned to leave, heading in the direction opposite to the elevators.

Original photo taken in 1917 when Winfield was first built

Woolworth designed this family crest in 1916 which appears above the fireplace in the Main Hall, and it shows him looking regal at top, his poor wife in the middle under a steel mask, and his three daughters, Helena, Edna, and Jessie. The crack running through Edna's face appeared on the night she took her life. (Monica Randall 1968)

The Ballroom, at a cost of more than two million dollars, was built in the home of F. W. Woolworth. It is complete with solid gold fixtures, gilded ceiling, sumptuous furnishings, and a built-in pipe organ. (Monica Randall 1960)

Detail of the gold Ballroom ceiling with open filigree above fireplace, which conceals secret rooms where guards would watch the guests below. (Monica Randall 1960)

The Empire Room with Napoleon's sleigh bed and canopy, where Woolworth died. (Monica Randall 1958)

The Empress Josephine Room. (Monica Randall 1958)

Detail of the god Neptune flanked by sea "horses" in the fountain. (Monica Randall 1960)

Full view of the marble Neptune fountain. (Monica Randall 1968)

The West façade of Winfield, during the Girls' School years. (Monica Randall 1968)

Cast of a movie called *Lost Voyage* posing at the front entrance of Winfield. Taken during the time of the Girls' School, it was then known as the Glamour Manor. (Monica Randall 1968)

Another shot from the filming of *Lost Voyage*, this is an antique car rented for the shoot. (Monica Randall 1968)

The William Woodward Estate, "The Playhouse," scene of the famous shooting tragedy in October 1955, on Halloween eve. Originally built by Helena Woolworth McCann, the owners at the time of this picture were Mr. and Mrs. Norris. On the left is the indoor tennis court where Cinerama was developed during the early 1950s. Monica lived on the second floor. (Monica Randall 1966)

The Grand Hall at the Playhouse, during Helena Woolworth McCann's day, in the 1920s. The two small paintings on the wall are Rembrandts. (Photo from collection belonging to Helena McCann, loaned to the author by her daughter, Woolworth's granddaughter)

November 1975, the well-attended auction where all of Woolworth's prized possessions were sold for a mere fraction of their worth. (Monica Randall 1975)

Aerial shot of Winfield taken in 1978 from the front of the house. (Monica Randall 1978)

Marble garden ornament with Napoleon's Imperial bees and an ominous mask.
(Monica Randall 1962)

Two-million-dollar main staircase, solid marble. (Monica Randall 1978)

The Empress Josephine room, as decorated in 1978 with original furnishings. (Monica Randall 1978)

The haunted Marie Antoinette Room, where the temperature was always 20 degrees colder. (Monica Randall 1977)

Woolworth's Empire Bathroom, with the secret door behind the mirror on the left, which leads to the Napoleon Room. (Monica Randall 1978)

The Edwardian Room, Woolworth's study. The fireplace was encrypted with Rosicrucian and Freemasonry symbols. The secret vault was found behind a panel in the southwest corner of the room. (Monica Randall 1978)

The West façade staircase. A 1930s silk gown rescued from the greenhouse, probably originally owned by Edna Woolworth. (Monica Randall 1978)

One of the many garden parties in period dress, this one was held at the Morgan Gazebo at Salutations. (Monica Randall 1978)

Another garden party, this one at Crescent Beach, and the participants here were posing to re-create a painting by Eugène Louis Boudin. (Monica Randall)

The shooting for the vodka commercial complete with Czar. The animals were still outside. (Monica Randall)

One-hundred-thousand-dollar Egyptian Woolworth Mausoleum in Woodlawn Cemetary in the Bronx in New York. It wasn't completed until a year after Woolworth's death. (Monica Randall 2001)

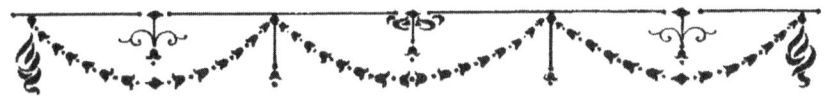

Chapter Fourteen

The Graphologist

A few days later I got a call from Richard Wettereaue, an investigative reporter for the *New York Post*. He had worked with me on a story on the Gold Coast earlier and knew about Winfield. Somehow he had managed to get a copy of Woolworth's handwritten will. It had been on file in the probate court, in Mineola, since the 1890s. According to the document, Woolworth left everything to his wife, Jennie Creigton, but later he had her declared mentally incompetent.

Once I had the handwriting sample, I contacted Mrs. Margaret Boettger, a professional graphologist who taught at a local university. She was regarded as one of the best in New York and was often called in to work with the police on difficult cases. It was several days before I could see her. She lived on the South Shore in a charming old brick house. I knew I was in the presence of a very special person the moment she opened the door. She was an attractive woman in her forties, with a beautiful speaking voice that sounded as though she might have trained as a singer. Her blond hair was brushed back neatly in a bun. We talked for a while about the subject at hand over tea. I was surprised to learn that graphology was a very old science, dating back thousands of years, and that large corporations, such as IBM and General Motors, as well as the FBI, employ graphologists to study the handwritings of prospective executives to discover in advance how they might hold up under pressure or how motivated they might be at their jobs.

"Handwritings vary greatly from country to country, but the basic principles apply whatever the language. The science of it derives from how we deviate from the way we're first taught to write as children. As our personality forms and develops when we're young, all our experiences and traumas are recorded in the brain and in time reveal themselves by the pressure of the hand and the direction of slant and by the angles, sharpness, height, or roundness of the letters," she said with indigenous calm, as though she believed the subject could help a lot of people understand themselves better if the study were put into practice. "Handwriting is very logical once you know what to look for. It's like a code to the unconscious.

"Extravagant flourishes in the upper zone often reveal an insecure person who is trying to impress others, or cover up his or her real feelings of low self-worth. Con artists and other dishonest people who are out to take advantage of others are easy to spot," she said, bringing out some samples she had on her desk to show me.

"People who write with very tiny controlled letters are often good at math or at projects requiring high levels of concentration. But it's not always that simple; there are hundreds of things to look for and crosscheck. There is very little about the character of a person that does not show up in the handwriting, and an expert can tell all. It even reveals hidden talents. Your handwriting is very much like a fingerprint, as there are no two alike. You really cannot forge someone else's signature. An expert would spot the deception every time, no matter how skilled the forger. If you take a photograph of it and blow the image up on a screen, there is a vibrational pattern visible that is unique to the original writer," she said, showing me some examples. I told her a little bit about where I was staying and some of the things that had been happening since I arrived. Finally she looked up with serene eyes and asked, "What have you brought for me to look at?" I showed her the copy of Woolworth's will. She stared at the paper for a very long while with an indecipherable expression before saying anything. Then she looked up and shook her head.

"I've never seen handwriting quite like this before."

"Do you think it was written with a quill pen?" I asked.

"That wouldn't matter all that much. What makes it so unusual are the extremes—the personality traits and character go to such extremes." She readjusted her glasses to get a closer look. Then she ran her hand lightly over the page several times as if to draw something from it.

"It's too bad this is only a copy. You lose a lot of information by not having the original. The pressure is difficult to tell. He has a heavy downstroke, making him a very creative person, a genius of a sort. This is a very materialistic man, grasping, persistent—one who would stop at nothing to attain his goals." Margaret was silent for a while. Then she nodded, pointing to some characteristic in the writing I was unfamiliar with—sharp, thrusting angular strokes that almost looked like daggers.

"Here there is a tendency towards cruelty. He could be almost sadistic at times. This was not someone to cross. He trusted no one and would go to any length to find out everything he could about people before he had any dealings with them. He would investigate everything about them: their private lives, their past, their weaknesses—especially their weaknesses and failings," she said in a grave tone. "He kept himself aloof and was very secretive. His own family would never know what he was thinking," she said, scanning the page with her fingers. "He did things in twos."

"Yes, he had two Empire rooms, two private studies, and often two entrances to a room, one that people knew about and another that only he knew about," I added while she held the page up to the light. I was dumbfounded by the accuracy of the process; I had told her nothing about this man other than describing the house that he built. But she went on and continued to amaze me.

"He was most suspicious of his coworkers. If he thought they gained too much information about his operations, he quickly disposed of and replaced them. He ran on fear and was unsteady emotionally and driven by his insecurities. He pursued his goals to the point of megalomania. My guess is, he was probably bipolar, given to sudden mood swings and prone to deep spells of depression, then soaring with some fantastic ideas that would be almost impossible to attain."

She continued to run her hands over the page again and again as though drawing something from it that revealed layer after layer of information that perhaps he himself would not have been aware of. "He controlled others like they were puppets on a string. Simple things, petty things, triggered his vindictive nature, and he would find clever ways to turn one person against the other. This gave him the feeling of power that he so desperately needed," she said.

"You're giving me chills," I said.

She looked up finally. "Yes, if he were to walk into this room, I suspect he would give us chills, but in reality this was a very sad, very lonely, frightened individual," she said solemnly. "But there is always some good in everyone," she said, looking back down at the paper.

"He had a great love for the arts, for music, and history. I see a passion for extravagance, but mainly to show off, although it seems to go much deeper than that."

At that point I told her about the rooms he had created that memorialized the great leaders throughout history.

"Yes, he would be fascinated by the lives of those people, as long as they were dead and no longer a threat. If they were still alive, he would regard them as rivals and would fear them. This fascination comes not so much out of admiration as out of a longing to draw something from them to enhance his image of power and wealth," she said, drawing her blue cardigan sweater tighter around her shoulders.

"I was told he believed he was the reincarnation of Napoleon," I added, feeling at this point it was okay to start revealing some information that I had withheld from her.

"Yes, I could see he would want to believe that. Again, he would go to extremes to indulge that belief," she added.

"What effect would all this have on his family?"

She sat up straighter as her shoulders seemed to stiffen.

"I shudder to think. He was incapable of giving emotionally. He put a price on everything, even emotions, even with his own family," she said almost primly.

"I get the feeling he hated women," I said, showing her the photo of the coat of arms he designed for the entrance hall of his house. "That's him on top, portrayed as a great warrior, and that's his wife below him, with the steel mask covering her face," I said, pointing to it.

"My word, it's unthinkable," she said, adjusting her glasses to get a closer look.

"And that was the first thing you'd see when you walked in the door, but that was all you got to see of poor Mrs. Woolworth."

"It would seem that he feared women, so he'd have to control them," she said as she flattened her palm down on the paper, as if studying some formation of letters in his style of writing. Then she reached over for a pencil and a small plastic ruler and began drawing thin vertical lines along the uppercase letters.

"Is he capable of murder?" I asked, remembering what happened the night of the séance. Margaret looked up at me inquisitively, though the question didn't appear to surprise her. She studied the paper a while longer, then shook her head slowly.

"No, not directly. He might arrange the demise of anyone who might get in his way, but he would find someone else to carry out such deeds for him." Then she paused and said, "I do see blood on his hands, but only as a symbol. He was not a happy man." She moved the paper back towards me to indicate that she had gone as far as she could.

"He had a daughter named Edna who took her own life, but the cause of her death was covered up," I said.

"Do you have any writing of hers?"

"No. I never found anything in the house, and I never thought to ask the Woolworth heirs when I knew them, and now they're gone."

"Without knowing anything about her, I wouldn't imagine she had a very happy childhood. Strong and driven personalities like this one rarely make good parents. However, a man like Woolworth would always maintain a proper image. He would keep up appearances, go to church, and be seen smiling with his family at his side. Any kind of scandal would be suppressed at all costs," she said as I pulled out the folder and showed her the rest of the photographs of Winfield. She shrugged, half in amusement. "It's all there, isn't it? A perfect reflection of everything he was. The intensity of this personality is so strong, you can almost feel it, even in this piece of Xerox paper."

"I'd like to show you the house sometime. I think you would find it interesting."

"Yes, I'd like that," she said while I rummaged around in the folder looking for the paper with Mrs. Reynolds's poem on it.

"I recently found this. It was written by a woman whom I'd known briefly a long time ago. She was the second owner of Winfield. Could you tell me what you see in her personality?" I asked, handing her the piece of stationery. She took the fragment with the poem on it and studied it for a long while.

"She has a warm, outgoing, trusting nature, is concerned with doing the right thing and has strong spiritual convictions and a love for the arts, music, color, and beauty. This is the writing of someone who likes order in her life and appreciates fine things, in people and in her surroundings."

"It's amazing that you can see that. Mrs. Reynolds was very friendly towards me, and I was trespassing the first time I met her. Does she appear to have any kind of delusions or irrational feelings about anything?" I asked, noting what I perceived as a change in her writing at the end.

Margaret turned the paper to the side as if to study its slant or rhythm. "Well, from what I can see, it is written by the same person, and she seems to be well-adjusted in general, but her mood changed. She has an artistic nature and is very intuitive and highly imaginative. Creative people are often misunderstood. They can be spontaneous and have wild bursts of energy and jump from one thing to the next. Uncreative people sometimes perceive them as unstable."

"I'm just amazed at what you can pick up from just a page of scribbles. It almost seems like pure voodoo, what you just did," I said.

"No, not at all. You study this in college, and it's admissible in a court of law, though you cannot convict anyone of a crime from the way they write, except in forgery cases."

"Is there anything you can't tell about a person from their handwriting?"

"Not much," she answered, but not boastfully. She had made it all seem so simple and logical, explaining each point as she worked in a way that was easy to understand, as though she didn't want me to think it was some kind of magic but the result of long, dedicated study.

I thanked her for the reading, and as I was turning to leave, a curious thought turned in my head.

"Do you believe people can be taken over by another . . . sort of like possessed by another person?" I was fumbling awkwardly for the right words. "And if they were, would it show in their handwriting?" I asked somewhat vaguely. She looked up with a puzzled expression.

"I don't really know. My training is more from a psychological standpoint. I've never come across a case such as that, but I have seen people with multiple personality disorders show different handwritings for each of their alternates. But it's very rare."

Chapter Fifteen

A Lion in the Ballroom

I felt differently entering the house after learning intimate secrets about the person who built it. Now the stairs, the walls, and the curious carvings that covered everything seemed gaudy, as though tainted somehow by what I'd learned that day. It felt different being there that night, and I realized that the romance of it was somehow ebbing away.

When I reached the top of the stairs, there was an envelope on the floor outside my door, and I gathered Pete must have put it there and was somewhere in the building. I picked up the envelope and noticed it had been stamped with red sealing wax, with a dragon gracing the center. Inside was a black-and-gold invitation to a costume ball being given in a few weeks by my friend Lori Summers, who had an estate in Locust Valley. Tucked inside was a thin sheet of tissue paper, an RSVP card, and a return envelope. I signed it immediately, adding André's name as my guest, and I left it on the dresser to mail the next day.

There was no answer at Katia's apartment, so I spent the night writing André a long letter telling him about the upcoming party and about the graphologist's revelations on Woolworth's handwriting, wondering if he would be the slightest bit interested.

There was a location shooting at the house the next morning. The film crew arrived at dawn with the usual truckloads of props, cables, and towering lights in endless rows. The ad was for a sixty-nine-dollar fake Persian rug sold by a rival chain. The slogan for the ad was: "Your home can look like a million." It was going to take a miracle and a lot of soft-focus filters to create the illusion of quality in the shabby reproduction. The art directors decided to distract would-be buyers by surrounding the rug with a fortune in priceless objects.

I had not been told that the star model was a wild jungle animal, and I was surprised when the familiar animal talent truck pulled up to the front entrance. A full-grown lion on a gold leash stepped out with his trainer and headed into the ballroom. A portable steel cage measuring six feet by six feet was quickly assembled in the far corner of the room. The entire day was spent doing light tests, taking Polaroids, and repositioning baroque and rococo chairs, vases of flowers, statues, and palm trees. After several hours of tedious tests, the lion, whose name was Norman, was finally brought out and draped elegantly on top of the rug. The lion seemed content at first, but as the day wore on, he became noticeably bored and began to nibble playfully on the edge of the carpet. No one seemed to notice; all were engrossed in working out the details of staging the shot. At some point, one of the art directors let out a loud moan, having noticed that one corner of the rug was completely eaten away. Someone called for a replacement to be brought in from one of the trucks outside.

The studio finished their tests just before dark, then shut down the lights, covered the camera with a black cloth, and prepared to leave. The actual filming was to take place the following day, after all the tests came back from a lab in the city. For security reasons, an armed Wells Fargo guard was brought in to keep an eye on the expensive props and equipment and, I assumed, to see that the lion stayed in his cage.

The guard's name was George. He was tall, dark, and hairy and had a nervous twitch in one eye. He had the face of a boxer who'd been punched too many times, with an oversized jaw. He walked with a kind of old cowboy swagger and looked as though he lifted weights for a good part of the day. One of the production assistants chatted with him for a while in the hall while the rest of the crew was leaving, and I overheard him say that they were due to return at 7:00 A.M. George nodded, his face set in a serious expression, his hands resting on his gun belt in an attitude of a commando at the ready.

Pete emerged from somewhere out in the garden. Friendly as usual, he offered to give George a tour of the downstairs rooms. George silently followed Pete about, then walked stiffly back towards the ballroom, where he was stationed for the night. His eyes swept the room, and he snorted, not seeming to be the least bit impressed or curious about the large cage in the far corner of the room. Nor did he ask what might be inside. He appeared to be of the old macho school of thinking, but I had the feeling that he'd never been called on to take action, and that he had resigned himself to a life of waiting for that which never happened. If there were any burglars prowling around Glen Cove that evening, they were not likely to attack the marble fortress, surrounded by its eight-foot wall. However, George appeared to be ready if the need arose. He quickly made himself at home, sat down on the oversized couch with a newspaper, then reached into his pocket and pulled out a cigar. He began peeling away the cellophane and was about to light it when I all but pounced on him, grabbing it out of his hand.

"Please," I said. "Cigars are such revolting things. They smell up the house and cause nice people to throw up."

"Right," he said, eyeing me warily as he put it back in his shirt pocket. Pete stood in the hall, his eyes fixed with curious interest on the gun that hung from the guard's holster.

"You interested in guns?" he asked Pete with a kind of hauteur.

"Well, yeah, I got me one, but it's a shotgun," Pete responded, straightening up to his full height.

"This here is a thirty-eight," the guard said, pulling it out with exaggerated bravado. He snapped the spring, twirled the chamber several times, then, with a well-rehearsed flick of his wrist, popped the barrel back in place and cocked the trigger.

"Here, you try that," he said, handing the gun to Pete, who looked at it, not saying anything at first. I moved out into the hall to avoid a possible barrage of gunfire, then overheard Pete say: "Won't do ya no good here, 'cause you can't shoot 'em."

The guard eyed him with detached severity. "What do you mean?" he asked.

"You can't shoot the fuzzy people, and we've got a lot of them in residence," Pete said jauntily. I suppressed a giggle, but seeing where this was going, I stepped back into the room.

"Pete, can I talk to you a moment?" I said, trying to keep a straight face. "While you're up and about, I was wondering if I could ask your advice about something upstairs. You know that big round gold thing that's been sitting on my floor for weeks?"

"Can't say I do, ma'am," he responded softly. Then he scampered up the stairs two at a time and waited politely outside my door for me to catch up. We turned into the room, and I pointed to the large decorative piece leaning against the wall beside the dresser.

"It's kind of highfalutin," he said, picking it up to study it.

"Yes, it is, but it belongs here, though it was never meant for this room. I'll show you," I said, pulling the folder of original photographs out of the top drawer of the dresser. "That's how it looked in Woolworth's room hanging over the Empire bed, and this room we're in now was the Empress Josephine room. It had a similar gold canopy hanging over this bed, but it was sold at the auction. I just thought for the sake of history it might be nice to put this up there, if you don't think it would be too much trouble," I said. Pete kept staring at the photos as though mesmerized. "Never saw nothin' like this before. Looks like kings and queens lived here," he said, handing me back the photos.

"Yes, I guess that's what they wanted people to think," I said softly. He glanced up ceilingward in an effort of deep concentration. "These walls are two feet thick—you could hang an elephant from them," he said airily. Then he pulled out a nine-foot metal tape measure from his rear pocket, and it sprang out, hitting the far wall like a snake squirming and rattling menacingly.

"Will we need to buy any special tools to get it up there?" I asked.

"Hell, no. I can rig it up right now. All I need are two jackknife ladders—one to hold the thing still while I bolt it to the wall, another to hold me—some molly plugs, and I got a power drill in my truck," he said, his pale gray eyes suddenly seeming exhilarated at the idea of having some exotic chore to do.

"You sure you don't mind?"

"It's no trouble. I just have to go over to the carriage house to get the extra ladder, and I'll be right back," he said, moving towards the door.

"Do you want me to ask the guard to go with you?"

"No. Better leave that boghead where he is; he'll just get in the way," he said with an air of independence as he thudded back down the stairs.

An hour later Napoleon's canopy was hanging nine feet over my bed. It was a little too grand for my taste, but I figured since the whole house was being used as a kind of Hollywood stage set, a touch of drama couldn't hurt.

Around midnight I was writing lists of things that had to be done for the shoot the next day, along with a note to pick up a gift basket of fruit to give Pete as a gesture of appreciation for his help, when there was a knock on my door. It was George. He held the loaded gun at his side while waving his other arm about wildly.

"You got to come down here—someone's crawling around in the ceiling," he said, his dark eyes glaring into mine with a hint of anger. I stared at him for a moment—longer than I should have. He seemed annoyed and confused by the strangeness of the situation, but embarrassed as well. I decided to make light of it.

"It's probably Pete, replacing bulbs in the organ chamber above the room you're in," I said calmly. "There are passageways all over the house," I said, following him back down the stairs. When we got back to his room, all was quiet except for Norman, who was snoring softly in his cage. George looked up at the ceiling and shrugged.

"There was a lot of noise before—banging. It came from up there," he said, pointing towards the alcove. "But then it shifted and sounded as though it was coming from somewhere down in the basement."

"Have you seen Pete?"

"No, not since he left with you earlier."

"Well, he likes to putter around the house. I wouldn't worry about it."

"But how can he putter around up there," he said, pointing, "and in the basement at the same time?" he asked in a sardonic tone. I looked up at him, not quite knowing what to say, so I said something stupid.

"This is a very strange house. The people who live here are strange; the animals are strange. Would you like a glass of milk? It might help you sleep."

"I'm not supposed to sleep, ma'am. I get paid to stay awake and be on the alert," he said belligerently.

"For what?"

"Well . . . er, criminals," he said, looking around the room at all the chained French doors.

"You're in the country. Oh, you may hear things. The pipe organ might start to play by itself. Not to worry—lots of people hear it. The neighbors say they sometimes hear it. It's behind that wall over there, and up there, and all around you. The room has great acoustics," I said, pointing in all directions at once. "Don't let it get to you, 'cause it's not real. Just think of it as a kind of echo."

"An echo," he repeated flatly.

"Yes, an echo from . . . the past. It's like a seashell. You know how when you were a kid and you held a seashell up to your ear, you could hear the ocean waves playing back like it was a recording? Well, it's sort of like that: the seashell's not haunted; it just recorded what was."

He continued to stare, and his left eye was beginning to twitch again. I turned to leave, realizing I had done more harm than good. Then I called back, "There's a TV set in the billiard room you can borrow; it might help keep your mind off . . . things."

"Yeah, thanks," he said glumly.

The house was silent again. I went up to my room, locked the door, crawled under the covers, and lay there staring up at the gold canopy, praying that it wouldn't come crashing down during the night. I drifted off into a strange nebulous sleep in which ephemeral images floated by as if dissolving on a black screen, accompanied by the scent of smoke and incense and a low, pulsing, languid chanting of men's voices. Flaming torches flickered on granite walls the color of deadly nightshade. No clear images came into view, just vivid smells, sounds, and flickering golden light, yet there was something strangely reverent and forbidden about it. I was beginning to feel myself drift into another sphere when I heard a gun go off. The shot resounded down the long dark hall outside my room. I quickly reached for my robe, and moments later there was a frantic pounding on my door. It was George again. He seemed shaken and was waving his gun about at the ceiling.

"I shot it." His voice splintered the air as his dark-leather boots pounded across the floor. "I need to use the phone," he said, glaring down at it as though furious with himself. I stepped aside as he all but lunged like a lightning bolt for the phone.

"What happened?" I asked, feeling detached somehow from the moment.

"I shot it," he said, choking on his words and seeming dazed and in shock.

"Pull yourself together, and please put that thing away," I said, referring to the gun. His hands were shaking as he began dialing the rotary phone, then slammed the receiver down and began dialing again.

"Shit!" he said shrilly, and he began dialing again, finally reaching what I assumed was his dispatcher's office in the city.

"I'm not feeling well. You got to send a replacement immediately. Can't wait—I'm leaving now," he said, inching his way across the room towards the door, and going as far as the phone cord would extend.

"Did you shoot Norman?" I asked.

"Who's Norman?"

"The lion you were guarding."

"Hell, no," he said, dropping the phone down on the rug as he turned and scrambled hastily back down the stairs.

"Can I get you something?"

"No. Just unlock the damn door!" he all but screamed.

"What door?"

"The front door—it's locked from the inside," he said irritably.

"That's impossible—" I started to say, but I stopped, remembering the time I couldn't open it even with the key.

"I'll walk you out," I said to deaf ears as he took the steps two at a time, his jaw clinched tightly as he moved frantically towards the front door. When he reached it, he just stood there staring out at the driveway. When I finally caught up, I put my hand on the doorknob but didn't turn it.

"You've got to tell me what happened," I asked in as calm a voice as I could.

"Just open the door, please . . ." he demanded in a low, raspy tone. Then he rolled his eyes, seeming to resent having had to call upon me for help.

"What happened?" I asked again.

"There was someone in the room. I was reading the paper. Then I saw it, and then it was gone."

"Who?"

"Just unlock the fucking door!" I turned the knob, and the door clicked open. He gave me a startled look as though I were a witch. Then he bolted down the drive to his car.

"What about your replacement?" I yelled out after him. There was no answer, just the sound of tires squealing and gravel spraying the air as he spun the car around and headed out the gate.

I breathed a sigh of relief and felt much safer with him gone, but I wasn't quite sure what to do. The lights were still blazing in the ballroom.

I walked in and picked up a half-eaten banana that the guard had left on the chair. Then I walked over to the cage. The lion was resting peacefully, staring out at nothing. I kneeled before the beautiful creature.

"It's no fun being a star, is it?" I said, half-tempted to reach in and pet him as though he were just an oversized cat, but I thought better of it.

"Would you like a banana, Norman?" I said, holding it close to the cage. He blinked and sniffed at the fruit, showed no interest, then lay back on the floor of his cage.

I got up and looked about the room for signs of damage from the gunshot fired earlier. There were no broken windows and no obvious damage to the dark-paneled walls. It was possible that the bullet could just as easily have slipped through the open fretwork in the ceiling and hit one of the concealed walls on the other side. Then, off in the corner, I caught sight of a small glint of silver. It was a thirty-eight-caliber bullet. I picked it up off the floor, carried it upstairs, dropped it in a drawer, and went to sleep.

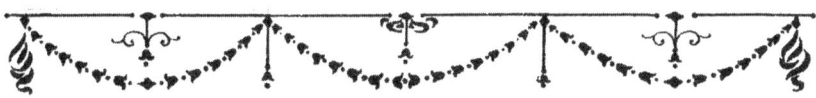

Chapter Sixteen

The Halloween Party

I can almost pinpoint the day when things took a turn. Everything after that seemed colored in a darker light. It was as if something that had been part of the house had finally taken over some part of me, like a virus that at first shows no symptoms, but one day you wake up, and you're not quite the same.

André returned for the Halloween party in one of his better moods. While he loved those gala events, a costume party alone would not have been enough to bring him halfway across the world. Judging by the constant phone calls that were coming in for him, it seemed there was some pressing business matter that had brought about his sudden appearance. I was glad to see him, but as the days passed without incident, I found myself growing anxious, no longer sure I knew who he was. He seemed like a different person each time he returned from abroad. He never mentioned his friend's death to me again, and I didn't dare bring the subject up. Everyone had a right to grieve in his or her own way.

André had a weakness for fancy-dress balls, but on the day of the party, he seemed preoccupied with running from one phone to the other. He used two former staff rooms on the main floor as offices and had two phone lines in each; he kept those rooms locked when he wasn't there.

We passed each other only once that day on the stairs, and he asked what time we were expected to arrive. "About ten would be fine," I said. Then I asked, "What are you going to be tonight?"

He stopped and glanced at me briefly. "A chipmunk, perhaps," he answered, not expecting to be taken seriously. "I don't really know. I'll decide later," he said, disappearing down the hall. Hours later I overheard him charming the owner of the costume rental shop into staying open an extra half hour. André was very persuasive and had a way of making the other person feel he or she had just made an important and desirable decision that would reap some nebulous reward in the netherworld. An hour before the party, he flew in the door out of breath and ran up the stairs, carrying a large gray box tied with a black cord. He stayed locked in his room until it was time to go. I took my time getting ready as no one ever got to those affairs on time. From the back of the mirrored closet I pulled out a 1914 gown of embroidered lace with a powder blue underslip and matching wide blue sash. A bunch of faded violets was bound at the waist.

Sometime later, when André emerged from the doorway, I heard myself gasp softly, but was rendered speechless. The whole atmosphere of the room changed as he stood there, a palpable presence in that dark gray uniform. It was what they once called a livery—a simple but commanding uniform that chauffeurs wore back when automobiles were first becoming popular. He stood there seeming almost surreal. Then I watched him walk across the room, graceful and assured, to gaze at himself in the full-length-mirrored door. He did a pivot and struck a pose like a general, his face flushed slightly at the sight of himself. He knew he looked good in the charcoal jacket with buttons down the front, high black-leather riding boots, and chauffeur's cap. I found myself enraptured by his appearance and drawn to him in a way that scared me, but at the same time I was overcome with a vague feeling that something terrible was going to happen to him. He was not aware of my change in mood, and I was determined not to ruin the evening.

"It was a toss-up between this and a squirrel costume. The place was cleaned out. How many people are going to this thing?" he asked, continuing to admire himself from all angles. Then he leaned close to the glass and made a face at himself.

"You make a very handsome chauffeur," I said, moving up to him and kissing him gently on the cheek. "Thank you for not escorting me to this party as a squirrel," I said, catching a glimpse of myself in the mirror standing next to him.

"You look fetching, my dear. . . . What are you?" he asked, running his hands down the length of the fragile gown.

"A ghost," I answered, turning to show him the back of the antique dress. "This came from the house and was probably one of Edna Woolworth's dresses."

"Well . . . you make a charming ghost," he said, taking my hand and leading me out the door and down the stairs. When we reached the front porch, he stopped for a moment.

"By the way, do you have any idea why there are huge clumps of grass missing from the front lawn?" he asked, not seeming too concerned.

"Gophers," I said, not daring to face him.

André was in good spirits and talked nonstop as we drove the short distance to the estate in Locust Valley. We knew we'd arrived when we spotted two huge black cauldrons on the side of the road, smoking with dry ice. A man dressed as a vampire stood outside the towering gates, flailing his arms around a long black cape with red-satin lining.

"Good evening," he said in a deep Bela Lugosi voice as each guest pulled up and showed their black-and-gold invitation. I recognized him as one of the gardeners who worked on the property. The staff were often asked to perform strange duties during special events, and most seemed to enjoy the change and took on their roles in good humor. We were waved to go ahead and pulled in past the gates. Hundreds of torches lined the long drive up to the house. Summercroft was a grand antebellum plantation-style house with four gleaming white pillars supporting a rounded portico. Outside on the lawn a cemetery with dozens of stage-prop tombstones was set up. I recognized some of the names on the stones, none of whose bearers were known to be dead yet. I scanned the graveyard and was relieved to find our names were not among them.

"Anyone you know?" André asked, pointing up at a skeleton hanging from a tree and covered with cobwebs. "Nice touch," he said. Then he drove on up to the house. You could hear the orchestra playing and the din of reveling voices.

Men in gorilla costumes were parking the cars of guests down by the stables.

"I'll take your keys, sir," one of the gorillas said to André.

"Like hell," he snapped. "I'll park it myself, Fur Face."

"As you wish, sir," the gorilla answered politely. Then he sauntered off to the next car in line.

"You didn't have to be so rude. They're just trying to help."

"I'm not turning this car over to a bunch of apes. How can they drive with those hairy hands, or paws?" André backed the car too fast and ran over one of the fiberglass tombstones. We both got out of the car to survey the damage as one of the hairy people ran over and propped it back up, not saying anything.

"Who's Maxwell Fenwick Stanford the Third?" André asked, reading the name on the gravestone he'd just flattened.

"One of the older guests," I answered.

"Not a good omen for old Max. He'll probably croak before the party is over," he said, totally amused with himself.

"That's not funny," I said as he got back into the car. I was about to follow, then asked, "Would you mind letting me off here? It's a long way back from the stables—I'll ruin my white satin shoes."

"Very well, madam. I'll meet you at the entrance," he said. Then he followed the other cars down the long circular drive, disappearing behind a high, ivy-covered wall. Above me, moths swirled around orange paper lanterns hanging low from the front porch as more costumed guests continued to arrive by the carload. Conversation and laughter coalesced in a haze of artificial fog and cigarette smoke. I didn't recognize anyone—not that anyone *could* be recognized. Some of the costumes and masks seemed grotesque. I felt out of place. Dressed in nothing more than a vintage gown, I looked perfectly normal but was surrounded by gory getups.

A gray Rolls Royce pulled up to the front of the house, and out of it stepped a woman dressed up as Marie Antoinette. She struggled with a wide hoop skirt and carried her fake head under her arm. Her real one was somehow concealed under a pair of artificial shoulders. Her date wore a black-hooded mask and was dressed all in black. After helping his headless lady out of the car, he walked to the rear of the car, opened the trunk, and pulled out a portable guillotine. Within seconds one of the gorillas ran over, jumped in the front seat, and drove off to park the car. Some of the other guests on the porch applauded the entrance of the fallen queen and the headsman. I smiled at them as they passed, but I wondered how they could enjoy the evening in such contorted outfits.

André was nowhere in sight, and I was beginning to wonder what was taking him so long. Just then I spotted a sea monster walking up the drive, dripping with yards of green cellophane made to look like seaweed. His partner, who was dressed as a squid, was trailing behind him, frantically picking up pieces of cellophane as they fell to the ground and trying to stick them back on. I thought it odd that they were walking to the party, but then I assumed they probably lived next door and had simply slithered through the shrubbery, as neighbors often did. I watched half-bemused as the guest's seaweed tendrils continued to fall to the ground. Then I reached into my beaded purse, pulled out several small safety pins, and handed them to the girl in the squid costume.

"Try these," I said. The girl looked out from her makeshift headpiece half-startled but relieved.

"Thanks," she said, and she quickly pinned her escort back together, then went inside to join the party. I kept searching the driveway for signs of André, but he was nowhere in sight.

"Got a light, baby?" I heard a man's deep gravelly voice behind me. I turned and saw a masked and hooded creature whom I took to be the Grim Reaper after noticing the sickle in one hand. A cigarette dangled loosely in the other.

"Got a light?" he repeated, putting the unlit cigarette to his mouth and swerving unsteadily while reaching for the pillar for support.

"No, sorry. I don't smoke," I said, turning away from him.

"Oh, but you should. . . . Everyone should smoke then everyone would carry matches," he said, babbling on drunkenly. He continued to ramble, but I wasn't listening. Moments later he put his hand on my shoulder, and I brushed it away, then ran from the porch down the driveway and headed towards the stables. There seemed to be a hundred cars parked along a high brick wall that ran along the stable-and-garage complex. The cobblestone courtyard was lit up by spotlights mounted along the roofline of the building. Several large catering trucks stood in a row with their generators running while staff ran with huge aluminum trays of food up to the house. I stood beside the open wooden gates that faced the carriage house, which was in the shape of a horseshoe, with the stables on the left and the garage and staff quarters on the right. All the lights were on in the garage, revealing a handsome collection of vintage cars. I moved towards one of the open bays and could hear two men talking. I recognized André's voice.

I was about to rush in but froze when I saw the car the two men were standing next to. For the second time that night, I had that strange overwhelming feeling, along with a slight pounding in my head. It faded quickly, but I was terrified at how suddenly I could find myself in such a state. It felt like a déja vu free fall. For a second an image passed through my mind. It came and went so quickly I could not focus long enough to make sense of it, but it apparently had something to do with that car.

I held on to the frame of the huge garage door, peering through the upper bank of glass windows, and caught part of their conversation:

"It cost a whopping eight grand back in nineteen-sixteen. You could buy a fine house for that kind of money," a distinguished silver-haired gentleman in a tuxedo was saying. André stood by, listening. He had a passion for old cars, and he kept walking along the side of this car, marveling at it as though it were a work of art. "You couldn't beat the twelve-cylinder layout for performance, smoothness, perfect balance.... Of course, it had a heavy crankshaft and rigid flywheel and more horsepower and torque," the older man said as though having a love affair with the vehicle. Then he moved to the front and opened the hood as though he were opening the case of a priceless Stradivarius. André looked in at the immaculate silver-plated engine and shook his head in wonder. When I regained my composure, I stepped into the room and called out to André. He turned and beamed brightly.

"There you are, darling. Forgive me—this is Matthew Billingsly. He's staying for the weekend and drove down from Rhode Island in this Packard Twin Six." I smiled and shook Mr. Billingsly's hand as we were introduced.

"It's beautiful," I said, moving closer to touch the car as though it were a living thing. It was in mint condition. Its black shiny surface gleamed in the glaring light of the old lamps hanging from the ceiling. André looked as though he'd died and gone to car heaven. I could almost feel the adrenaline surging through his lighted veins. His eyes shone with pleasure as he gazed longingly at the sleek automobile. I could easily forgive his having left me alone at the entrance.

I too was trying to hold fast to the moment, but for different reasons. Looking about at the bare, whitewashed concrete walls with their simple, well-maintained, varnished oak-wood windows, I realized that there was nothing in that setting that had changed since the place was built. Even Mr. Billingsly was of the old school, with the natural air and fluid courtesies that come with breeding. In the next bay there was a yellow Alfa Romeo, and beyond it was a red Stutz BearCat, but they belonged to the owners of the estate and were permanent residents of the handsome ten-car garage. Mr. Billingsly was quick to add that he was simply a guest, there for the weekend, and that he had been given the use of one of the units. Cars such as his were never left out to weather the elements. I looked at André. His sinewy frame took on an almost heroic bearing. In his gray livery, standing next to that black limousine the year could very well have been 1916, and that was where I suddenly ached to be, though I could not say why.

Mr. Billingsly opened the door of the car, and the rich sound of solid, well-oiled hinges resonated around the room. He then reached inside and turned on the headlights, and their fluted lenses flooded the open courtyard outside with light.

"Would you like to step inside?" he said, graciously extending his hand to me. "Your gown goes perfectly with the interior," he said, helping me onto the black running board. Then I noticed the cut-crystal vase mounted to the passenger-side wall with a silver bracket. Mr. Billingsly had gone to the trouble of putting a single red rose in the vase to enjoy on his long trip down to Long Island. It filled the small space with the cloying sweetness of its perfume. The rose nearly brought me to tears, but I fought to keep my composure. Our host leaned closer to André, tapping him on the shoulder gently.

"You know, we could take her out for a spin."

"We'd love that, but you'd never get out. You're blocked in by all the cars, and we'd better be joining the other guests up at the house." André reached in and helped me out of the car. "Would you like to walk up to the party with us?" André asked with a sudden sweep of his arm.

"Oh . . . I'll be along in a while—just need to polish things up a bit here," Mr. Billingsly said, turning off the headlights after we cleared the courtyard gates.

The house was ablaze with light, and you could hear the orchestra playing through the open French doors. Just inside the main entrance hall, an attractive young woman made up as a gypsy was checking names off a list. She waved us by, insisting we enter the party by way of the drawing room and saying in a contrived rehearsed tone, "You do want to pay your respects to Clifford."

"Who the hell is Clifford?" André asked, glancing at me briefly.

"They do this every year. Just go along with it," I whispered, taking his arm. Standing tall, as if on a stage, the gypsy girl recited:

"Clifford was our butler for forty years, but alas," she said, nodding her head towards the drawing room, "he hung himself last night from the stable clock tower."

"That's swell. Where's the food? I'm starving," André said, rolling his eyes. The girl pointed again to the drawing room, which it seemed we had no choice but to enter. We did as she asked, passing a bevy of bats hung from the ceiling on invisible wires. Lying at the far end of a heavily draped room was a brass coffin containing a very realistic-looking corpse. Surrounding it were masses of white lilies and a pair of iron standing candelabras lit with dozens of candles. There was organ music coming from behind the black-velvet drapes.

"Classy," André whispered to me, though there was no one else in the room. "Now can we eat?" he said as we rushed out into a large vestibule. Life-size plastic skeletons hung from the walls in various distorted poses. They had been theatrically cobwebbed and seemed real except for the flashing red eyeballs and tape-recorded comments they made as we brushed past.

In the ballroom, people in outrageous costumes danced wildly to disco music along with a strange mix of show tunes while a strobe light flashed annoyingly from the ceiling. No one looked comfortable in their bizarre costumes, which distorted their rhythm and movements, but everyone appeared to be having a good time. Several guests applauded when our hostess entered the room looking regal in a lavish Queen Elizabeth the First gown. She waved when she saw us and started to move in our direction, but was quickly whisked onto the dance floor by a man in a sequined dragon costume. She squealed with delight as he twirled her around trying not to trip on his long cumbersome tail.

Just then a red-bearded man dressed as Henry the Eighth came rushing across the dance floor, his eyes focused on balancing four glasses of champagne in his hands, when he bumped into André who was trying to get to the hors d'oeuvres table. The champagne and the man's hat went flying to the floor.

"Please forgive my clumsiness," the king said to the chauffeur as they both scrambled to pick up the plastic glasses. André reached down and picked up the gent's cumbersome velvet-and-gold-trimmed hat.

"A thousand pardons," the man said, apologizing again and placing the glasses down on a nearby table. He stood up facing André.

"Maxwell Stanford here," he said, extending his hand.

"Maxwell Fenwick Stanford the Third... you're alive," André said boisterously.

"Why, yes. Have we met?"

"Not really, but I ran you over on my way in." The man looked at him puzzled. "Your tombstone—I squashed it flat as a bug. But you're still breathing—that's good," André said, amused at his own private joke.

"Why yes, I believe I am still breathing, I'm happy to say," he said good-naturedly, with a hint of Locust Valley lockjaw, a cultivated local accent that gave his words a polished British tone.

"Well, let's say I help you replace those drinks," André offered, suddenly shifting his attention to the bar.

"Be back in a minute, love," he said reassuringly, but I got nervous. Moments later he drifted up behind me like a ghost and whispered, "May I have this dance." The orchestra had slowed down and was doing a medley of old movie tunes. I slipped into his arms and looked around the room as we began to glide around the floor.

"I wonder if Mr. Billingsly ever made it up here," I said.

"Don't be silly. He's probably still in the garage, making wild, passionate love to his car."

"Good for him."

The lighting in the room dimmed, and the band broke into a rendering of "Ramona," a haunting piece with the tempo of a slow waltz. As we floated around the room to that languid old tune, couples paired off and joined us on the dance floor. I rested my head on André's shoulder, finding comfort in the feel of the rough, heavy texture of his uniform, with its faint scent of cigars. André surprised me, as he often did, by knowing the words to the song. He sang them teasingly in my ear. "I'd rather die, then await to find you gone, Ramona. I need you, my own." André could not hold a tune, but there was a sweetness and something unnamable and perfect that transpired in that moment.

"Do you ever wish you could go back?" I asked, looking up at my partner.

"Back when?" he responded, giving me a withering glance.

"Back to a time when people kept roses in their cars and danced to music like this."

"We're doing it now, love," he said, holding me tighter.

"Yes, but this is a fantasy. Our hosts spent a hundred thousand dollars on this little party. It's hardly normal."

"If it were normal, you wouldn't appreciate it," he said. I closed my eyes as we continued drifting dreamlike along the dance floor while the old silent-film tune, with its message of simplicity and innocence, cast a spell over the room. When the song ended, the band shifted into something more modern, and the mood was broken. I opened my eyes and noticed the couple dancing next to us were locked in an embrace and swaying slightly. The girl was wearing a gray-silk 1940s gown, and her hair was turned up in what was known as the victory roll. Her partner was in a World War Two uniform of some kind, but as he turned, I caught sight of a grotesque addition to his costume. An axe was theatrically made up to appear to be embedded in the left side of his head, and the gaping wound had stage blood trickling down from it. The sight of it caused something in me to snap, and without thinking I pulled away from André and ran from the room, out the French doors, and onto the terrace.

The pounding in my head started up again with sickening force. Several pumpkins lit with candles stood along the balustrade, marking the exit points that led to the gardens beyond. As I ran past, one of the pumpkins fell and splattered on the terrace floor. I turned and saw André as he stepped out onto the terrace and looked around, but I was certain he hadn't seen me. While that horrible image of the axe burned in my brain, all I could do was run, but I could give no explanation as to why.

I found a long slate path covered over with latticed arbors, and as I ran, I could feel the fragile chiffon layers of my vintage dress catching and tearing on the thorns of the vines. The smell of damp leaves mingled with the fragrance of the last of the summer roses. At the far end of the path, in a secluded, overgrown spot, stood a small whitewashed brick cottage with a tower on one side. I ran towards it and was about to go inside when I heard André call out my name. His voice was low and seemed displaced and faraway. The pounding in my head continued. I was spinning out of control and experiencing a replay of someone else's nightmare, but I could do nothing to stop it. It came in subtle flashes and discordant images as if on a screen in my mind, but speeding along too fast to focus, image after image. I pressed my hands as tightly as I could to my temples, trying to crush the thoughts, but they continued for a few seconds longer then just as suddenly it stopped. I was out of breath and shaking when I heard the steady crunching of freshly fallen leaves and realized that André was right behind me. He put both hands on my shoulders and swung me around to face him.

"What's wrong?" he demanded.

"I don't know," I mumbled, feeling disoriented. Then I burst into tears, crying as if my whole world were coming apart. "You've got to get away from me before it's too late," I blurted out, having no idea why I said it. I held my breath for a second and took note of what I was saying and how crazy it must have sounded. He continued to stare at me, appearing compassionate, but there were doubt and discord in his expression. There were lines in his forehead that weren't there before.

"I'm taking you home," he said in a low, bereaved voice.

"Let's not go back there just yet," I insisted, feeling him draw me close to him. It was a warm night for October, and a slight vaporous haze clouded the air. I could hear the steady rise and fall of the foghorns drifting across from Long Island Sound. The noise and music from the party seemed very far away. André pulled himself away from me for a moment, then reached over to the heavy wooden door of the cottage and undid the iron latch. Some long strands of ivy had attached themselves to the outer frame, and they tore free when he opened the door. The room held the stagnant smell of the sea, and had not been used in years. André fumbled with the chain on a standing iron lamp next to the door, and the frayed amber-tinted shade lit up the tiny room. At the far end a tall stone fireplace stood in the corner on an angle where the two walls joined. On its ledge, an old ship model with faded canvas sails leaned awkwardly on the mantel, along with several hunt trophies in need of polishing. André took some newspapers and kindling out of a large oak box and quickly got a fire started in the hearth. The fire flickered with a feral golden light around the walls of the welcoming room. I sank into the oversized chintz couch that stood before the mantel while André remained standing.

"Do you want to tell me what's going on?" he asked in a mordant tone. I was still in a kind of fugue state, and I must have turned noticeably pale. His expression softened as he came over and sat down next to me, taking both my hands in his.

"This thing," I blurted out, my voice choking in my throat. Then I tried again. "It started before we got here, when you first came into my room, in that costume. I had this overwhelming feeling you were in some kind of danger, but not because of coming here tonight; it was something else. Then when I saw you again in the garage and next to that car, I knew that car, or one just like it—I knew I'd been in that car before, with you. But that's impossible—we both know that's impossible. But there were these images.... It was as if I had accessed someone else's memory. And then that hideous man with the axe stuck in his head." I lost control again, and André handed me a tissue.

"It was just a silly Halloween costume. People get to express their dark side once a year," he said, trying to help.

"I know how delusional this must sound to you, but part of me knows there's something real about it. I can feel that something horrible happened, but when or to whom is impossible to say. It may have something to do with this dress, it's more than fabric and thread, when I put it on I can feel things that are not part of me but someone else. It may be some kind of gift." I said shredding the tissue in my hand nervously.

"Gift," he repeated, getting up from the couch and lighting a cigarette—something I'd only seen him do once before in all the time I'd known him. He took a few puffs, then flicked it into the fire.

"You think it's a gift. Look at you: you're an emotional mess, just from the sight of a stupid costume," he said, sitting back down.

"It wasn't a costume I was seeing. You think I'm crazy, don't you?" I said in a whisper.

"No.... It's just unsettling when you run off into the night and try to hide in the woods alone. You can't blame me for thinking you were running away from me," he said, his eyes narrowing as they fixed on the flames in the fireplace. He seemed more wounded than confused.

"I'm so sorry I ruined the party for you," I said, trying hard to sound normal and wishing that we were back on the dance floor and that I'd never opened my eyes. The fire crackled in the hearth, creating a warm and soothing diversion from the chaos I'd created.

"What the hell—there's a party every week. That's all people do around here," he said, his demeanor softening.

"Yes, but you'll never get to be my handsome chauffeur again," I said with a note of hesitation in my voice. He ran his hand along my cheek, and I kissed his fingers as they passed over my mouth.

"How did you find me down here in the woods?" I asked softly.

"You left a trail of chiffon wisps. That's one good thing about your wardrobe of cobweb frocks," he said lightly, looking down at the damaged gown, which hung in tatters.

"What was I thinking?" I said, remembering the day Mrs. Reynolds and I rescued those gowns in the greenhouse. "I destroyed a little piece of history." I felt terrible. He reached up, and as he tried to undo one of the tiny pearl buttons on my dress, it broke free and rolled across the floor into the shadows.

"What is this building used for?" he asked, looking about the cozy room.

"To escape. All the estates around here have secret cottages or gazebos hidden somewhere off the beaten path. Even the rich get tired of being rich. Not far from Versailles, Marie Antoinette had a thatched cottage where she used to pretend she was a shepherdess. That's where they found her when they came to take her to the guillotine," I said sadly.

"How come Winfield doesn't have one?"

"It did once, at the end of the allée. I remember when it burnt down during the sixties."

"Maybe I should rebuild it. I'm beginning to like this place," he said, continuing to fumble with the antique buttons on the back of my dress while kissing me gently on the shoulder. We stayed in the tiny cottage that night, drifting in and out of a restless sleep as disconsolate sounds of night creatures kept us on guard. We found our way back to the car just as dawn was beginning to break in a milky haze of fog. A hushed stillness had settled over everything. Clouds of mist drifted across the lawn and the staged graveyard, making it look hauntingly real.

André disappeared after that. He left for Europe the following week and simply never returned. I wrote to him, and I received occasional postcards saying he was tied up with business problems in countries I'd never heard of. I continued to run the house as if expecting him to return any day.

Fall came and went as the gardens withered and died. The pool, left unattended, reverted to its original state, turning black as tar. Willard vanished from the house just as suddenly, and the door to his wing remained padlocked.

Chapter Seventeen

Gordon Merdock

By November the regular location shooting season had ended for the year. André's partner, Martin Carey, not wanting the house to sit idle during the long winter months, came up with the idea of renting it out to a fund-raising organization for a gala Christmas party. One of New York's top party organizers, George Paul Roselle, was to produce the event, recreating a turn-of-the-century Parisian setting. He and his team of twenty designers arrived one day in a long caravan of limousines. As they made their way through the house, they talked excitedly about their plans to fill each of the main and second-floor rooms with glittering trees and vintage holiday decorations.

In the entrance hall, they set up a thirty-foot tree that rose up the stairwell, and they covered it with thousands of gold butterflies and star-shaped lights. An antique gold sleigh shaped like a swan was brought in from an old estate in Millbrook, New York. They planned to use the sleigh to ferry arriving guests to and from their cars. In the event it didn't snow, they had a backup plan to bring in truckloads of artificial snow to cover the lawn, where six live reindeer were to roam, their antlers coated with a special glow-in-the-dark paint. The entire front of the mansion would be trimmed with bands of Plexiglas icicles.

I kept out of their way, but I was excited by each new idea they dreamed up. The upcoming event, set for December 16, 1978, took on the fervor of high drama as the designers tried to outdo one another.

Their plans were all very grand, but several weeks into the project something went wrong.

The men were both inspired and intrigued by their opulent surroundings, which seemed to awaken something within them. They were having the time of their lives, often working well into the night like driven little elves. It wasn't long before they began to discover unusual things. One production assistant hanging garlands of roping over one of the doors came upon the first of many secret passageways. Then they found the hidden vaults behind the mirrored panels in the bedrooms. On their breaks they began playing a game of hide-and-seek inside the chambers of the pipe organ, with its dark twists and turns and dangerous, steep drops. In the heedless ordinance of their curiosity, they found things no one else had in places no one had ever thought to look — little inconsequential things, most likely left behind by the students of the charm school: an earring here, a scrap of paper there, an empty pill bottle, a hair clip. Fueled by these mundane discoveries, which nourished and inflamed their already fertile imaginations, they began to weave tales about the building's eccentric features and possible history.

I was spending most of my time in the city doing research at the New York Public Library, so I'm not exactly sure what happened after that, but one day when I returned, there was a sudden change of management, and the person who had been in charge was no longer there. I began to hear stories secondhand; it appeared that something very odd was going on. One of the workers on the crew had suddenly lapsed into a coma and was in the hospital. The following day another was injured while going down the stairs. A third woke up one morning and found his left arm paralyzed, but doctors could find no physical cause for his condition. A painter left the job after some photographs he had shot came back from the photo lab with someone standing in the room he'd been painting, although he knew he had been there alone. It turned out to be the same room that had been kept locked during the school years.

Gordon Merdock, a tall, heavyset man in his early forties, was one of the coproducers on the project. He stood out from the others; and seemed to fill a room with creative zeal and manic energy. His face was covered with a thick, red, bushy beard from which a pair of cherubic, but frantic, brown eyes sparkled with a curious elfin gleam. He reminded me of Smokey the Bear, or someone you'd likely meet at a lumber camp in Vermont. The three-piece suit he wore seemed out of character, as did the overstuffed briefcase he carried as he ran nervously from one end of the house to the other. Doors, walls, and furniture got in his way, and he was always crashing into things. His voice was raw, edgy, and froglike, and whenever he was losing it, he would lean his head back and pop a peppermint lifesaver into his mouth. Whatever he was thinking registered clearly in his expression, and despite the friendly smile, he was a bundle of anxiety. People liked him, partly because he took himself so seriously. He worried about everyone and everything, and if nothing went wrong, he held his breath in anticipation of disaster. He didn't have to wait long.

One afternoon there was a knock on my door. Before I could answer, Gordon entered the room and asked to use the phone. His hands were shaking.

"Is something wrong?" I asked.

"No," he snapped, more to the wall than to me. He dialed several numbers, and, getting no answer, he threw his hands up in frustration. He rose abruptly, and the phone wire got tangled around his foot, knocking the phone off the table along with several standing picture frames.

"It's okay," I said as he scrambled to set everything back in order. "Any news about your man in the hospital?" I asked to divert his attention.

He glanced at me briefly. "I don't understand what's going on around here," he said, turning and heading back out the door. I followed and was about to say something when a moment later, his breath caught and he stopped dead still on the staircase landing. I moved towards him and saw that the palm of his hand was bleeding. His eyes were fixed in disbelief as he quickly pulled a folded white handkerchief from his jacket pocket and wrapped it around his hand. Several drops of blood fell on the marble steps.

"What happened?" I asked. He didn't answer but continued to gaze at his hand while turning it slowly. "Does it hurt?"

He looked at me as though in anger. "I didn't cut it," he said gruffly. "You can see there's no wound; there's nothing I could have cut it on," he said as fear crept into his voice and his beard began to twitch. He ran his hand along the smooth marble banister several times to show me there was nothing that could have caused his hand to bleed.

"Stigmata," I said, as if to dismiss it. "It's the first case of it I've ever seen, but it seems like you're under a lot of stress, or perhaps you were a saint in your last life," I said trying to make light of the situation. He glared at me as though I had somehow caused him to bleed, and I started to explain what I thought the word *stigmata* meant, but he cut me off.

"I know what stigmata is, and this is not it!" he snapped in a sardonic tone.

"Then what is it?"

There was a long silence, and I could see he was gathering his forces to make a move or difficult decision. But he turned and began to move back down the stairs, wrapping the white cloth tighter around his hand as though he were really injured.

"It's off," he snapped suddenly. "The whole thing is off. I'm pulling everyone out of here in the morning." With his other hand he punched the finial post as he passed. "Bad vibes," he grumbled, his voice breaking as he stood at the bottom of the stairs. "I knew it when I first walked in that door. I told them—I did tell them—I had a feeling about this place. But all they could see was how beautiful it would be. Now I have one man in the hospital and two others down with no explanation," he said morbidly, looking up at the mantel that towered over the hall. "There," he said, pointing up to the coat of arms with his bandaged hand. "That says it all. What a statement that makes." He looked back at me, his eyes squinting suspiciously.

I held his gaze, then walked past him heading towards the kitchen. "You'd better wash that blood off; you'll feel better." He didn't resist but followed me into the servants' wing. He walked over to the sink, turned the water on, and held his hand under it for a long time. Then he rinsed out the handkerchief and spread it out to dry on the counter, which I took to be a good sign. I began to fumble with the pot on the stove, thinking he could use a cup of coffee before he left. "Do you want anything in it?" I asked. He shrugged indifferently.

"Look! Will you look at this?" he said, holding out his hand. "Like nothing ever happened, but you saw it bleed."

"Yes," I said, handing him the coffee and noticing his hand was still shaking.

"I had to play psychic hostess, so I put milk and two sugars in it. See if it's okay," I said, watching as he took too big a gulp. Half of it backed up and dribbled down his beard as he lurched forward, grabbed the still-wet handkerchief off the counter, and started coughing.

"It's that bad!" I said, running over with some paper towels.

"No. It's . . . just the way I like it," he said in a wheezing voice.

"What do the others think about all this?" I asked, trying to get his mind off what happened on the stairs.

"You know how creative people are—they get so wrapped up in what they're doing, they can't see past their nose," he said, taking another sip of coffee.

"Do you believe in haunted houses?" I asked.

"I do now. Is that what this is?"

"I've been doing a lot of research on the subject of late, and yes, I think it just might be," I responded.

"But can you explain to me why every time you hear about a haunted house, it's always an old creepy mansion out in the middle of nowhere. You never hear about ghosts lurking in split levels, or a Levittown ranch or splanch or whatever," he asked, moving his hands about wildly as he spoke.

"You have a point. . . . It may have something to do with greed. Wealth and power seem to breed a certain form of desperation. If you have it, you'll do anything to keep it or get more, and more is never enough. You'd be amazed what goes on around here in this part of Long Island. The rich have the power to cover things up. Wives shoot their husbands as they're stepping out of the shower. Husbands strangle their pesky wives and bury them in the rose garden. Shrinks poison their rich patients and run off with their jewels, and puff . . . it all goes away; nothing happens; no one gets caught," I said, noticing Gordon staring at me as though I was bonkers.

"You're just making this up, aren't you?" he said, downing the last of his coffee.

"No. I'm dead serious; I keep files on all this stuff. It's sort of a hobby of mine. Then there are all the butler stories."

"Please spare me," he said, hiding his face in his hands, more from exhaustion, it seemed, than anything else. I ignored his plea and kept babbling, convinced it would get his mind off his troubles. "The butlers around here are a breed unto themselves. They take charge of the household, keep the ladies of the manor zonked on sleeping pills, and get them to sign over their fortunes. It was a way of life around here, but they're dying out. Butlers are a thing of the past."

"I bet there's a pip of a story to this place," he said, looking up and glancing around the room.

"I'm working on it, but I haven't cracked the case yet."

"That might be why we're having all these problems, 'cause I don't believe you can ever cover things up. It makes for bad Karma . . . and this house has a little Karma problem, and I'm not about to stick around and be pulled down with it," he said edgily. He sat slack jawed at the kitchen counter for a while, then pulled a small leather notebook from his breast pocket and began scribbling on a page that was already filled to capacity. I noticed that his hand was still trembling as he began making tiny notes to himself along the side margins.

"Do you put events like this together often?"

"No," he grumbled, not looking up. "This was my first. I'm really an environmentalist, trying to save the planet—the rain forest, the seas, the whales. That's what all this was for. I got talked into overseeing this because the producer is a friend of mine. But I'm in over my head. My men got carried away with this place, distracted. . . . They were like kids on a treasure hunt—more interested in snooping around than getting any work done," he said, sounding vaguely beaten and abused.

"I wish there was something I could do. We've been filming here all summer and we've never had a problem on production. Aside from this prima donna pooch that lost most of his hair, and a lion that ate the rug," I said, then noticed he'd looked up from his notes in a quizzical way.

"Why did the dog lose his hair?"

"You don't want to know," I said, offering him another cup of coffee.

"No," he snorted, stuffing his notepad back into his pocket, his eyes narrowing as he gazed at his oversized watch, which had what looked like a rainbow arching across the face.

"I'm going to be sorry to see everyone leave. I'm sure it would have been a great party."

"Yeah, it would have been great," he said bitterly, banging the cup down on the counter. He frowned angrily, and then he turned abruptly and headed out into the hall, picking up his briefcase from the table. He left without saying good-bye. *What a strange man,* I thought to myself, though it crossed my mind he might be thinking the same thing of me. I walked over, and bolted the front door, and watched as he sped down the drive in a red utility van with a bumper covered with decals: "Save the Whales and Dolphins" and "Adopt an Emu" and "Have You Hugged a Tree Today?" These were all causes I would eventually come to embrace in time, but in that moment I thought, *A hippie has left the building.*

The house was silent again. I suddenly felt a terrible emptiness, which may have been there all along, but I managed to avoid thinking about it. I should have left along with the others, but there was this fog in my head, a kind of terminal vagueness that clouded my judgment. I began to have bad dreams.

I went up to my room and noticed that the gown I had worn to the party several weeks before was still hanging in tatters on a hook on the back of the door. I hadn't put it back in the closet, knowing it could never be worn again, but I couldn't bring myself to throw it away. I took it down and studied it for a while, wondering if there was anything I could do to restore it but knew it was useless. Exhausted, I drifted off to sleep with the dress still in my hand.

The dream I had that night took on a waking clarity. It seemed formed of a memory not my own, and the images and sounds seemed part of an ongoing nebulous drama that had played itself out again and again. Light took on a strange intensity as a scene formed, as if on a screen, of a lush, tree-lined road with a shiny black, old-fashioned Packard car. It pulled up and parked at the lower west gate outside of Winfield. Behind the wheel sat a handsome young man in a dark gray livery. It was almost dark as a heavy fog rolled in off the sound. The gates were chained and bound with a padlock. Hanging from the gate was a memorial wreath of laurel leaves and white lilies. The sight of it seemed strangely familiar. The driver sat there in the car unmoving, staring straight ahead, his jaw fixed, as though he was gathering strength to perform some mission known only to himself. After some time, the car began to move again, slowly at first. It backed away from the gate as though he'd changed his mind about something. He continued to back away from the entrance until he was about forty feet away; then he stopped the car again. After a moment the car suddenly jolted forward with such force that as the car sped ahead it tore open the gates, shattering the chain and lock. The flowers from the wreath splattered across the windshield.

Out of the fog vaporous shapes formed and faded, then cleared for a moment as the lawn to the right took on the appearance of a graveyard. Ghostly cloaks of moss hung over statues of winged angels and hooded figures. The house loomed ahead, the white marble walls shimmering as though phosphorescent in the dim light. The car slowed down but continued cautiously up the long drive as the clipped rows of linden trees arched over it, forming a canopy. Finally, when he could go no further, the driver stopped at the base of the wide marble stairs and waited.

Though a dream, I was aware of the still and pungent air while silvery-winged birds who flew only at night sang their canticles of insensible gloom. Suddenly a young, angelic woman appeared from the house and ran across the terraced lawn like a frightened forest creature. The pallid light robbed her face of color as she wove her way past the maze of clipped boxwood hedges. She was dressed in faded blue, her ankle-length gown fluttering like waves of ethereal light. She moved silently towards the pavilion, then paused purposely and looked around as if to make sure no one had seen her. Her hand rested on one of the stone pillars as her eyes fixed on something or someone nearby. There was the muffled sound of a car door slamming off in the distance. Then the young uniformed man moved into view and quickly ran towards the teahouse. It appeared that the girl was motioning for him to go back, but his eyes shone with innocent determination, and with his powerful arms he reached out to embrace her. She appeared to pull away, not rejecting his touch, but as if fear outweighed her ability to trust herself and take what she wanted. They began speaking, but I could not hear their voices. It seemed she was trying to warn him of something as her eyes darted about the darkened garden.

Then he grabbed her hand, and they both turned towards the waiting car, but in that instant a third figure appeared in the shadows. A security guard had apparently heard the gate crash open and come to investigate. An argument broke out between the two men, and the girl was pushed aside by the guard. The chauffeur struck out at the other man, and there was a struggle. I saw a hand reach for a garden tool, or what looked like a sledgehammer, lying by a garden wall. Then in one swift motion the guard struck a blow to the left side of the young man's head. Something the color of deadly nightshade splattered across the white marble balustrade, and I realized it was his blood, flowing from his wound onto his dark gray jacket. He fell to the ground, then tried to raise himself but could not. The girl stood there, frozen in terror, screaming soundlessly into her hands as she dropped to her knees at his side. The guard grabbed her and pulled her violently away from him. Suddenly a heavyset woman in a nurse's uniform appeared in the doorway of the house, rushed down the stairs, and took the sobbing girl away.

While still in shadow, the guard began to drag his dying victim across the tiled floor of the teahouse then down a flight of narrow stone steps that led to a steel door set into a concrete wall. The door opened into what looked like a tunnel hidden beneath the earth. The young man's body seemed to convulse when he saw where he was about to be taken. The door slammed shut, and everything was still for a while . . . and then the silence was broken. Slowly at first, there was a rhythmic sound coming from inside the wall, and then it turned into a loud banging. It was the horror of that sound that jarred me awake.

I didn't expect to see Gordon Merdock again after he left that night in December, but about a month later he called from New York. He neglected the usual courtesies, like saying hello, but got right to the point. "I've got to talk to you about something, but not out there. Would you be willing to come into town?" he said with a certain urgency.

"Yes, but give me some idea . . . ?"

"Not on the phone. I'll tell you when I see you," he said emphatically.

"Okay, I'll meet you in Central Park, at the skating rink tomorrow at two."

"Fine. See you then," he said, hesitating for a moment as though he was going to say something else but changed his mind.

It was cold and windy in the city, but I found it invigorating and welcomed the chance to get away from the house, which seemed desolate now with no one around. Gordon was waiting outside the skating pavilion when I arrived. He didn't smile when he saw me but remained stone faced and somber while rubbing his hands together to fight off the cold. He was wearing a tan, suburban town coat and a black, Russian-style fur hat.

"Why all the mystery?" I asked, following him into the coffee shop, where we could watch the skaters through the tall glass doors. The skate house was old and weathered from nearly a century of use. The smell of coffee and fresh popcorn filled the air. Gordon didn't answer but remained silent as we watched a young couple leave. Then he moved towards their table at the far corner of the room. I tried another question.

"How are all your people, the three men with the mysterious illnesses?"

"They're fine," he said in a gravelly voice. "Every one of them recovered almost immediately after we dropped the project," he said, shaking his head slightly as though still baffled.

"Strange that something like that should happen all of a sudden," I said, still not disclosing what I knew about the past.

"Well, the whole thing shook me up more than I wanted to admit," he said, looking down at his hand and flexing it.

"So what made you call after all this time?"

"After we pulled out of there, I couldn't seem to shake the whole thing from my mind. I started to have troubled dreams for the first time in my life, and I kept thinking about you staying out there alone," he said, looking around the room and noticing the long line at the concession stand. "Anyway, I went to see this psychic a friend told me about. I figured it couldn't hurt to get someone else's slant on things. She's only a few blocks from here, over on Seventy-second Street. Her name is Marge LaJudas. I was told she's one of the best in New York. Well, I went to see her yesterday and told her nothing beforehand. She—" He stopped mid-sentence. "Why are you looking at me like that?" he asked, frowning.

"Sorry . . . the idea of a man visiting psychics . . . I always thought of it as a woman's preoccupation," I said, feeling embarrassed that my reaction showed.

"I'm open to anything. I've always taken an interest in occult history, lost civilizations, and obscure religions. Throughout history, the most powerful and successful people took an interest in the subject, so it's nothing new. Besides, it makes life more interesting," he said, maintaining a serious expression.

"In what way?"

"Well, if a psychic tells you something good is going to happen, you look forward to it, and if she tells you something bad, like you're taking a trip and the plane is going to crash, you feel you have the power to prevent disaster by simply not getting on the plane. Or you take the trip in a hot air balloon, or on a pogo stick for that matter, but you don't get on the fucking plane," he said, raising his voice enough to attract the stares of the group of people sitting next to us.

"Interesting viewpoint. Did you visit a fortune-teller before you planned that Christmas party?"

"No. That was my one big mistake," he said, waving his hands about. "Anyway, about this woman Marge that I went to see. She has this kind of chapel, with this elevated altar that she sits on. I was instructed to light a candle and write down a question on a piece of paper and slip it under the candle. There was no one else in the room except me, so she couldn't have known what I asked."

"What did you ask?"

"I'll get to that in a minute. Anyway, she's wearing this long white silk robe, and she has this long blond hair, and she closes her eyes and goes into this sort of trance for a few minutes. I'm just sitting there looking at her, not knowing what to expect, and finally she takes a deep breath and starts to describe the whole house."

I must have given him a questioning look because he put his hand to his head and said, "Winfield . . . I mean, she starts to describe Winfield in detail. I mean everything—the stairs, all those strange rooms, the gold ceiling, the gardens. She even said there was an astrological observatory on the roof! Did you know about that?"

"No . . . there is something up there, a lookout tower or something," I said, wanting to hear more.

"Well, after she goes through every little nook and cranny of the place, she's really got my attention, 'cause that was my question—only she never saw what I wrote. Then she comes out and says there are negative spirits in the house that can drain you—cause mental confusion or something. The way she's telling it, it's not like in the movies, where ghosts are going to jump out of the walls and strangle you in your bed. It's not like that, she says. It's more subtle, more insidious than that. She said it's what it does to you emotionally. It beguiles you; it taunts and charms you—lures you like a spider's web."

"Then what?" I asked, wondering if he was trying to scare me.

"I don't know," he said absently in a far-off voice. "She mentioned an older man, a brilliant, driven, but bitter and unhappy, man capable of achieving extraordinary things. She said he was trying to attain the impossible."

"He did attain the impossible. He started out with nothing and ended up one of the richest men in the country. Then he built the tallest building in the world. Did she know his name?"

"No, and I never told her, but even I knew who she meant. The only thing that was strange was that she was describing him as though he were still alive and living in the house!" he said, a little flushed.

"Really," I said uneasily, shifting my attention to the skaters outside. There was a long pause. I found myself holding back information, and I wasn't sure why. Gordon was such a strange person, and I didn't know what to make of him at that point, but as he continued with his story, it became clear to me that he was telling the truth.

"You're talking about Woolworth. Sometimes I get the feeling he's alive out there too, but it's just a feeling. It's hardly logical. Look how long I've been there, and nothing's happened to me," I said, sounding a little smug. "What else did she say?" I asked tentatively.

"According to my psychic friend, you put yourself at risk whenever you go digging into the past or into things that don't concern you."

"What happens out there does concern me," I said defensively.

"Why? It's not even your house," he said, raising his voice.

I just looked at him, unable to respond at first. "I can't explain it—why I'm there, or why I've stayed so long. It's just something I have to do. Just once, I have to know that I saved something. It was almost bulldozed. If André and his partner hadn't come along when they did . . ."

"You're possessed," Gordon said, cutting me off.

"Stop talking stupid. I'm immune to that mumbo jumbo," I snapped.

"Apparently you're a trigger, or catalyst," he said, his voice stiffening.

"Me? I tried to bring the place back to life. I even brought the original furniture back and put it in the rooms where it belonged. I brought hundreds of people out there to film all summer, and nothing bad ever happened to them," I said, flustered.

"Apparently you did something—opened Pandora's box, stirred things up. Can you think of anything?" he asked, his mood darkening.

I sat there mute and wondering. "There *was* a scary moment. A few months ago we held a séance. At first, I thought it was some kind of game—that the people involved were a little melodramatic, but things happened that night that I can't explain. . . . It was real, too real and frightening, and we ended it," I said, not wanting to say any more about it.

"Anything happen after that?"

"No, nothing. Like I said, we had a great summer. Everything was fine."

Gordon searched the room with his eyes as though looking for a waiter, then saw that the line at the concession stand had gone down. He jumped up from the table. "I'm going to get us some hot chocolate," he said. I stared out the window and watched a group of skaters as they gathered to form a human chain. One of the skaters fell and laughed, trying to grab onto the end of the whip as they sped along the ice. I longed to join them, but Gordon returned with the steaming drinks.

"Thank you," I said, warming my hands on the cup. Gordon took several quick gulps. "What made you go see a psychic after all this time?"

"I couldn't sleep, and when I did, I had disturbing dreams," he said grimly.

"Your dream didn't involve a man getting hit in the head with a sledgehammer, did it?" I asked cautiously.

"No. There was no violence in my dream. I was just trapped in a chamber in Egypt."

"What's that got to do with Winfield?" I asked.

"Nothing, except it was the same dream my worker was having when he came out of the coma. It made no sense, so I figured I had nothing to lose by seeing a psychic."

"What was your man doing before he took ill?"

"All he remembers was snooping around in the basement." Gordon sat quietly, stirring his hot chocolate with a popsicle stick.

"What are you thinking?" I asked, noticing the puzzled frown on his face.

"I'm thinking I should have brought a tape recorder yesterday. There was so much stuff that this woman told me, I couldn't follow half of it. Remember, I don't know who any of these people are," he said, taking another frantic gulp of his drink.

"Like who besides Woolworth?" I asked, growing impatient.

"I don't know. She just gave me descriptions—no names. She mentioned a woman with reddish blond hair."

"His daughter Edna had blond hair. The one who died," I said.

"No, not a member of his family—someone he called his empress."

"I've never heard that before," I said, feeling he was onto something that I didn't know.

"There was something very strange and complicated that went on out there," he said, his eyes filled with pinpoints of confusion. He began to fumble with a paper napkin, then looked up at me. "Oh, I remember now. She said the thing that pushed the old man over the edge and turned him bitter was that he did love someone, a woman—not his wife, of course. This woman lived with him under the same roof. She was by his side day and night."

"Miss Salters," I said, interrupting him.

He looked up. "She didn't give a name other than the empress, but she did say that this woman had blondish hair, was slender and soft-spoken, and gave up most of her life to be with him."

"It had to be Miss Salters. She stayed in the Empress Josephine room, the one I'm in now. I have all her furniture—I mean the furniture Woolworth bought for her. I had to recover most of it, but I remember her name was scribbled in pencil on the back of each piece. I never knew who she was—in fact I know nothing about her," I said, thinking for a moment. "There's supposed to be a way to get from what was her room to the Napoleon room, Woolworth's room, but I never found it," I said, starting to feel a chill in the room.

Gordon looked amused. "Has a certain charm to it. Where was Mrs. Woolworth in all this?"

"She was locked in her cell, all the way down the hall at the other end of the house."

"Well, that's one way to deal with a wife who gets on your nerves," he said, smiling wryly. "How did people get away with that sort of stuff?"

"It happened all the time. I wasn't kidding about the things I told you back at the house in December. It was all true. Did your psychic friend say anything more about this mystery woman?"

"Only that this woman he called his empress got tired of waiting for him to dump his wife and marry her; that after many years of waiting on him hand and foot, she ran off to marry someone else. Apparently it destroyed him. For all his wealth and power, he was lost without her and couldn't bear to see anyone else happy in love, not even his own daughter, whom he married off to a rich philanderer. The psychic did mention that the daughter bore a striking resemblance to the woman who left him, and that the old man was so full of hurt and vengeance at that point, he didn't always know what he was doing. He ended up ruining his daughter's life. The daughter was apparently in a miserable marriage, but there was someone else she wanted to be with."

"Everything that your psychic told you makes sense. I mean, it fills in a lot of missing pieces. I've only gotten fragments of information about the daughter, Edna, over the years. From what you're telling me, it sounds like there was one tragedy after another. Edna's only child was Barbara Hutton," I said sadly.

"The one who was married a hundred times?"

"I believe it was six times. Poor thing! I read somewhere that it was Barbara Hutton who found her mother's body after she'd killed herself. She was only four years old at the time. You don't recover from something like that. You know, it's ironic how one tragedy can set up a chain reaction within a family, and one broken life leads to another, and on to the next generation. Everything I ever read about Woolworth's granddaughter, Barbara Hutton, indicates that she never knew a completely happy day in her life."

"Powerful families have always bent the rules, but it comes back to haunt the living," Gordon said, stopping to move his chair away from the drafty window.

"Do you remember the Woodward case?" I asked.

"The one about the beautiful showgirl who shot her millionaire husband in their Long Island mansion? That was back in the fifties, wasn't it?"

"Fifty-five. People out there still talk about it as if it happened yesterday. Two suicides resulted from that covered-up tragedy. That was a Woolworth house too, you know."

"Is there any connection between those two families?" he asked.

"None, the Woodwards bought the showplace from Woolworth's surviving family back in the forties. People always confuse the two names."

"I have no idea who any of these people are," Gordon grumbled.

"I'm as lost as you are at this point. Every owner, every person who worked there, even some of the students, described seeing a ghostly woman floating about in the garden or one of the rooms upstairs. I just assumed it was the daughter because she took her own life. But there are conflicting accounts as to where she ended it. Her aunt said it was at the Plaza Hotel, not Winfield. The whole thing was covered up, of course—suicides always were. Everything I've ever heard indicates that in order to have a spirit manifestation, or whatever you want to call it, there has to be a traumatic death associated with it. Some sudden, unexpected, tragic end to one's life, and the trauma, and intensity of emotions, somehow cause the whole thing to imprint somehow. That's as far as I've gotten. The research is out there but not easy to find." I said, feeling frustrated at my inability to find the right words.

Gordon leaned forward and asked, "Have you ever seen a ghost?"

"No, never. That's the weird part. I know they exist. I believe I've gotten them on film. But no, I've never actually seen one," I said.

Gordon seemed to be running something through his mind before he spoke again. There was a long pause. "Are you familiar with Sir Arthur Conan Doyle, the nineteenth-century writer, the one who created the Sherlock Holmes series?"

"A little bit. I know of him, but I've never read his books."

"Well, he was obsessed with the occult, despite his portrayal of his star detective, who dismissed such subjects as a lot of bunk. In real life Doyle stated in the press that he went to séances all the time, communicated with the dead, and had shot quite a number of photographs of his little spirit friends. He set out on a one-man campaign to tell the world about his theories and to prove there is life after death. On April twelfth, in 1922, at Carnegie Hall in New York, he gave a slide presentation of actual photographs of ghostly apparitions that he had taken during séances he attended. His presentation was so convincing that three people in his audience committed suicide shortly after, just to experience the afterlife." Gordon seemed to enjoy making this revelation.

"Is that really true?"

"All you have to do is go to any library and scan the New York papers for that year. It's all there," he said just as someone turned up the volume on the sound system for the rink and a Strauss waltz began to blare over the loudspeakers. We had no choice but to listen to the music and began watching the skaters glide past on the frozen pond.

"So, did your psychic friend give you any suggestions on how to restore peace at Winfield?" I asked after the waltz ended.

"She said there was something hidden out there . . . some link, something that holds the old man there, and that if it were found, its secrets exposed, all the negativity would go with it."

"Like what? I've gone through every inch of that place over the years, and so did your inquisitive Christmas decorators. They got into things even I didn't know about."

"It's not something obvious, or anything you would think to look for."

"I love a challenge. When do we start looking?" I asked excitedly.

"It's not that simple. You're not to have anything to do with this!" he said, with a finality that unnerved me. "I mean, you have to wait outside while I search around."

"Might I ask why?"

"Woolworth hates you. He'd kill you, given a chance," he stated, as though this were in the realm of possibility. I sat there frozen in my chair, not wanting to admit that what he'd just said scared me. I could feel the memory of that night in June sneaking up on me like an unwelcome shadow. For a second, through the aroma of coffee there in the café, I remembered the scent of incense. Gordon's eyes were now fixed on my hands, and I realized they were trembling.

"Something wrong?" he asked dispassionately.

"No . . . nothing," I said, slipping my hands under the table as he continued with his disturbing revelations.

"According to Marge, my psychic, it's got nothing to do with logic or with you personally. It's that you look like the woman who scorned him, and you're living in her room."

"You're talking about someone who's been dead for sixty years—just to put things in perspective," I said irritably.

"He doesn't know he's dead. In his mind, or spirit mind, or whatever, this is all playing out like it were nineteen-sixteen, or whenever it was that this traumatic event took place in his life. He's stuck in some loop, but if we're to change things for the better—break the spell, if you will—we have to snap him out of the loop," he said emphatically.

"Is it really that simple?"

"Hell, no. I have no idea what I'm doing, or what to look for, but there's a clue hidden in the house behind a wall, or at least I think that's what she said. I'm getting confused again; it was all too much to remember at once. Let's go for a walk. I can use some air," Gordon said, jumping up from his chair. He paused just long enough to pop a Lifesaver into his mouth and was out the door of the skate house before I could gather up my things. I quickly put on my gloves and braced myself for the cold. We walked around the park for a while, not saying too much. Off in the distance, I could see the Dakota, looming dark and ominous through the bare trees. Gordon walked faster than most people, and I had difficulty keeping up with him. I followed him down a steep path that led to a stone underpass. Gordon stopped suddenly to pick up a silver key chain someone had dropped on the cobblestones. He dangled it in the air as though it were a valuable prize. "I'm always finding things other people miss," he said, smiling like a ten-year-old boy. I didn't have the heart to tell him it was just junk.

"Good. You're just the person I'm looking for. So when do we start poking around Winfield?" I asked.

He looked up with his inscrutable owlish eyes, removed his hat, and ran a hand through his hair. "I already told you, you're not to get involved in this search."

"I *am* involved, and after the things you just told me, I'm more determined than ever. Besides, you can't get in the house without me," I said, pulling out my set of house keys and dangling them teasingly before his eyes. "So it's settled. Can we start tomorrow?"

"I guess," he responded as though his frantic walking had drained something out of him. A cold, bitter wind blew across the park, churning up dead leaves and dust from the city. Gordon put his hat back on, looked at his watch nervously, and grunted. "Got to go."

He was halfway across one of the park roads before I could ask, "What time?"

Without turning his head, he yelled back, "Late."

Meeting Gordon had come as a surprise, and though I regarded him with a certain wariness, I enjoyed his eccentric, but forthcoming, manner. There was something haphazard and unfocused about him, and his attention span seemed to be limited to fifteen minutes. He was wound up tight as a spring and ready to jump at any moment, but more at his own shadow than anything else. He could be exasperating and rude, but I sensed instinctively that he was sincere and well-meaning. I could relate to him as a sister would to an older brother, but more than that, I was beginning to suspect that he too was now caught up in the undergloom and beckoning mysteries of Winfield. In the short time he'd been there, the house had gotten to him, and I entertained the idea that I might have found a fellow searcher to share my quest for answers.

Chapter Eighteen

The Library

I caught the commuter train at Penn Station and was back in Glen Cove in less than an hour. My car was waiting in the parking lot. There were no lights on in the house when I pulled into the drive a few minutes later. The light that was always kept on in my room had apparently blown out, making the house seem abandoned. When I opened the front door, the temperature inside seemed to have dropped, and I wondered if there might be something wrong with the heating system. If there was, there was nothing I could do about it till morning, so it seemed like a good night to make a fire in the fireplace. There was enough wood to last the winter, piled ceiling high on the back porch, and more logs and kindling were stored in the library closet. I turned on the lights, loaded several logs into a wide canvas bag, and was about to carry them upstairs when I stopped to gaze about the small, ornately carved Gothic room.

Floor-to-ceiling bookcases with walnut-framed glass doors surrounded a cozy marble fireplace. This had been Woolworth's private sanctuary, where he came to be alone and pursue his scholarly interest in history. I had the feeling that he actually read the books in his library, unlike most of his neighbors on the Gold Coast, who ordered expensive gold-and-leather tomes by the yard that were strictly for show. As I gazed about the rows of oversized volumes of world history, I wondered if perhaps the key to his obsession with the historic rooms on the second floor could be found somewhere on those shelves. Sometimes the thing you're searching for turns out to be right under your nose. I quickly made a fire and began looking over the books.

There were the predictable collected works of Mark Twain, and *David Copperfield*, followed by a handsome set of volumes entitled *History of the City of New York*, by Martha Lamb, Robert Browning's *Poetical Works*, and a rare, cordovan-leather first edition of Pepys's *Diary and Correspondence*. Next to it was the *Complete Trotting and Pacing Record* by Chester. The bookshelves rose twelve feet or so, and I needed the tall mahogany ladder that was leaning against the far wall to get to the top row. Those shelves were filled with texts on European history and its leaders, like Alexander the Great and Charlemagne, and with works on obscure areas of science, such as *The Soul of Things* by William Denton (1888) and *The Law of Psychic Phenomena* (1893), Next to them was a handsome red-leather book, dated 1908, called *The Life of Napoleon*, by J. T. Herbert Bailey. I began leafing through it and noticed several pages had been torn out. Checking the index, I found that the missing pages concerned Napoleon's time in Egypt. I put the book back on the shelf, then spotted a black-and-gold volume titled *The History of the Supernatural*. I pulled it out, curled up on the thick Oriental rug in front of the crackling fire, and began reading.

One of the chapters was on a man named Joseph Rhodes Buchanan, whose name I'd never heard before. Buchanan became world-famous during the 1850s after making an astonishing discovery. He was able to prove scientifically that every object, or piece of clothing, touched by man has the person's history imprinted on it. He claimed that the human mind has the power to access and play back this electromagnetic recording of history, very much like a videotape or a daguerreotype photo of past events. This curious faculty he called psychometry, and he believed that it was possible to develop this ability with practice, though in his experience only the very rare and gifted person seemed able to master it, and those who did came by their ability under extreme and bizarre circumstances. At the time of his discovery, Buchanan was a respected man of science. His works and lectures had been published in scientific journals throughout the world. Buchanan, like Franze Anton Mesmer, who pioneered the field before him, believed that by nature we are pervaded by invisible vibrating electrical energies, and that the secret of being psychic—being able to see beyond the five senses—comes from the ability to tune into these energies. He believed that one could develop an attunement to this vibrating aura that he claimed lies in the electrical system of the brain.

Is the past entombed in the present, as Buchanan claimed? He stated: "The world is its own enduring monument, and with the discovery of Psychometry, it will enable us to explore the history of man." He further stated: "The mental telescope is now discovered, which may pierce the depths of the past, and bring us in full view of all the grand and tragic passages of history."

I put the book down for a moment, realizing I had never read anything like this before. In all my years in college, nothing even remotely related to this subject had ever come up. And yet it all seemed so plausible, even consistent with known laws of nature, if not with those of science.

There was no way to know for sure whether Woolworth had studied this subject or these books had been left by one of the following owners. It seemed just as probable that one of the inquisitive students, bent on holding séances and playing with Ouija boards, might just as easily have slipped them on the shelves during the girls'-school years. But the students weren't traveling about the globe, searching out and paying huge fortunes for the former possessions of Napoleon and other great leaders and people of power or influence in history. If indeed it is true that all objects, once having been owned by an individual, vibrate with that person's own unique frequency and continue to give off a residue of his or her energy, then could they transmit that energy to another? Did Woolworth, who no doubt had an extraordinary mind and a ceaseless curiosity about historic objects, search out and relentlessly collect things that had once belonged to rich and powerful people for a reason? If this were true, what had he planned to use that power for?

Intrigued by this, I scanned the shelves and came across *The Prodigal Genius,* a biography of Nikola Tesla by John J. O'Neil. By the turn of the last century, Tesla was generally regarded as the greatest inventor the world had ever known. Though considered eccentric by some, he created and discovered world-transforming devices, often without theoretical precedent. I was surprised to learn that Tesla gave us the alternating electric current that we use today and that he also invented the radio—not Marconi, as many American encyclopedias still mistakenly claim. Intriguingly, J. P. Morgan, Sir John Jacob Astor, and George Westinghouse had financially backed this nineteenth-century wizard up to a point.

The book noted that when not inventing, Tesla enjoyed attending lavish dinner parties; on several occasions he would have passed Winfield on his way to J. P. Morgan's sprawling estate only a few doors away. Tesla built his most famous laboratory, Wardencliff, on Long Island's North Shore. On it stood a revolutionary two-hundred-foot tower for wireless transmission across the Atlantic. But Morgan, who had financed the project, suddenly withdrew his support after Tesla made an astonishing announcement, claiming he had received a transmission signal from extraterrestrials within our own galaxy. Morgan called him a nut, and withdrew financial support. Wardencliff and the tower were abandoned and eventually destroyed.

Tesla was devastated, and for a time he turned his attention to a revolutionary approach to the study of ghosts and time travel. In 1892, at Columbia College in New York, Tesla gave a much-publicized lecture on some unique experiments he was conducting on photographing spirit entities. He also claimed he was able to get color images of the human aura, a phenomenon that had been visible to psychics for centuries. A hypersensitive vacuum tube he invented turned out to be not only an excellent detector of human electromagnetic fields or auras but also able to capture images of long-dead persons, who mysteriously showed up as ghosts on film. There was no mention of whether or not Tesla had ever met Sir Arthur Conan Doyle, although they made similar claims. Tesla's research papers on these and other experiments were missing from his files. It was reported later that the FBI confiscated all of his records from the basement of the Penn Hotel in New York after his sudden death in 1943.

While I did not fully understand the workings of such complex devices, I would have given anything to get my hands on that equipment for just one night, or even an hour, during the time I was at Winfield. For surely I would have captured the whole kingdom of spirits, perhaps all the great and infamous ones that the man of the house seemed to be trying to link up with. But from my own limited experience, you do not need anything special—no electrical charge or complex vacuum tube. I have on very rare occasions gotten mysterious ghostly images with nothing more than a vintage Rolliflex box camera and ordinary film from the local drugstore.

The fire had dwindled down to burning embers. It was late. I put the books back in their places. It struck me as interesting that this kind of information was more available in Woolworth's day than today, and that these remarkable men all lived and made their astonishing discoveries in the last century.

I would not learn until many years later that a top-secret U.S. government project called STARGATE was already underway in 1978, investigating this very subject but keeping their findings under wraps.

It was cold in my room that night, and though it was late, I quickly lit a fire in the hearth to stay warm. Just before falling off to sleep, I caught a reflection of the gold canopy in the mirror opposite the bed. Its carved gilt surface seemed to take on a life of its own in the dim fanfare of light. I thought about all the things I'd just read and wondered, Was it really possible that its history was somehow imprinted in that ornamental prize that had once been one of Woolworth's proudest possessions?

With these thoughts I drifted off into a deep and peaceful sleep. Sometime during the night, I became aware of a slow creaking noise, like that of a door that had not been opened in some time. After a moment it stopped, and my attention shifted to the sound of the wind blowing outside, funneling through the hairline cracks of the wooden window frames. As I lay there, I began to have the unsettling feeling that something had entered my room and was stalking me with knowing instincts. A moment later I became aware of a live weight on top of the bed—a weight that was moving slowly, stealthily along the side of the bedcovers, coming towards me one measured step at a time. I looked up and saw a pair of tiny, red, glittering eyes. The moon outside shone pallidly enough that I could make out the dark moving form of what was unmistakably a large ugly rat, its snakelike tail squirming loathsomely on the white satin bedspread. It swayed for a second, baring its nasty little teeth. I stared at it, unable to move at first. Then I was about to hurl it across the room away from me when I jolted awake and realized it was just another bad dream.

I reached for the chain of the bedside lamp and turned it on. Everything was as it should be, along with the comforting sound of the soft burning logs dying down to embers in the hearth. But just to make sure, I looked under the bed, got up and checked the shower stall, and looked under the couch in the dressing room. There was nothing. I was not afraid of rats but did not welcome the idea of one crawling around in my bed, even in a dream. It was just unnerving. I shook the thought from my mind, walked over to the sink, and began to splash cold water on my face. When I reached for the towel, it slipped from my grasp and fell to the floor. Bending down to get it, I spotted something on the rug at the base of the mirrored wall that my room shared with the master suite. Moving closer to get a better look, I saw what looked like ashes on the floor and smelled the faint odor of cigarette smoke.

I wasn't in the habit of calling my friends at four in the morning, but I ran to the phone and dialed Katia's number, rationalizing to myself that she'd welcome hearing all about Gordon's intriguing revelations in Central Park. I waited, but there was no dial tone. I clicked the receiver frantically several times, hoping to shake the phone into operation. I soon realized why I couldn't reach her. After following the cord, I saw that the wires had been severed by knowing little teeth. This was not a good thing. No indeed, it was right up there in a long list of not-so-good things.

I was not raised to be a wimpy female. In fact, I spent a good part of my days proving to myself and to anyone who would take notice that I was one of the bravest of creatures to be living in what was undoubtedly a haunted house. But to stay there for one second longer was beginning to seem idiotic even to me. I had up until that moment convinced myself that there were perfectly logical explanations for every weird thing that had happened so far. I went back to my room, sat on the bed, and began chewing the edge of the bedspread, trying to think of a logical explanation. Then it hit me. This was the country, after all. Animals fall down chimneys all the time. Everyone who lives in an old house knows that all kinds of creatures—squirrels, birds, weasels, everything short of King Kong has been known to tumble down a chimney. How stupid of me not to have remembered that fact. But I couldn't recall ever seeing one light up and smoke. I sat there holding the dead phone in my hand, waiting for dawn to break. As the room slowly filled with the comforting glow of blue light, I slowly opened the door to my room, ran downstairs, and made a strong cup of coffee. Then jumped in the car and drove to the nearby train station to call the phone-repair service. They sent a man out within the hour.

"Looks like you have a rodent problem," he said matter-of-factly.

"Looks that way," I responded in an exhausted tone. "I don't suppose you could install the new line through a bolex cable, or something less tasty?" I asked.

"No, ma'am. We just have one kind of line for resident phones," he said dryly.

"Fine. Then you can attach it with a removable clip so I can lock it up in the safe when I'm not here?"

"I can do that," he said, and the job was done in less than twenty minutes. Everything was back to normal again, or so I thought.

Gordon arrived at the house later that evening, dressed in a pair of faded blue jeans, a plaid flannel shirt, and a navy pullover sweater. The look suited him.

"What exactly are we supposed to be looking for?" I asked, after enjoying a cup of tea and some stale peanuts we found in the kitchen.

"Something . . . something tied with a string. I'm not sure what, but whatever it is, it's hidden behind a wooden panel," he said, gazing about the room as though we'd find it in the kitchen.

"That tells us a lot," I said, sensing it was going to be another long night.

Gordon seemed jumpy and restless as usual. Then, without saying anything, he sat himself down on the floor and struggled to adjust himself into a lotus position. His powers of concentration seemed fragile and tenuous, as though he were going through the motions but could not completely calm his own inner demons.

"What are you doing?" I asked.

He answered with his eyes closed. "I need to find my center, harness my energies . . . focus on my purpose, before I can begin." He took a deep breath, then let the air out slowly. He no sooner appeared to get his rhythmic breathing down than he jumped up from the floor and said, "Oh, I almost forgot these." He reached into his briefcase and pulled out a rainbow-colored candle and a small bottle of saltwater. "We'll need these later. It helps to create peaceful vibrations," he said in a serious tone. I smiled to myself; his behavior was sometimes foreign to me. But deep down I was grateful that he took an interest in whatever it was that was plaguing the house, and that he was willing to spend the time on what was beginning to sound like a good old-fashioned treasure hunt. I decided not to say anything about the dream I'd had or the disturbing events of last night.

Gordon went back to his meditations, then after a few minutes opened his eyes. "Well, we might as well get started. We should probably check out the downstairs rooms first," he said, struggling to raise himself from the floor. "How many of the rooms have paneling?" he asked.

"There're at least five, plus all the storerooms and the servants' pantry."

"We can save time by each taking a room. I'll start in the library while you check out the billiard room. I have a feeling that what we're looking for wouldn't be in a place where servants had access," he said, taking the candle and lighting it, then turning and walking out of the room and towards the hall. I followed close behind.

"Are you taking the good-luck candle with you and leaving me here alone to fight off the banshees unarmed?" I asked, trying to make light of the moment.

"It's all about intent," he responded, placing the candle on the floor in the center of the hall. "Remember: just keep moving along the walls and tapping until you hear something that sounds like it might be hollow on the other side." He turned and disappeared into the library, seeming very much at home. I went into the billiard room, checked the walls and side cabinets, and found nothing except for a pile of papers held together with a paper clip. They were just records of menus and recipes dating back to the school years. Then I noticed an empty envelope cut neatly along the top. I was about to put it back when I recognized the name Sunny Gwynn. Underneath the name was "care of the Grace Downs school," and there was a return address from Aitken, South Carolina. I put the envelope in my pocket, thinking I would try to make contact with her.

I was suddenly distracted by Gordon's incessant pounding and tapping and feared he might be damaging the walls. The sound echoed through the marble hall. Then all was quiet for a while. A few minutes later, Gordon was standing in the doorway to the billiard room, holding a well-worn leather book.

"Did you see this?" he asked, leafing through the yellowed pages.

"Oh, you found them. Which one have you got there?"

"This one is on mind-altering drugs, ancient ritual potions, and Egyptian embalming fluids. I've never seen a book like this, and some of the others look like heavy-duty stuff," he said, gazing at one of the wood-engraved illustrations.

"I was up half the night reading the ones on the supernatural, but I missed seeing that one."

"You find anything in here?" he asked while continuing to leaf through the book.

"Just some old menus from the sixties."

"Well, I covered the library. I think we'd better start tackling the ballroom. I'll need your help in there." I followed him down the hall. Then he paused at the tall mahogany doors and took a deep breath.

"This isn't going to be easy. This room has layers of paneling, and half of it's hidden," he said as he walked around the outer edges, where the walls seemed to take on a new meaning for him. He was able to identify the origins of many of the carved symbols and adornments, and he made note of every detail, molding, cartouche, embellishment, and insignia as though it were part of a puzzle.

"That's interesting," he said, pointing up to something near the white marble fireplace. I moved closer but could not make it out in the dim light of the chandelier, which had some of its bulbs missing.

"What is it?"

"Occult symbols. They're not in keeping with the Renaissance theme of the room," he said. Then he began tapping the wall with his ear up against it, listening for any changes in sound. He took his time, moving slowly inch by inch as he worked his way towards the alcove. Then he stopped.

"I thought I heard something," he said, pointing up to the organ chamber.

"Like what?"

"The patter of feet."

"Mice," I said absently, not wanting to alarm him.

"Has anyone been up there lately?" he asked, nodding his head up towards the gold-filigreed ceiling.

"Not that I know of. Why?"

"Remember the man on my decorating crew, the one who went into a coma? . . . When he came out of it, he said he remembered hearing something up there. But when he went up to check it out, he said some of the planks from the ledge had been removed. Because of the dark he couldn't see, but he knew his way around up there; they all did at that point. But when he stepped forward, he fell down the narrow shaft. He was able to grab onto something, but he hit his head, breaking the fall. He could have fallen all the way to the basement, and that probably would have killed him."

"That's horrible," I said, wondering why he hadn't told me that before. "But what about the others, and your hand?"

"I don't know, I just don't know, and bringing it up makes me wonder what I'm doing to myself coming back. . . . Anyway, I'm not going up there, and it seems useless to continue searching this room." He turned to leave and headed out into the main hall. There was something about the angry way he walked that made me think that our searching mission was over, and that he'd changed his mind or given up. But then he paused at the bottom of the stairs and looked up.

"Are there any paneled rooms upstairs?" he asked, squinting his eyes.

"One — Woolworth's private study," I said.

"I thought we just passed it."

"That was his private library. His study is in the master suite. The paneled walls have been painted over, so it's hard to tell."

"We probably should have gone there first," he said, heading up the stairs with a surge of renewed energy. The Edwardian room, as it was called, was at the far end of the house in the west wing, opposite the Empire room. First, a huge oak door led into a small vestibule with a walk-in closet. Then another door led to a large spacious room dominated by a massive carved wood fireplace. Over the mantel was a medieval coat of arms, which I was told Woolworth had designed himself. Gordon was already engrossed in exploring the walls in the dark when I switched on the lights. A pair of ornate lion-crested wall sconces suddenly gave off a faint glow of light, but not enough to really see anything. Tall floor-to-ceiling windows were draped with rich wine-red colored drapes with silk tassels running along the side. The wide planked floor was covered by a deep burgundy rug, and except for a pair of dragon-shaped bronze andirons and a high Gothic chair and writing desk I had brought, the room was empty.

Gordon scanned the room with his eyes. "I have a feeling about this room. These squared-off panels make it easy," he said, running his hands along the beveled moldings.

"These walls are solid walnut underneath the battleship gray paint," I said.

"Who would do such a thing?"

"The designer showcase people. Painting over priceless paneling is one of their trademarks. At least it's not Kelly green or bubblegum pink, like the other houses they did up in the area."

"This paint's no help. It's covered up any hairline cracks or openings," he said as he began tapping and pounding. I watched him work, wondering why he never seemed to get tired. "Do you know what this room was used for?" he asked as he made his way around the mantel.

"It was Woolworth's private office away from the city, but I was told he often held court here with his inner circle. I'm not sure who they were or what they did. Most likely it had to do with his business, but it could be something else. There was a rumor about a secret society."

Gordon stopped what he was doing. "You know, he might have been a Free Mason or a Rosicrucian."

"What's that?"

"It's a secret fraternity, officially the Ancient Mystic Order of the Rosae Crucis. Goes back to Egypt. Some of the most powerful men in the world have been members, including Mozart, George Washington, Theodore Roosevelt, and Napoleon. They do a lot of good, but behind the scenes, and they're into the occult sciences big-time. Those books downstairs gave me an inkling. Look at the fireplace. The symbols are all obscured, so they don't register except to a trained eye," he said, walking over to get a better look. "There's the cross—looks like it's just part of the design, but in the center is the rose, the Rosae Crucis. Up there on top—the carved pyramids over the temple—another sign. You don't just become a member; it's a lifetime of grueling study. You move up the ranks in stages," he said, running his hands along the ornate carvings that I'd never noticed before.

"So why is it a secret?"

"In our twinky, Disneyesque society, who'd understand?" he said sarcastically, turning back to his tireless searching of the walls. When he got to the closet, he gave the mirrored door an especially hard whack that rattled the glass.

"That mirror's been replaced," I said, walking towards it. "When I first saw this room back in the sixties, the mirror was black. You could still see your reflection in it, but it was strange. I think the school had it replaced."

"Interesting," Gordon said, running his hands along the edge of the door as though it might conceal something. "There's an old belief that if you concentrate on your own reflection in a black mirror long enough, you can transcend time and space and connect with your past lives and such. I don't know of anyone who's tried it, though."

"I'm not sure I follow you."

"It's a kind of mental exercise, or discipline, depending on what you believe. . . . Maybe it's like staring into a crystal ball—you see what you want to see. If you focus your energy on something long enough, you can make almost anything happen. It's all about energy," he said while checking out the mahogany draws in the large walk-in closet.

"We need more light in here. Do you want me to get a lamp from my room?"

"No. I'm okay for now," he said, showing no signs of getting tired. He continued to pound and tap monotonously as though nothing else in the world mattered. I lost track of time, but after about an hour or so, he finally spoke, clearing his throat several times first. "Do you hear that?" he said in an exhilarated tone as he hit the wall just opposite the fireplace.

"Hear what?"

"There's a faint echo. There . . . listen. When I tap this panel, there's a vibration that follows, like the rattling of metal," he said, his face flushed and glowing with unwavering determination. "To hear it, you have to come closer and put your head right up to the wall." I moved towards the panel, and he tapped it again. This time I heard a faint sound coming from inside the wall.

"We're just above the fireplace in the ballroom. It could be an open flu or something. The chimney must be right behind this wall," I said, beginning to feel a chill of excitement.

"There's got to be some way to get behind there. These panels are all sectioned off like they could be a door of some kind. One of them might open at some pressure point, or there could be a hidden latch behind all this paint," he said, feeling along the grooved edges of each panel. "Do you have a screwdriver?"

"There's one in my closet down the hall. I'll go get it," I said, turning to leave.

"I'll go with you." He followed close behind as we made our way down the darkened hall to my room.

"It's in here in a steel box on the floor," I said, bending down to rummage through the clutter of hammers, saw blades, bolts, and nails. I spotted what we needed and was about to grab it when I heard that creaking noise from my dream again, followed by a quick gasp from Gordon. Before I could turn around to see what was happening, something ran past my legs. I looked down and froze. Below me was the rat standing tall on its haunches. It was hissing menacingly, with teeth bared.

I remember being yanked from the closet by the shoulders and hearing the closet door slam shut with such force, it shook the room. I began to shake all over and saw terror in Gordon's eyes. He stood with his back up against the closet door, his full weight against it. His mouth was gaping open and he was twitching slightly beneath his beard. With his left hand he reached back awkwardly and turned the key in the lock. Then, without saying a word, he rushed out into the bedroom, returned with a heavy chair, and tilted it up against the door.

"What are you doing?" I asked, not recognizing my own voice.

"I'm not taking any chances. That thing's not getting out of this closet," he said hoarsely.

"It was trying to stop us, wasn't it? That thing knew what it was doing. How could a rat—" I stopped mid-sentence, and as I turned, I noticed that the mirrored wall next to the sink was gaping open at a curious angle. "Oh my God, that's . . ." I started to speak but could not find the words. Gordon moved towards the opened mirror and peered into the dark room beyond. It was the Empire marble bath. In the dim light we could make out the gilded carvings of Napoleon's sacred bees of Egypt encrusted along the upper moldings above the pink marble walls and, beyond them, the room where Woolworth had died.

"Did you know this wall opened?" he asked.

"No," I muttered, feeling my throat constricting. "I heard a rumor years ago about a way to get from that room to this one, but you hear all kinds of things about a place like this." I stood there staring at the open wall. "It's been there all this time. I think that thing came in my room last night, but I thought it was just a bad dream," I said, trying to stop myself from shaking. There were beads of perspiration on Gordon's forehead as he checked around the door frame, trying to discover its secret.

"It's some kind of trick mirror. Look here," he said, pointing at the base. "It pivots at a hinge in the center, but the latch that holds it is on the other side of the wall." He pushed at the brass-rimmed frame, and it closed again with the rusty sound of metal scraping.

"All this time anyone could have come into my room," I said, thinking in horror about the false sense of security I created by installing locks on the hall door.

"Well, if you didn't know about it, then no one else did. No one human, that is. I wouldn't get too worked up about it now. It doesn't matter anyway," he said, swinging the mirrored wall back in place, then turning to leave.

"What are we going to do now?" I asked.

He gave me a look that was unnerving. "We're getting out of here, now."

"But we're so close."

"Get whatever you need to take with you. You're not staying here another night," he said grudgingly.

"What about the rat?"

"That's no rat!" he said as I followed him down the stairs, taking only my journal with me.

Chapter Nineteen

Snowy Night in the City

Gordon and Katia were finally introduced. They hit it off immediately and never ran out of things to talk about. They were both near scholars on certain subjects, and I had trouble following their areas of expertise at times, but when they were together, I learned a lot and knew I had a lot of catching up to do. I stayed at Katia's apartment in the city for the next few days, and she proved to be a true friend. In an effort to rejoin the real world, Katia and I went skating in Central Park, saw at least a dozen new movies, went shopping at Bloomingdale's, and visited the Metropolitan Museum of Art. But my mind was still at Winfield. We talked till all hours of the night, discussing every possible explanation for the recent events. Katia worked very hard at convincing me that some things were better left alone, and that no logical answers or solutions were likely to come along. So I resigned myself to not going back to Glen Cove just yet.

One night it was too cold to venture out into the city. At 2:00 A.M. we couldn't sleep, so we watched on TV the forties classic *Gaslight* with Ingrid Bergman. The sets were lavish and grand, but the story was so depressing. I could identify with Miss Bergman's character and knew how she must have felt as her hold on sanity began to ebb away. Only it wasn't the man in my life who had slowly chipped away at my grasp on reality, but the house itself, with the help of some aberrant, possibly hallucinated, pesky little rodent. When the film ended, Katia got up and turned off the TV set. "God, what some women go through with their men," she said, waving her hands in the air. Then she turned to go into the kitchen to make us some herbal tea.

"Still no word from André?" she yelled out from the other room.

"Nothing," I said listlessly.

"Maybe you should report him as a missing person, but I get the feeling he knows where he is. . . . I have a vision of him surrounded by water. He could be lost at sea . . . or at Alcatraz," she said, laughing at her own humor. "Just kidding," she said, coming back into the room with two cups. "But I really do see him on the water. Maybe he's on an extended cruise."

"André is a workaholic; he doesn't take cruises. Without a phone glued to his ear, he'd go nuts." Katia placed the cup of tea on the table before me. "Thank you," I said as she took hers over to the window and sat down on the window seat. The flickering lights from the city framed her face softly.

"Your life must be very interesting, knowing everything that's going to happen to you ahead of time," I said.

Katia looked up and laughed. "I only wish. It never works for me. I can only use my abilities to help others, and then it's iffy. It comes and goes, and what I do only appeals to a small percentage of people. It wasn't always like that. Most people don't realize that during the last century, and well into this one, psychic activities were standard fare. We were very much accepted and popular in polite society. Think about it: There were no TVs, computers, or video games. People had to entertain themselves. On any given Saturday night, half the homes in America brought in fortune-tellers and clairvoyants. It was all part of their parlor games. Séances were all the rage, especially during wartime, when you wanted to find out if your boy was going to come home alive or if he'd been killed in action. It was a way of communicating with the dead. I think people were more spiritual, or humble. They seemed to have faith in things you can't always see. Maybe it gave them hope in a situation that was beyond their control. The practice of holding séances and seeing clairvoyants didn't end until all this other garbage was invented. Then Hollywood movies tainted the whole subject with sensationalized nonsense and gave us all a bad name."

"You have to admit, though, there were a lot of charlatans taking advantage of trusting and gullible people, too," I added.

"That's true, but there's also a lot of science out there that validates some of the weirdest elements, and it's being ignored by our educational system and the government. You take the whole Kirlian photography phenomenon. It pretty much proves that we are not just our bodies; that we have an electrical core that cannot be destroyed," she said in an animated tone.

"I found a book on that in Woolworth's library at the house last week. Apparently the Kirlians stumbled on it by accident. It started out with a simple maple leaf. They cut off a small piece of it, laid it down on a sheet of unexposed film, then took a photograph of it. Only, when they developed the film, the whole leaf showed up with the missing piece intact."

Katia's eyes lit up, as she leaned closer. "Here's the weird part," she said. "They later performed the same experiment on a deformed human hand. A young man they knew had lost his index finger in a fireworks explosion as a kid. They photographed his hand, exposing it to a high-frequency current while taking the photo. When the photo was developed, the hand showed up perfect, with all five fingers intact, and no one can explain it. But we're not hearing about it on the six o'clock news, nor is anyone investigating the phenomenon. Doctors have known about this medical anomaly for centuries. There are hundreds of accounts where a soldier has lost a limb on the battlefield but claimed to feel pain or tingling in the missing body part years later. Medical people don't know what to make of it, but they know it happens."

"So do you think there's any connection between this and ghosts?" I asked.

"Who knows? It's been going on since the beginning of man, and we still don't know how to explain it."

"I bet someone like Tesla could explain it if we could ever get our hands on his research. Katia, you want to hear something really crazy? I think they all knew each other," I said, the thought just popping into my head suddenly.

"Who?" Katia asked.

"J. P. Morgan was right next door, and Tesla and he were working on some very secret stuff, when for some reason Morgan pulled the plug on him. Tesla was not only doing research on ghosts; he was also working on some time machine; he even hooked up with Einstein on it. There are photographs of the two of them together. Tesla, from what I've read, wasn't one to give up on anything. When he lost one backer, he went to someone else. He even got support from John Jacob Astor for a time.

What if he went to Woolworth? For help, I mean. Talk about a perfect match. Woolworth was searching for immortality. He studied constantly. I think he would have been open to anything."

"You're going off the deep end again," Katia said, getting up and pacing the floor.

"I'm just thinking out loud, that's all. They were such amazing people, so full of life and ideas. Where are they now? All we have left are the buildings they left behind, and we destroy them," I said, suddenly feeling tired and defeated.

"I know it's still bugging you, but you should be glad to be out of that place. You have to know you can't possibly save everything. Their time came and went. It was a great party while it lasted, but it's over," she said, her face studying mine as though she already knew it was useless.

"You had to be there, Katia, to know what it was like. I tried to paint them on canvas but failed. I took tens of thousands of photographs, but I was never really able to capture it, nor could I find the words to describe how magical those places were. Even as ruins, they just took your breath away. They were an unrecognized, unappreciated art form that embodied an indefinable kind of poetry. All those fortresses buried in vines, everything coated in dust and cobwebs. They were more haunting and evocative when I saw them than when they were first built. Just knowing they existed made life seem more exciting. Then there were all the wonderful things left behind, waiting to be discovered—the old steamer trunks filled with fabulous gowns and letters and old photographs. The mansions came and went so fast—in the blink of an eye. But the one thing that never occurred to me until I read about it just recently in those old library books was that, aside from all that visual beauty, there was this whole new element coming into play but never touched on before. That part of their magic may come from their being alive in some curious way. They are vibrating with an energy that you cannot see, and if what I read was true, they have their whole history imprinted in each slab of marble and in every plank of wood and pulsing through those corroded walls. Whatever it is, whenever I was around them, I felt alive and full of wonder. To experience them was as uplifting as any symphony or work of art that you go back to see again and again in a museum because it nurtures something deep within your soul."

Katia sat quietly staring out the window, and I wasn't sure if she'd been listening. There was an overtone of melancholy in her silence, but then she turned, her eyes lucid and solemn, and she said, "I wish I'd been around to experience them with you. It changes things to look at them in that way, but I don't think you have to understand or even believe in any of this to be affected by those places or any dwelling where people have lived. I have a friend who's a real estate agent on Long Island. She told me there's a house that she's sold eight times in eight years. Seemingly happy married couples would buy the house and within a few months they would break up. Everyone called it the bad-luck house. But they were probably being affected by some dissonant energy that you can't see or define. No one could figure it out. Apparently it had nothing to do with ghosts or spirits because no one ever died in the house. Of course, it works the other way, too. There are happy houses, where you feel good the moment you walk in the door," she said.

Then, finally realizing it was after two in the morning, we said good night.

The next night, February 26, 1979, Gordon called and offered to come over and cook an Italian meal for the three of us. It was snowing heavily and too cold to go out so we welcomed the idea. Gordon was often unpredictable, but he always did what he set out to do. It was his nature, however, to either be two hours late or two hours early. This time he was two hours late, explaining that he had to drop his friend Francesca Hilton off at the airport and put her on a plane to Morocco so she could meet her mother Zsa Zsa Gabor for lunch. Katia and I were still not sure if Gordon was prone to delusions or was in fact telling the truth. It would take us some time to realize that, odd as his stories and excuses sometimes seemed, he always told the truth. Gordon attracted the unusual, and life around him was never dull, but he also had a talent for turning ordinary situations into chaotic ones.

Dinner that evening was no exception. Gordon was unhappy with the choice of wine Katia and I had contributed claiming that it did not go with his squid and kumquat entrée. Without saying anything more, he left the building and set off into the storm to find the right wine. When he returned sometime later, he took over Katia's small apartment kitchen, turning everything upside down rearranging the pots, pans, and groceries. Gordon was one of those people whose whole chemistry seemed to change whenever he was around food. He moved about in a frenzied state as though his life depended on producing this one meal, which required the use of kitchen utensils Katia and I had never heard of. He grumbled at Katia for not having a garlic press or cheese grater or kumquat peeler, but when he discovered there was no strainer to drain the pasta, he slammed a bunch of scallions down on the countertop, mumbling under his breath. Before anyone could stop him, he emptied a dying plant from a flowerpot that stood unwatered on the windowsill, rinsed out the dirt, and used it to drain the spaghetti. Katia entered the kitchen just as some of it went slithering down the drain.

"I don't believe what you just did. Worms crawl around in flowerpots," she screamed, looking around at the mess in her kitchen.

"Good. It'll add to the flavor," Gordon said, dumping the drained spaghetti into a large bowl.

We dined by candlelight and made a toast to future adventures.

"How's the wine?" Gordon asked imperiously.

"Great. It has that warm zingy aftertaste, like battery acid," I said.

Katia cut in, giggling. "I thought it was more like dinosaur urine." Gordon was not amused at our teasing.

He glared at us, then shot back, "You girls are something. Between the two of you, you can't boil an egg."

"We're career goddesses. We never set foot in the kitchen," I said haughtily.

Gordon gave me a disapproving glance. "You're both going to end up old maids," he said.

Katia giggled again. "Here, here! I'll drink to that," she said, raising her glass in a liberated gesture. Gordon shook his head and stuffed a mountain of pasta into his mouth, devouring it heartily. It was a very pleasant evening, though I was aware that they were making a concentrated effort to steer clear of the one subject that was still on my mind. But that was all about to change.

Around ten o'clock Katia got up from the table and turned on the TV set to watch the news, but without the sound. It was a ritual she always performed, but she never really paid much attention to what was happening on the screen. As Katia and I cleared the table, Gordon, once having eaten, became animated and talked with crackling enthusiasm about the joys of levitation. Figuring the wine had gone to his head, we ignored his rambling and went on to something else. I left the table and walked over to the window. The snow had tamed and quieted the city, and I realized I was seeing New York in winter for the first time. I don't know what made me turn around when I did, but had I waited a second longer, I would have missed it. My eye caught the image on the TV screen, and I gasped so loud that both Katia and Gordon froze where they stood. They followed my gaze and saw why.

There on the TV screen was Winfield, covered with the day's newly fallen snow. I lunged across the room and turned up the sound. A news reporter stood on the lawn with a microphone in his hand. He was interviewing some public official who stated that the owners had failed to pay over $160,000 in back taxes, and that the bank was about to foreclose. "This mansion is a white elephant. If it can't be sold by the end of this month, it would be within the best interest of the public to have it bulldozed." A second later the image was gone, and a hockey game appeared on the screen. I stood there as though I'd been struck by a train. There was silence in the room as Gordon switched off the TV set. Then something snapped in my head. I ran for my bag and grabbed the car keys. For a second I couldn't remember where I'd parked the car for the past week, but I knew it would come to me as soon as I got to the street. I frantically grabbed my coat and stumbled about, trying to pull on a pair of leather boots. Katia, looking alarmed, came over.

"What are you doing?" she asked softly.

"I'm going out there."

"Are you crazy? There's a foot of snow! It can wait till morning!" Katia shrieked, backing away from me as though I'd lost my mind and might prove to be contagious.

"You're not going out there tonight," Gordon said, blocking the door. I was suddenly reminded of those public-service ads you see on TV, about advising friends who drink not to drive—only I wasn't drunk, and I resented being treated like a child.

"Gordon, move away from that door," I demanded.

He just stood there with that impenetrable aura of defiance of his that made me want to strangle him at times. "Just sit down and get hold of yourself," he said condescendingly.

"Move away from that door!" I screamed, taking on the demeanor of a bulldozer. Gordon stood his ground, all three hundred pounds of him.

"Do you understand, I can't just let this go. It's not about me, or us against a bunch of ghosts, or that pain-in-the-ass rat. There's something out there, some mystery. I don't know what it is, but I've known that house since I was a kid, and I felt it from the first moment I laid eyes on it. No matter how hard I tried to stay away, weird circumstances kept drawing me back, and there has to be a reason. This is real. It may be beyond our comprehension, but—I don't care if it kills me—I'm going to get to the bottom of it," I said, feeling the adrenaline rush through my veins.

"Let her go," Katia said. "You're not going to stop her." Then she removed a silver chain with a charm of some kind, set into a crystal.

"Here, put this on for protection," she said, placing it around my neck.

Gordon hesitated, then rolled his eyes as he backed away from the door. "If you're going, I'm going with you. Though I don't see how going out there during a blizzard in the middle of the night is going to help save anything. You heard the news: your mysterious fiancé and his partner haven't paid the taxes on the place since they bought it. How are you going to change that?" Gordon asked, his voice charged with tension, though it was clear he'd already given up the fight as he moved about the room nervously gathering up his things. For all my forced bravado, I was secretly relieved. Katia walked into the kitchen and started putting dishes away. I followed her.

"Aren't you coming with us?"

"I don't know. This is all too crazy. I just can't handle that rat business," she said, covering her face with her hands. Gordon yelled out from the living room.

"That creature is in rodent heaven by now."

"Did you have to say that?" I said, not wanting to be reminded. "Katia, I used to spit at people for wearing fur coats. Now *I* feel like a murderer. What if that thing turns out to be just some poor little animal who fell down the chimney?"

"Yeah, right," Gordon fired back from the other room. "And he just happened to saunter through a passageway that even you didn't know about and pop in to borrow a screwdriver so he could open a jar of peanuts to serve his little rodent friends over cocktails. Well, he didn't fool me for a second. Boy, that was something," he said, slamming the kitchen door so hard the dishes rattled. "I thought you handled it rather calmly," he said, turning towards me.

"I'm no screaming ninny," I snapped, knowing I was not being completely honest.

"He's not dead," Katia said in that knowing tone of hers that suddenly gave me chills.

"Don't start getting creepy on me now, Katia," I said in a rasping tone.

"Disgruntled spirits have a way of taking over anything and anyone to do their bidding, even a fly, if that's all that's handy. They need a physical form to enter this dimension. You remember what happened the night of the séance?" Katia asked.

"How can I forget? You said we were protected that night."

"We were, up to a point. We just underestimated the power of whatever is out there."

"Stop it, Katia! This is the wrong time to be sharing these little cosmic tidbits," I said, putting my hands over my ears. "All we're trying to do is finish what we set out to do while there's still time. We were so close, so close. Gordon's psychic was right about that hidden panel, so she's probably right about everything else, and you can tell us what we can do to protect ourselves from anything negative."

"Yes, like staying home tonight and watching the Late Show, and maybe sending out for a pizza later," she said flippantly.

"We're wasting time. You heard the news report: they're going to seal the house in the morning. This may be the last chance to get back in," I said, opening the front door to leave as Gordon picked up his briefcase. "Hold on, I'm coming, but I'm driving, 'cause you're hysterical." I bit down hard on my lip, but didn't argue.

"Katia, are you sure?" I asked, as if I could change her mind about going. She hesitated for a moment, looking towards the kitchen.

"I never go out during the full moon. Besides, someone needs to stay behind in case you need help," she said nonchalantly.

"How is your staying here in your toasty apartment going to help?"

"I'm going to light candles and pray for your swift return," she said with her dry sense of humor. "Speaking of candles, there are some things you might want to take with you," she said, rushing across the room to the hall closet. When she opened it, several boxes tumbled out onto the floor. She pulled out a black plastic duffel bag and handed it to Gordon.

"You'll need some of these," she said, removing the white candles from their holders on the dining room table. "Oh, and some sage, to ward off . . . whatever, and a flashlight," she said, racing across the room to the kitchen. "Oh, and I think you're going to need this," she said, looking up at Gordon, handing him a new screwdriver, and holding it as though it were a dead mouse.

"Do you have a portable tape deck I could borrow?" Gordon asked.

"One tape deck coming up," she said in a chipper tone as she fumbled around in her closet and more boxes and clothing came tumbling out. "Well, I guess that's everything. Remember: call me when you get out there."

Chapter Twenty

Woolworth's Vault

Gordon and I didn't speak during the forty-minute drive out to Glen Cove. I sat in the passenger seat like a stone, my teeth clenched so tight, they hurt. Feelings of panic merged with anger as I realized that André had to have known about the tax situation all along and that he never said anything about it. I was also worried about what would become of the rooms full of furnishings I'd brought in, many of which were quite valuable because of their history. There was no way to get them out of there by morning. The drive seemed to take forever. Though the main roads had been plowed, once we got to the little hamlet in the cove, the car began to skid in the slushy wet snow. Finally we pulled up to the entrance arch, and Gordon got out of the car and opened the gate. There were fresh tire tracks along the drive leading up to the house, where the TV crews and reporters had been earlier.

Winfield had been transformed into a winter fairy-tale castle. I was reminded of the frozen Siberian palace in the movie *Dr. Zhivago*: icicles hung like fringe along the balustrades and roof while the life-sized statues were garlanded with mantles of snow. There was a hushed silence about the place that carried the muted sounds of birds fluttering unseen in the snow-drenched pines.

We got out of the car, and I opened the front door feeling as though we were trespassing. The moon shone like a laser on the shiny marble floor, flooding the hall with an eerie blue light. The house was freezing cold, and judging by the temperature, the furnace must have been off for days. Gordon followed me up the stairs to the door to my room. "You go in first in case that thing got out; you can wrestle with it," I said officiously.

"It would have frozen to death by now," Gordon said, shrugging his shoulders. As he opened the door, thousands of tiny white feathers billowed up, swirling tauntingly around us as we entered the room. A strong, pervasive fragrance of rancid perfume invaded our nostrils, and a wave of nausea came over me. My bed and dressing table were overturned; everything that had been on it strewn about on the floor. The down pillows had been slashed with a knife. Through the doorway of the dressing room and bath, I could see that all the crystal and perfume bottles had been swept off the shelves and lay shattered on the floor. The phone wires had been cut, and for a second I thought I'd gone mad.

"Who could have done this?" Gordon asked while his eyes darted about the room.

"Vandals probably. All the publicity—the story must have made the local papers days ago. Kids are drawn to these places like a magnet," I said woodenly.

"But how would they have gotten in?" Gordon asked, bending down to pick up a lamp that was overturned on the floor.

"They can always get in. There's probably a broken window somewhere."

"Look, it's not broken," he said, standing the lamp back on the night table.

"I don't care, I just don't care about any of it," I said, then walked across the room and opened the glass doors to the terrace to let some air in as the feathers sprang to life again.

Gordon went into the dressing room first while I sat wearily in one of the chairs and buried my face in my hands.

"It's gone!" he croaked a second later. "Whoever did this must have let it out. You'd better have a look in here," he said as though preparing me for some new calamity. I hesitated, then walked into the dressing room and gasped. The closet door was flung open, and strewn about the floor in chaotic heaps were my prized vintage gowns, lying about like crumpled rags. I bent down and clutched at them as though they were living things, and wept. Gordon began to gather them up in his arms, rummaging through them as he worked.

"They're not so bad really, just a little wrinkled, but they're okay.

Look," he said, holding one up to the light. "You'd better take them with you this time." He draped as many as he could carry over his shoulder. "I'll take these down to the car," he said, his voice straining under the circumstances.

"No, I'll do it. You go make the biggest fire you can down the hall in Woolworth's study. I'll be back in a minute," I said, gathering up the heap of clothes in my arms.

"Why make a fire?"

"Because it's freezing, and we're going to finish what we came here to do."

"I was afraid you'd say that," he said, sounding unnerved but up to the challenge. I ran down the stairs with the gowns and returned a few minutes later. Halfway up the stairs, I heard the strangest-sounding music coming from the west end of the house. As I moved closer to it, I could hear that it wasn't really music—there was no theme or harmonic order to it. It sounded more like a primal, dour, moaning sound, with a clanging of chimes in the background. When I got to the top of the stairs, I ran down the hall and entered the dimly lit Edwardian room. All the windows were white with frost, and lacelike patterns were etched across the glass. The massive fireplace looked like an apparition carved out of ice. Most of the pipes in the house had burst from the cold, and a frozen pool of ice covered the floor outside the bathroom door. By the sink, a spray of ice shot out from a broken faucet and formed an arch in midair. Gordon sat on the floor in the lotus position, seeming content with the eerie sounds coming from the portable tape deck Katia had given him.

"Gordon, what the hell are you doing?" I asked, taking in the surreal surroundings.

"Going into an alpha state," he answered with a calmness that bothered me.

"We've got work to do, and what's that godawful noise?" I asked irritably.

"It's to ward off evil spirits. This is no ordinary tape. I recorded it myself while in a Himalayan cave. That's the sacred ritual chant sung by two hundred celibate monks while in an illuminated state of consciousness. Believe me, no harm can come to us with that playing."

I stared at him, utterly flabbergasted. I was about to say something stupid but was rendered speechless as I realized I wouldn't have made it past the front door alone that night without him. Gordon was full of surprises, and from the look on his face, I could see he was sincere in his beliefs; but, clearly he was one of the weirdest people I had ever known. He was unaware of his own theatrics; nothing he did was for show. It was just the way he was.

I glanced at the smoking fireplace and saw that he'd made a feeble effort to get it started, using some crumpled newspaper. But the wood hadn't caught, and the charred paper had burnt itself out. I added some more twigs, logs, and paper from the closet, and within minutes the hearth was blazing, splashing golden rays of color on the mythological carved faces glowering down from the mantelpiece. We both gazed at the fire, welcoming the warmth, while the incessant chanting and beating of chimes played on in the background. After a while it seemed to penetrate the walls, and the air in the room began to seem strangely charged, though probably more by our own nervousness than by anything to do with the house.

Gordon reached into his bag and pulled out and lit two candles, then fished out whatever tools he needed and walked over to the corner of the room where he'd been searching the week before. He leaned against the wall, squinting his eyes, then tapped it once or twice, the rhythmic expulsion of his breath visible in the cold room. Outside I could hear a dog barking in the distance. Gordon began tapping gently with the screwdriver, chipping away layers of old varnish and gray paint. As the room began to warm up, the frost slowly began to melt on the windows, and I could see the moon, hanging low in the Western sky. While Gordon was chipping away at the panel, I noticed how the moonlight reflected on the two pyramids carved high above each end of the mantel. The light shone through the portal or temple at the base and rose up through a shaft in the seven tiers. I called Gordon's attention to it, and he turned away from the wall to look at it. "I've never seen anything like it," I said. "Do you suppose it means something?"

"I think everything in this house means something," he said, sounding distracted, as he continued to chip away at the panel one inch at a time. "There's a theory," he began, "that when the pyramids were built, they were used for higher consciousness training. The pharaohs, from what I remember, studied for as long as twenty years before they were ready to do whatever it was they did once they got to the king's chamber. They had to go through seven stages of intense and dangerous training, and many of them died along the way. Only after passing these tests were they allowed to enter the pyramid's secret chamber. The theory is, once there, they could travel into the fourth dimension and go back or forward in time. Some say the pyramids were giant time machines, but a lot of it was timing. You could only do certain things when the planets were in the right position," he said, continuing to work on the wall. "Can you hold the flashlight? I think I found the screws." Excitement registered on his face. Holding the light as steady as I could on the wall, I moved closer and watched as he removed two long thin screws that penetrated deep into the panel. "Look—there's a metal latch holding the whole thing in place," he said, picking up a thin pocketknife and slipping it along the top of the panel. We both heard a faint click from inside the wall as a portion of the wooden panel, measuring about two by three and a half feet, popped open, cracking a rusty hinge at the same time. We exchanged triumphant glances. You could feel a disturbing disquiet in the room as we held our breath. We were entering uncharted territory, and with it came a vague knowledge that we should not be there.

Gordon lifted the panel and placed it on the floor, revealing a two-foot-wide black metal vault with a brass handle on it. We just stared at it for a moment, as it gave the eerie appearance of the narrow end of a coffin. Outside, a sudden flurry of galelike winds shook the tall glass windows, and for a second the cold swept through the room, chilling us. I could see Gordon's hand was shaking as I held the light on the metal box.

"There's writing on it," he said, clearing his throat nervously. Scrawled across the front of the vault in red grease pencil was "F. W. Woolworth." Gordon reached in and pulled on the handle while I held my breath, half expecting some poltergeist mischief to ensue, but nothing happened. The wind continued to moan outside, and the world beyond that room seemed far away and irrelevant. All of our concentration was on opening that vault as Gordon continued to pull on the handle. It stirred just a bit, about an inch or so, but it would not open.

"It's jammed. The mortar and bricks around it have settled over the years, and it won't budge. I could pry it open with a crowbar, but that's the one thing Katia forgot to pack," he said, seeming to glow with determination, but now there was a disturbing air of recklessness about him. He reached into his bag for a hammer and used the screwdriver as a chisel to chip away at the dried-out mortar. Pieces of it flew out into the room as he worked, while the vault casing vibrated with each blow, making a high-pitched pinging sound as it inched out only a tiny bit more. Gordon cursed under his breath when the screwdriver snapped in two. He looked back at me in frustration, holding up the severed handle.

"No, don't even think about it. . . . I'm not going back to my room for more tools."

"I didn't say anything," he said, poking the flashlight down into the two-inch space at the top of the vault. "There's something in there," he said excitedly. "Look down—I'll hold the light. It's something wrapped in brown paper with a string around it." His voice registered nervousness. Silence and tension broke the mood of adventure, and something told me to rethink what we were doing. The odd, unfamiliar, and rhythmic sounds on the tape recorder droned on, causing my mind to drift and think of things like eternity and what I should be putting in my will.

"What are we going to do?" I asked, watching as Gordon kept trying to reach into the narrow opening, but his hands were too big. "Let me try. I've got these skinny little fingers," I said, wiggling them in front of him, trying to break the tension.

"No. See if you can find a coat hanger instead. You don't know what else might be in there," he said, still fumbling with the flashlight. I ran to the nearby closet in the room and returned in a second, handed him the wire, and watched as he bent and contorted it in all seemly positions, then lowered it down in the vault.

"Don't pull out a shrunken head," I said trying to make light of the moment.

"A shrunken head I can handle; it's that grouchy fur ball I don't want to deal with," he responded as beads of perspiration began to form on his forehead.

"Well, if he was around he would have made his presence known by now," I said, as the wind rose again, blowing snow and sleet at the windows.

"Can you hold the light for me?" he asked finally, his face contorted in concentration. Gordon poked several times at what was in the vault, trying to get a hold on it, but each time it slipped from his grasp. Finally the wire caught, and slowly he pulled out what looked like a roll of papers tied with a yellowed string. I reached over towards him and slipped the rotted string from the brown paper covering and watched it crumble in my hand. It crackled faintly as it fell to the floor. Inside were several pages of paper folded over once and then again. When I tried to open them, fragments crumbled and dropped from my hand. Built alongside the brick wall of the chimney that ran from the main floor to the roof, the vault had been exposed to a lot of heat over the years.

I continued to fumble through the pages, handing them to Gordon as they disintegrated and turned to dust with the touch of our hands. After peeling away several tissue-paper-thin sheets tucked away in the center, where they had been protected, I unfolded several old discolored lithographs of Napoleon. In one, he crouched menacingly on his throne at Fontainebleau, his eyes seeming strange and aberrant. I recognized the throne that had once stood in the Empire room opposite the hall from where we were. There was no way to know if it was the original or a copy. There was another illustration under it with some faint handwriting along the border, but so faded, it was almost illegible. At the bottom, it was identified in French. "Visite aux Pyramides de Gizeh." This was followed by the tag: "C. Matte after Granier." There was a date, April 12, 1799, scribbled in pencil and circled several times. The illustration showed Napoleon standing before a sarcophagus in the king's chamber of the Great Pyramid. He was illuminated as several of his men and savants stood around him, holding flaming torches.

I handed it to Gordon. "This is just a copy of a well-known painting. I've seen it before in a museum in France," he said absently.

"This might have been torn out of one of the books on Napoleon that's downstairs in the library," I said, taking it back. I turned it over, noticing something was written on the other side, but again it was unclear and faded. It was written in a shaky hand in faint sepia-colored ink. I attempted to read it out loud:

"All that I created, all that was mine. These walls were my bones, my sweat, and blood. I transcended all boundaries of time and space. This was my celestial instrument where . . ."

It faded out where the fold had exposed the paper to heat. It was unsigned, but I thought I recognized the handwriting.

"I can't make out the rest of it," I said, turning back to the illustration, unable to take my eyes off it. Something about it and those words struck a chord as chills ran up my spine. An idea so fantastic was beginning to take form in my head as bits and fragments of information that had been collecting in the back of my mind for years were somehow recalibrating and coming into focus, and by the time it hit me, there was no doubt. I looked up at Gordon.

"What are the dimensions of the King's chamber in the great pyramid?"

"I think it's seventeen feet by thirty-three—something like that," he said with a baleful stare.

"That's it," I said, and shivered involuntarily.

"What . . . what is it? You look like you've seen a . . ." He didn't finish.

"Gordon, did you ever suddenly know something, even though you may not be able to prove it and you know that no one will believe you—but you just know," I said, feeling my intuitive senses becoming strangely charged and lucid. "The secret room . . . there's another room in this house that no one knows about. Your psychic mentioned it, and I saw those dimensions in the blueprints, and that room is a replica of the King's chamber."

"Where is it?" Gordon asked, bending down to fumble with the cassette machine.

"It's right below us . . . well, not quite," I said moving toward the window. "It's out there below the west staircase," I said, pointing out the window. "I remember seeing lines marked on the blueprints, like an entryway or a tunnel leading to what must have been a room built off the basement."

"It's too preposterous," Gordon said, looking out the window and seeing nothing but a clean blanket of snow covering everything except the two giant marble lions that stood guard like sentinels at the base of the now-hidden staircase.

"It doesn't end there," I said as threads and fragments rose out of my memory and streamed through my consciousness faster than I could piece them together. "For years I've heard things—a little comment here, a revelation there. I can't even remember where I first heard that Woolworth had somehow managed to bring back a sarcophagus from Egypt, but that no one knew what became of it. I know this sounds crazy, but I think that it's downstairs in that secret room and that Woolworth is buried in it. Do you remember that when we were in the park, you kept telling me that your psychic was talking about him as though he was still in this house. I think she's right," I said, catching my breath. "I don't believe for one second that he's buried at Woodlawn cemetery next to his wife, whom he avoided at all costs in life. But by the way, that crypt at Woodlawn is Egyptian and has the same dimensions, and Woolworth always did things in twos. This house meant too much to him to ever leave it or allow anyone else to live here in peace. If I'm right, that would explain the dream you had and that man who went into a coma. Remember—your dream about being trapped in a chamber in Egypt? Only it wasn't in Egypt, it was right here," I said.

Gordon kept staring, seeming vaguely off balance. "But how could we have picked that up if we didn't know?" he asked.

"Electromagnetic imprinting. The whole house is playing back its history. I only read about it last week in a book on psychometry. Woolworth might have been a sensitive. All those things he collected—Napoleon's bed, the gold canopy, the thrones, and the paintings—followed by what we know of his beliefs and actions could have all been the result of psychometry. It's almost as if there was a complete transference of mind energy. Napoleon's thoughts and beliefs, grandiose as some of them were, became the thoughts and beliefs of Woolworth, right down to wanting to die on the same day that Napoleon entered the King's chamber in seventeen-ninety-nine."

"What did Woolworth die of?" Gordon asked while still gazing at one of the lithographs.

"According to the official report, septic poisoning—basically an abscessed tooth. He was told he would die if he didn't seek medical treatment that could have saved him. But he refused and chose to lie there in his room in Napoleon's gold sleigh bed for days, eating only rotten bananas and oatmeal."

"How do you know that's what happened?" Gordon asked skeptically.

"I interviewed the housekeeper, a Mrs. Oslenski. She was ninety-two when I located her a few years ago. She was living only a few blocks from here. Also, you have to remember that when I was living in the Woodward Playhouse, our immediate neighbors were Woolworths. They drank a lot and talked a lot, and I kept records of everything I heard. Then there was Mrs. Reynolds. She owned this house when I first wandered over here. She showed me the Empire room while it was still intact. Everything was just as Woolworth had left it. She kept it as a kind of shrine. I'd never seen anything like it, but I was too young to understand half of what was in there. I remember there was a painting of Napoleon hanging on the wall. It was a dramatic image of him in his royal robes, standing on a grand marquee, distributing bronze eagles to his army."

"Eagles are a symbol of immortality," Gordon added somberly. "That's how Napoleon got hundreds of thousands of gullible young men to go to battle with him—he convinced them they would be immortal if they followed him to glory."

I still had the lithograph in my hand. "This date of April twelve is circled over and over for a reason. I think Woolworth staged his own death; that it was all part of some master plan that went wrong."

"But why would he do it? He had everything!" Gordon said.

"He had everything, but he wanted immortality. That came out the night of the séance. Maybe that's what your psychic meant when she said he strove to achieve the impossible. He was so obsessed at that point that something must have convinced him that if he died on that date and juxtaposed his death with Napoleon's entry into the tomb of the Great Pyramid, he could somehow enter the fourth dimension and link up with the emperor. Who knows what he was thinking? He talked about having transcended time and space as though he believed he could do it, but he actually died on April eighth."

"That might explain why he's stuck here, like he missed his connection," Gordon added as he leaned his head against the carved mantel, his eyes closed as though he was lost in thought. "Well, this madness has got to stop," Gordon said in an icy tone, and before I realized what he was about to do, he grabbed the drawings and papers from my hand and flung them into the fireplace.

"Have you gone mad!" I shrieked, lunging down to retrieve them, but it was too late. The hearth seemed to open its iron mouth like a ceremonial altar as flames began to lick at the dried-out pages, which sizzled, turned black, and crumbled as a whirlpool of flames formed and faded. Shadows flickered on the brooding walls around us. Whatever else those papers might have revealed their secrets were lost forever. Moments later, gray tendrils swirled about as ashes blew in wisps about the room and landed silently on the floor.

"You had no right! They belonged to the house!" I said, half-hysterical.

Gordon seemed jumpy as a cat. He made an inarticulate sound and cleared his throat. "It's what the psychic told me to do. That's why I didn't want you to be here the first time we came out. She said if I destroyed whatever was found in the vault, the house would stop trying to protect it."

"Psychics, even the best of them, are often wrong," I shot back irritably. There was a deathly stillness in the room, and I realized that the tape Gordon had brought had suddenly stopped playing. We were no longer protected. For a long while, we stared at the burning embers, feeling the heat ebbing away. The wind continued to howl outside as it whipped at the windows, sending chilling currents of air through the room. I sank down onto the floor, suddenly feeling more drained and exhausted than I'd ever felt before.

"Gordon, I think we should leave right now. I don't think we were meant to know any of this," I said, suddenly feeling like a fugitive caught in a trap. The room seemed to sway for a second as another strong wind blew in off the sound, sweeping snow and ice from the trees and rooftop. It made a low, thunderous sound as it landed below in huge drifts that all but engulfed the house. This noise continued and seemed to take on a pulsing, fearful resonance long after the wind died down. We both turned and glanced at one another, then realized the sound wasn't coming from outside the house. Gordon moved towards the door, looking as pale as a spooked vampire.

Somewhere off in the house, we heard a loud banging. Gordon picked up the flashlight from the floor and held it as though it were a weapon. I followed him into the darkened hall, then down to the stairwell landing, where he paused to lean over the rail.

"It's coming from the basement," he said, recklessly running down the stairs, taking care not to make contact with the marble railing.

"You're not going down there, not now," I called after him. It was as if he didn't hear me. His eyes seemed far off and distracted. He turned left at the bottom of the stairs and disappeared through the basement door.

"Don't be crazy. There are no lights down there," I said, hearing my voice rise in panic. The banging continued. With each throbbing blow it picked up speed, and the echoes reverberated throughout the house. The chandelier appeared to sway for a moment, then stopped. I ran to the basement door and looked down and saw Gordon's light flashing haphazardly across the gray marble walls.

"You coming with me?" he yelled up, blinding me with the light.

"I don't do basements."

"But you know your way down here."

"No, I don't. I was only down there once. Pete, one of the gardeners, showed me around and tried to convince me that he was communicating with spirits via Morse code with the pipes. Old houses often have banging pipes," I said, trying to convince myself that's all it was.

"That's only if the heating system is working. Judging by all the ice down here, I'd say it's been off for a week."

Again we heard the noise, but we could not tell where it was coming from. It seemed to be shifting directions, illusively evading its source, repeating the experience I'd had when I first moved in.

"Gordon, it's a trick," I screamed down to him. "The house is playing with us." He shrugged his shoulders and continued to play with the electric switch box at the bottom of the stairs, to no avail. He seemed animated with excitement, like a kid challenged by a new and dangerous quest. That recklessness had always been in him, but now I was worried. Holding on to the brass rail, I moved halfway down the stairs to join him.

"Did you ever hear the theory about what really took down the *Titanic*?" I asked, trying to distract him.

"I thought it was an iceberg. . . . The whole world, including all the experts, has unanimously agreed it was an iceberg," he said in a loud voice, flailing his arms and the flashlight about dramatically.

"Yes, of course it was an iceberg, but what never came out in all the stories and books that have been written about it is that one of the millionaires on board had brought along an Egyptian coffin that was down in the storage compartment. It was passed off as just a coincidence, but you wonder. There's another well-documented case. An English archaeologist, a Colonel Vyse, was having the Basalt sarcophagus shipped to England in eighteen-thirty-eight when the boat mysteriously sank off the coast of Spain," I said, knowing how much Gordon liked to banter historic anomalies.

"What's your point?" he said, looking up impatiently.

"Food for thought, Gordon—just something to ponder."

He ignored my revelations, then a moment later shot back, "We're not on a boat."

"I know, but the very disturbing thought just popped into my head that it might not be the old man who's causing havoc around here. It could be something far more sinister, something we don't want to know anything more about, like some pesky little curse that might have come along with whatever he brought back from Egypt." He threw me a look of irritation, and I inched my way back up the landing.

The wind was still blowing outside, and from where I stood I could see a six-foot snowdrift piled up against the glass door on the north side of the house. For a second I thought I smelled cigarette smoke. Then it was gone. I could hear Gordon moving around in the basement, opening and closing doors. His light darted about the walls in jerky movements.

"There must be a hundred rooms down here," he yelled in a muffled voice that sounded far-off. The banging sound grew fainter and seemed to shift from one end of the house to the other. I was growing more restless and fearful by the second and decided to try a different approach.

"Gordon, I'm leaving. I'm going to count to ten, and if you don't come up here by then, you can take the train back to the city."

"Wait," he yelled up. Then he reappeared in the darkened stairwell. "I think I found something."

"What?"

"That banging's not coming from inside the house, it's coming from outside the basement walls," he blurted out excitedly.

"Listen," he said, motioning me to follow him down the stairs. "There's a room down here—looks like the base of the organ chamber. You can see the bellows and the pipes rising up through the ceiling to the main floor, but the outer walls in here are wood," he said with coiled intensity.

"I don't want to go on with this, Gordon. Please, let's leave."

But he went on. "I found a steel door that leads to somewhere outside the building's walls. I'm sure it's a tunnel."

My curiosity got the better of me, and I found myself inching my way down the marble stairs while he held the light on each step I took. I followed him down the long hall, and we came to a section of the basement where the floor was covered with raised wooden boards like the kind you'd find on a beach path. They creaked and moaned like an old ship as we walked over them, splashing icy water up from around the planks. Gordon winced when he bumped his head on a raw light fixture that hung down from an exposed wire in the ceiling.

I watched him move in shadow as he made his way along the narrow boards, brushing cobwebs from his clothes. Then he flashed the light on the far end of the wall, where there was a steel door with a long barlike handle.

"What are you going to do?" I asked dully.

"Break it down." His answer didn't surprise me.

"You've done enough demolition for one night, and I don't recall seeing Katia pack a pneumatic drill or an air compressor in your bag, so let's call it a night," I said.

"Aren't you just a little bit curious? I mean, if you're right about a king's chamber, it would be mind-boggling—a first."

"It would, but collecting Egyptian coffins was all the rage on the Gold Coast back then. Stanford White had a sarcophagus on his front lawn that he filled with geraniums. William K. Vanderbilt paid three thousand dollars for a little mummy and kept it in the middle of the living room as a conversation piece. There was another sarcophagus used as a fishpond at Ferguson Castle, and one at the Garvan estate was used as a horse jump. But you're right—an entire Egyptian tomb would be a first," I said miserably, realizing I was babbling to the walls at that point—Gordon was busy yanking a piece of steel rod from one of the organ pipes. When he freed it, he began to use it as a crowbar. The hinges on the steel door were rusted out and brittle, so it didn't take long before he snapped the top hinge. The rest of the door gave way as Gordon tumbled backwards, almost knocking both of us to the floor. The banging sound that we'd heard from upstairs began to fade into a different sound altogether as the room filled with a strong damp odor of rotted earth, intermingled with the pungent smell of decay. I lit matches while Gordon fumbled around on the floor for the flashlight that had slipped from his grasp.

"Let's get out of here. This is too creepy."

"I'm going in there. Wait here." There was a look of exultation on his face. Before I could stop him, he disappeared into the gloom of the tunnel, taking with him the only source of light. I lit one match after the other, and then two at a time, but each in turn was snuffed out by a draft coming from the tunnel. There was a deathlike stillness in the air as I stood there alone, wondering what manner of madness had brought me to this place of nightmares. The banging had stopped completely, but I became aware of a faint rhythmic sound like a steady beating of a jungle drum: thump . . . thump. I recognized the sound from the one we picked up on the tape recorder the night of the séance, which sounded very much like a human heartbeat. The memory of that night came rushing back in a vivid flood of images. I continued to light matches, shielding them with my hand, not daring to breathe, afraid to go back, afraid to follow. Off in the distance there was a faint shadowy glow of light.

"Gordon," I called out, but there was no answer. I called again but got no response while striking another match that quickly blew out. Between the cold and darkness I began to shiver violently, then took several steps backwards to get away from the draft as I struggled to light the last of the matches. It held and flickered. Just then I backed into something heavy and breathing in the doorway. I turned to face it. If ever there was a scream loud enough to fill that house, it was the scream I let out at the sight of Willard standing there, his eyes demented, his face unshaven, his teeth bared like those of some wild thing. Clinging to his shoulder was the rat. Its eyes shone like mirrors as they caught the orange light of the tiny flame. I felt its fur brush against my face as it lunged towards me, and the room began to swim in sickening, terrifying circles.

Gordon reappeared in that instant, swinging the long rod he'd torn from the pipe organ. While it was too dark to know what happened at that point, Willard was somehow struck off balance and hurled into the maze of the organ pipes. A high-pitched series of discordant notes erupted as the bulk of his weight crashed through the long wood-and-tin organ chambers, and they were accompanied by an eerie twang that sounded like a thousand violin strings snapping at once.

"Run!" Gordon yelled, though he'd dropped the flashlight in the confusion. Enough light streamed down from the upstairs stairwell to guide us back down the long hall. We ran up the stairs, skidding on the polished marble floor, then catching our balance again as we hit the far wall. As we ran out the front door, we listened for footsteps behind us. There was nothing for a moment, but then we heard them coming. I don't remember getting into the car or the engine starting up. Gordon was driving across the lawn through a half-foot of snow, zigzagging between the trees and heading towards the front gate. We were about twenty feet from it when I yelled, "It's locked!" Gordon seemed unfazed, with his eyes focused on the gate.

"What is this we're driving?" he asked, not bothering to slow down.

"It's a sixteen-year-old Caddy," I answered, gripping the dashboard.

"Great, you can't kill a Caddy!" he said exuberantly as he slammed through the mass of steel grates. The gate made a pinging sound as it snapped off at the hinges. He then turned left, and we headed towards Crescent Beach.

The full moon made everything seem like daylight. We just sat there still shaken, quietly watching as it hovered like a mirage over the Manhattan skyline in the distance. To the north you could see the lights flickering along the shoreline of Connecticut.

"Are you okay?"

Gordon didn't answer but nodded unconvincingly.

"Why didn't you answer me when you were in the tunnel?"

"I became disoriented and confused. There was this strange humming sound. It sounded like a thousand bees were swarming all around me, but there was nothing there. It blotted everything out, and for a second I couldn't remember where I was. I just ran out as fast as I could," he said, in a still-shaken voice.

"Did you find anything at all?"

"Just bare walls, with what looked like granite beams overhead. At the end, there was a solid wall where a door or portal once was. It was sealed up with cinder blocks, so I guess we'll never know what was on the other side."

"I don't have to see it to know. All the pieces fit. It has to be the last thing he did," I said, staring out at a huge freighter as it sailed silently along the sound, heading towards New York.

Gordon was about to start up the car again, then stopped and looked up. "I remembered something I read a long time ago in some history book about Napoleon's experience in the Great Pyramid. According to one account, he bribed the guards to allow him to lie in a sarcophagus, because he'd heard that Alexander the Great had done it before him. He believed that he could access the future and foretell the outcome of battles beforehand. You could go back and forth in time and divine your destiny. But Napoleon is said to have gone into a state of complete suspended animation. He seemed neither to breathe nor register a heartbeat. It was as if he were dead. When he came out of it, three days later, he was so shaken by what he saw that his face was ashen and his hair had turned white. He ordered his men never to speak of the incident again. But years later, when he lay dying in exile at St. Helena in eighteen-twenty-one, he seemed on the verge of revealing what had happened to him to an aide who stood at his side. Then he shook his head and said in French: 'No. What's the use? You'll never believe me.'"

"Do you think anyone will ever believe *us*?"

"Probably not," Gordon said, mumbling under his breath. "I don't think we'd better talk about it."

"Maybe in the year two thousand."

"Why then?" he asked.

"I don't know. I just have a feeling people will be more open. By the way, that was some driving you did back there," I said, getting out of the car to survey the damage. "You bashed my car," I said, getting back in out of the cold.

"I thought we were running from a madman," he said.

"You know, Willard has always been a little strange, and I do question his taste in pets, but I really don't think he was going to harm us. He is or was the caretaker, after all. We just spent the night smashing through a paneled wall in the study, set fire to possibly valuable artifacts, and pulled apart half the pipes in the organ, and we were about to tear down a concrete wall in search of King Tut's tomb in Glen Cove. Can we blame him for looking just a tad askew?"

Gordon appeared to be laughing out of control suddenly.

"Then, to top it off, we drive through the front gates when we could have stopped and opened them with the key, but . . . Gordon, this is not funny. Willard is probably calling the police. We broke every law in the books, and the ASPCA will be after us for cruelty to rodents. We'd better take the back roads through town. We can cut through the Welwyn estate and drive through Ghosts Gulch. That will bring us out on Lattingtown Road," I said, still caught up in the stress of the evening.

Gordon gave me that look as he started up the car, but he didn't speak for a while.

"I think we'll avoid Ghosts Gulch, if you don't mind," he said as he plowed through the snow, heading south towards the Long Island Expressway.

Epilogue

Of the six hundred estates that once existed along the island's North Shore, only about a hundred remain. This was the story of just one of them. I never returned to the house after that night. The following day Winfield was seized for back taxes. My furnishings were safely transferred to a warehouse nearby, and after a month or so I was allowed to pick them up.

Things seemed to take a turn when a large corporation stepped in at the last moment to lease the property, saving the house from possible demolition. A short time later the marble swimming pool and tennis court were bulldozed to make way for a large parking lot that took up much of the east lawn. Many of the second floor's historic rooms and fireplaces were destroyed to make offices, and the basement was gutted, rewired, modernized, and fitted with a massive air-conditioning system. Security guards watched the place day and night, but the rumors of its being haunted continued. In 1995 Winfield was abandoned again.

I never saw André again, but some years later I ran into an acquaintance of his on the Long Island Rail Road. It was his belief that the elusive Mr. Von Brunner, in need of funds, had sold his share of Winfield, returned to Europe for good, and reunited with his fifth wife. I had no way to verify this. Gordon, Katia, and the former cook Sunny and I have remained friends through the years.

Around the turn of the century, Woolworth's five-and-ten-cent stores made him a household name. The public never knew of the secret life of the eccentric genius at home on Napoleon's gold throne, trying to infuse his life and death with the late emperor whom he worshiped to the point of obsession. We will never know the details surrounding Woolworth's death, but it is my belief that the sarcophagus he is said to have brought back from Egypt, though never found, was buried with him in an underground secret room that has been sealed since his death in 1919.

However, according to family members, Woolworth spent over $100,000 to have an elaborate mausoleum constructed at Woodlawn Cemetery in the Bronx. It too appears to be a reproduction of the king's chamber found at the Great Pyramid, measuring thirty-three feet by seventeen and eleven feet high. The entrance is guarded by a pair of Egyptian sphinxes and supported by granite pillars carved with bands of bees, scarabs, and horns of Isis. Inside is an elaborate stained-glass window of what appears to depict an initiation undergone by those chosen to learn the secrets of the chamber reserved only for kings.

Woolworth died before the mausoleum was completed, and he was said to have been temporarily placed somewhere else. But where?

Winfield remains an enigma. Despite my efforts to keep a record of everything that happened during my brief time there, I did little to change things for the better, and the rumors continue. Taking all into consideration, I believe there is a much larger picture that goes beyond chasing ghosts or the circumstances that brought them about. The greater challenge may lie in our learning to better understand the entire spectrum of subtle energies, or soul essences, that appears to linger long after we're gone and continues to affect others in a positive or negative way. This light force lies within all of us and appears to be eternal. Something of our essence does remain, not just in the houses we leave behind, but in everything we touch—our clothing, the objects we use everyday. There is a resonating imprint, or recorded memory, of everything we do. So as you go about your daily lives, smile—you're on some kind of cosmic camera, and all your actions are in some way recorded in the ethers for all time. Perhaps we need to take a closer look at the long-lost works of the nineteenth-century scientist Joseph Rhodes Buchanan and the mastermind Nikola Tesla, who is alleged to have patented a device that caught the endless effluvia of these silent hosts on film.

It is interesting to note that while Winfield was being rebuilt after the fire in 1916, at the same time Nikola Tesla was experimenting with time travel and lecturing on the subject at Princeton University. It may seem far-fetched to us now, but, at the time, his work was widely accepted, and he even appeared on the cover of the *New York Times* when he was nominated for the Nobel Prize. Basking in the glow of celebrity but desperate for funding, Tesla approached a number of powerful and wealthy men to back his many projects, including John Jacob Astor and J. P. Morgan, Jr., who helped him get started, but then both turned him down. Woolworth, who knew Tesla, would have been a prime target, considering his interest in history and other esoteric subjects. Tesla's name was found on one of Woolworth's guest lists at Winfield. Woolworth was a man of many secrets, but it seems fair to assume that he would have been more than just a little intrigued with the idea of time travel and the chance to go back and relive the glory days of the little general. However, after years of searching, I could find no records of Woolworth having invested in any of Tesla's innovative ideas, which is not to say that Tesla didn't try.

So, in essence, all I have is a theory that Woolworth was dabbling in time travel in his home in Glen Cove. It is not an easy theory to prove. But if Buchanan was right, the information is not lost, and all is recorded ethereally in the crystalline structure of the very walls of Winfield. Perhaps more accessible is the physical evidence found in the puzzling cryptography encoded in the complex carvings that cover the main-floor rooms and Woolworth's private study on the second floor. In the end we are left with more questions than answers, and that is perhaps as Woolworth intended.

Winfield stands abandoned and is slowly being engulfed with creeping vines and relentless plant armies. But it remains a shining symbol in the mythos of the Gold Coast's final days. Winfield is owned by Mr. Martin Carey and is now listed on the National Register of Historic Places. One can only hope that its marble walls will continue to stand gleaming beneath the sun and stars in the centuries to come.

Author's Note

For those of you who may have read my first book, *Mansions of Long Island's Gold Coast*: for the record, in Chapter 5, on page 65, I describe having spent one night at Winfield. That night was in December 1977, and it was an uneventful evening. I did not move into the house until the following spring, on May 23, 1978. Photographic coffee-table books generally spend a year or two in production, and all materials had to be turned in by winter of 1977. The book was finally released in December 1979.

Anyone wishing to share their own experience or thoughts may write to me at:

"Timberwood"
Box 75, Oyster Bay
New York, 11771

Acknowledgments

This book would not have been possible without the support and generosity of many people, beginning with Woolworth's granddaughter Connie McMullen, who gave me access to a rare collection of photographs, and Mr. H. P. Smith, who oversaw the Woolworth archives on the twenty-fourth floor of the Woolworth Building in New York. I wish to thank all those who responded to an author's query published in the *New York Times,* and to all the estate workers who shared their experiences and bits of history, which otherwise would have gone unrecorded.

Carin Siegfried, my insightful editor, and Julia Lord for believing in this story
Dorothy Borges of the Grace Downs School
Janice and Richard Diana
Austin O'Brian
Mrs. Connie McMullen, F. W. Woolworth's granddaughter
Philip Van Rensselaer
Mrs. Richard S. Reynolds
C. W. Post College research department
College of Psychic Studies, London
H. P. Smith, Woolworth Building Records Department
New York Public Library
Parapsychology Foundation, Inc.
Eileen J. Garrett Library

Jim Dunne, former Woolworth worker
W. Dale Cramer
Peggy and Howard Katzander
Sunny Quinn
Marge LaJudas
Church of the Universal Brotherhood
Andrew Merlow
Wilma Carroll
Norman Green, Pall Corporation architect
Mrs. Pat Santora
Joyce Cain
Lori Summers
James Darrow
Mrs. Steven O'Slansky, former housekeeper to F. W. Woolworth
Mrs. Ethel Schroder, former secretary to Mrs. R. S. Reynolds
Margaret Boettger, graphologist
Lisa Fontinetta
Ray Attonito, former Winfield caretaker
Mr. Richard Wittereau, investigative reporter, *New York Post*
Mrs. Florence Norris
John Alitis
Joe Mazer, former Woolworth worker
Alicia Zizzo Salinger
Edna Heagney
Bunny Minsky
George Dixson, scientist
Mr. Martin Carey
Dominick Dunne
David Moorhouse
The late Howard Metz, Egyptologist, scholar of Egyptian history
The American Dowsing Association, Lindenville College, Vermont
Bridget Fontana
Dale Reed
Janet Chino
Nancy Ruhling
Syosset and Oyster Bay Library
Bob Frissell

Nikola Tesla
Erwin Gordon
Mrs. Atwood F. Sedgwick, Woolworth relative
Noel Wisdom, artist
Pete Secara, former Winfield gardener
Nick Samardge, film director
Jean Quinn
William Stuart Nimmo

Selected Bibliography

BOOKS

Anderson, George, with Joel Martin and Patricia Romanowski. *We Don't Die*. New York: the Berkley Publishing Group, 1988.

Andrews, Ted. *How to Develop and Use Psychometry*. St. Paul, Minn.: Lllewellyn Publications, 1995.

Bagnall, Oscar. *The Origins and Properties of the Human Aura*. Old Tappan, N.J.: MacMillan, Inc., 1970.

Baily, J. T. Herbert. *Napoleon*. London: Carmelite House, the Cranford Press, 1908.

Baker, Nina Brown. *Nickels and Dimes: The Story of F. W. Woolworth*. New York: Harcourt, Brace & Company, 1954.

Barnothy, Madeleine F., ed. *Biological Effects of Magnetic Fields*. Plenum Press, 1964.

Brough, James. *Woolworth*. McGraw Hill, 1984.

Buchanan, Joseph Rhodes. *The Manual of Psychometry*. 1885.

Burr, Harold Saxton. *Blueprint for Immortality: The Electric Patterns of Life*. London: Neville Spearman Ltd., 1972.

Cheney, Margaret. *Tesla: Man out of Time*. New York: Laurel Books at Bantam Doubleday Dell Publishing Group, 1981.

Christopher, Harold J. *Bonaparte in Egypt*. New York: Harper & Row, 1962.

Denton, William. *The Soul of Things*. Dorthhamptonshire, England: the Aquarian Press, copyright 1863, reprint 1988.

Draper, Wanetta W., and Inez Hunt. *Lightning in His Hand: The Life Story of Nikola Tesla*. Denver: Sage Books, 1964.

Dunne, Dominick. *The Two Mrs. Grenvilles*. New York: Crown Books, 1984.

Finucane, R. C. *Ghosts: Appearances of the Dead and Cultural Transformations*. Amherst, N.Y.: Prometheus Books, 1996.

Fiore, Edith. *The Unquiet Dead*. New York: Ballantine Books, 1987.

Fodor, Nandor. *The Haunted Mind*. New York: Garrett Publications, 1959.

Freeland, Nat. *The Occult Explosion*. New York: Berkeley Publishing Corp. 1972.

Holzer, Hans. *Ghosts: True Encounters with the World Beyond*. New York: Black Dog & Leventhal, 1997.

Hudgings, William F. *Dr. Abrams and the Electron Theory*. New York: Century Co., 1923.

Hudson, Thomson Jay. *The Law of Psychic Phenomena: A Working Hypothesis for the*

Systemic Study of Hypnotism, Spiritism, Mental Therapeutics, Etc. London: G. P. Putnam's Sons, 1902.

Jung, Carl Gustav. *Memories, Dreams, Reflections.* New York: Vintage Books, 1989.

LeShan, Lawrence. *The Medium, the Mystic, and the Physicist.* London: Turnstone Press, 1974.

Lethbridge, T. C.. *The Power of the Pendulum.* London: Routledge & Kegan Paul, 1976.

Long, Max Freedom. *The Secret Science Behind Miracles.* Marina del Ray, California: DeVorss, 1981.

Lorimer, David. *Survival? Body, Mind and Death in the Light of Psychic Experience.* London: Routledge & Kegan Paul, 1984.

Mackey, Albert G. *An Encyclopedia of Freemasonry and its Kindred Sciences.* New York: Mason History Co., 1873.

Mead, Robin. *Haunted Hotels.* Nashville: Routledge Hill Press, 1995.

Moody, Raymond. *Reunions: Visionary Encounters with Departed Loved Ones.* New York: Villard, 1993.

Moore, William L., and Charles Berlitz. *The Philadelphia Experiment: Project Invisibility.* New York: Fawcett Crest Books, 1979.

Morehouse, David. *Psychic Warrior.* New York: St. Martin's Press, 1996.

Moss, Dr. Thelma. *The Probability of the Impossible: Scientific Discoveries and Exploration in the Psychic World.* New York: a Plume Book, New American Library, 1974.

Nichols, John P., *Skyline Queen and the Merchant Prince.* New York: Trident Press, 1973.

O'Donnell, John. *Thought as Energy: The Science of the Mind.* 1973.

Okonowitz, Ed. *Possessed Possessions.* Elkton, Md.: Myst and Lace, 1996.

O'Neil, John J., *The Prodigal Genius: The Life of Nikola Tesla.* Hollywood, Calif.: Angriff Press, 1944.

Parapsychic Acoustic Research Cooperative. *The Ghost Ghost Orchid CD.* Winston-Salem, N.C.: Wake Forest University Press, 1999.

Permutt, Cyril. *Photographing the Spirit World: Images from Beyond the Spectrum.* Cambridge, Mass.: Patrick Stephens, 1983.

Playfair, Guy. *The Indefinite Boundary: An Investigation into the Relationship Between Matter and Spirit.* New York: St. Martin's Press, 1977.

Prince, Walter Franklin. *Noted Witnesses for Psychic Occurrences.* New York: University Books, 1963.

Rawlings, Maurice S. *To Hell and Back: Life After Death—Startling New Evidence.* Nashville: Thomas Nelson, 1993.

Richet, Charles. *Thirty Years of Psychical Research.* London: W. Collins Sons, 1923.

Rogo, D. Scott, and Ray Bayless. *Phone Calls from the Dead.* Englewood Cliffs, N.J.: Prentice-Hall, 1979.

Seifer, Marc J. *Wizard: The Life and Times of Nikola Tesla: Biography of a Genius.* Sekaukus, N.J.: Carol Publishers, 1996.

Sheldrake, Rupert. *The Presence of the Past: Morphic Resonance & the Habits of Nature.* Rochester, Vt.: Park Street Press, 1988.

Sinclair, Upton. *Mental Radio. Does It Work and How?* London: Werner Laurie, 1930.

Thurston, S. J. Herbert. *Ghosts and Poltergeists.* London: Burns Oates and Washbourne, 1853.

Tompkins, Peter. *The Secrets of the Great Pyramid.* New York: HarperCollins Publishers, 1978.

Tompkins, Peter, and Christopher Bird. *The Secret Life of Plants.* New York: Harper & Row Publishers, 1972.

USA Weekend Editors. *I Never Believed in Ghosts Until. . . .* New York: Contemporary Books, 1992.

Van Rensselaer, Philip. *Million Dollar Baby: An Intimate Portrait of Barbara Hutton*. New York: G. P. Putnam's & Sons, 1979.
Vaughan, Alan. *Incredible Coincidence: The Baffling World of Synchronicity*. New York: Signet Books, 1980.
Wilson, Colin. *Afterlife*. London: Harrap, 1985.
——. *The Geller Phenomenon*. London: Aldus Books, 1976.
——. *The Occult: A History*. New York: Random House Publishers, 1974.
——. *Strange but True Ghost Sightings*. New York: Robinson, 1997.
——. *Strange Powers*. New York: Random House Publishers, 1975.
——. *The Mammoth Book of the Supernatural*. New York: Carroll & Graf Publishers, Inc., 1991.
Wilson, Colin, with Damon Wilson. *The Encyclopedia of Unsolved Mysteries*. London: Harrap, 1987.
Winer, Richard, and Nancy Osborn. *Haunted Houses*. New York: Bantam, 1979.
Winkler, John Kennedy. *Five and Ten: The Fabulous Life of F. W. Woolworth*. Freepard, N.Y.: Books for Libraries Press, 1940.
Woolworth, F. W. *The Dinner Given to Cass Gilbert by F. W. Woolworth*. New York: privately published by F. W. Woolworth, 1913.

NEWSPAPERS
Newsday weekend magazine, "Once Upon a Gold Coast" by Harvey Aronson, 6 April, 1968, p. 1.
Long Island Press, "Haunting Return of L. I. Grandeur," 20 October 1967, p. 29.
World Journal Tribune (New York), "So Many Mansions" by Anne Anable, 22 January, 1967, Sec. 2, p. 3.
New York News magazine, "Gatsby's Long Island" by Russ Chappell and Monica Randall, 17 March, 1974, cover story.
Newsday's Long Island magazine, "Why the North Shore's Estates Are Vanishing" by Joseph Treen, 14 January, 1973, p. 8.
Newsday's Long Island magazine, "The Gold Coast: from Grandeur to Ruin" by Robert Marten, 2 December 1979, pp. 28–34.
Newsday's Long Island magazine, "Why Long Island Flunked Its Gatsby Screen Test," by Al Cohn, 24 March 1974, cover story.
New York Post, "Months Among the Whispers" by Richard Wettereau, 5 January 1980.
New York Times, "Old Long Island Mansions Are Her Haunts" by Jane Geniesse, 1 December 1979, style section, p. 48.
Newsday's Long Island magazine, "A Romantic Look at Long Island Past" by Marilyn Goldstein, 12 June 1977, p. 1.
New York Times, "A Carey White Sheep—the Story of Wooley," 6 February 1976, p. 33.
Dayly News, "These Cops Really Give a Ram!" by Donald Singleton, 1 February 1976, p. 47.

www.ingramcontent.com/pod-product-compliance
Lightning Source LLC
Chambersburg PA
CBHW070737170426
43200CB00007B/550